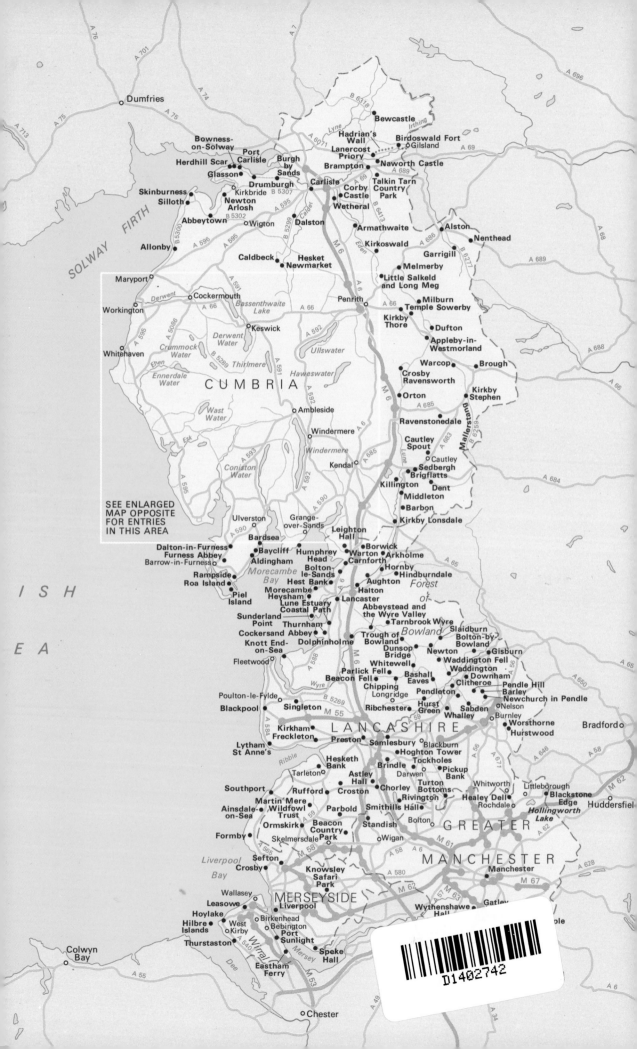

BEAUTIFUL BRITAIN

AA

THE LAKE DISTRICT AND LANCASHIRE

BEAUTIFUL BRITAIN

THE
LAKE DISTRICT
AND LANCASHIRE

Published by the Reader's Digest Association Limited, London for the Automobile Association,
Fanum House, Basingstoke, Hampshire RG21 2EA

THE LAKE DISTRICT AND LANCASHIRE
was edited and designed by
The Reader's Digest Association Limited
for the Automobile Association,
Fanum House, Basingstoke, Hampshire, RG21 2EA.

This book contains material from
the following titles originally
published by Drive Publications Limited:
*Treasures of Britain, Discovering Britain,
Hand-picked Tours in Britain, No Through Road,
Book of the British Countryside, Book of
British Towns, Illustrated Guide to Britain,
Book of British Villages, Illustrated Guide
to Country Towns and Villages of Britain,
250 Tours of Britain, Book of British Coasts,*
and from the following titles published by
The Reader's Digest Association Limited:
*Folklore, Myths and Legends of Britain,
The Past All Around Us, Nature Lover's Library,
Food From Your Garden, The Cookery Year.*

ISBN 0-86145-724-2

Filmset by MS Filmsetting Limited, Frome, Somerset.
Separations by Scantrans Pte Ltd, Singapore.
Printed and bound by C & C Joint Printing Co. (HK) Ltd, Hong Kong.

Printed in Hong Kong

Cartography by Thames Cartographic Services, Maidenhead
and the Automobile Association, Basingstoke based on
mapping by John Bartholomew & Son Ltd, Edinburgh.

A name printed in bold type on the endpapers map
or underlined and printed in capital letters on
the tours maps indicates that the place is featured
in this book.

Cover photographs: Rydal Water
by Noel Habgood/Derek Widdicombe Picture Library (top);
Cregneish Folk Village by *Trevor Wood* (bottom left).
Introduction (pages 6–7) Lake Windermere by *Patrick Thurston.*

CONTENTS

This is England's scenic wonderland, a place of craggy mountains and green dales, of chuckling streams, foaming waterfalls and, above all, lakes. Its half-tamed landscape, which has changed little since it inspired poets like Wordsworth and painters like Turner is now protected in the largest National Park in the country. The 16 lakes which give the area its enchanting name are but part of the attraction. Above them soar the highest mountains in England whose grandeur is doubled in the waters below. Waters which are fed by a myriad tumbling becks that have carved fern and flower clad gorges where waterfalls plunge and sparkle. All this was not discovered by the Lakeland poets – they merely told the world about it. Stone Age man was there more than 3000 years before them and built the great stone circle at Castlerigg; the Romans and Norsemen, too, knew the lakes and left roads and villages. Later, monks came in search of peace which was frequently shattered by Scottish raids across the Border.

Lancashire, which once included the southern lakes, still has its share of the windswept slopes and moors of the western Pennines. Beneath them, a flat black-soiled plain of rich farmland with cosy villages and fine houses stretches out to a sandy shore. The great northern playgrounds of Blackpool, Morecambe and Southport – and many smaller resorts – line this shore. Beyond them lies a dot of green set in the Irish Sea, the Isle of Man, a scenic gem in its own right.

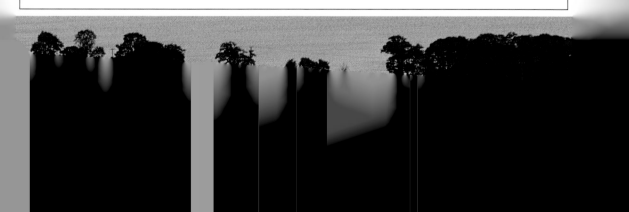

ABBEYSTEAD AND THE WYRE VALLEY

Lancashire
7 miles southeast of Lancaster

A steep descent between neat beech hedges leads to Abbeystead in the sheltered valley of the Wyre. Built on the site of a long-vanished Cistercian abbey, the village has some farms which look like manor houses, a fine school, an ornate horse trough and a colourful tangle of cottages. Surrounded by heather moors, Abbeystead is noted for its fine grouse and its bees – many of the farms and cottages have honey for sale.

The two arms of the Wyre, Marshaw Wyre and Tarnbrook Wyre, meet at the village. Where they converge, the woods crowd right across the junction – a domain of green shade in summer and a crisp, golden world in autumn. No sooner have the two Wyres met, than their combined waters swell broadly across the valley, impeded by the dam of Abbeystead Reservoir half a mile below the village. It was constructed in the 19th century to provide water for textile factories downstream at Dolphinholme and beyond. The still water reflects the woods that crowd upon its eastern shores. A path runs along the north bank of the reservoir, first among the trees, and then through the open country beside the river as it emerges from the dam. This is fine strolling country, crisscrossed by a network of easy paths. Many wildfowl can be seen gathering on the slowly silting shores, particularly in the winter.

About a mile beyond Abbeystead is Christ Church-over-Wyresdale, known locally as the Shepherds' Church. This is because its porch faces rich green water meadows – ideal grazing land for sheep. The inscription over the church door reads: 'O ye shepherds hear the word of the Lord.'

ABBEYTOWN

Cumbria
15 miles north of Cockermouth

Abbeytown is well named, for not only did it grow up around the 12th-century Holme Cultram Abbey, but also many of its buildings were constructed of stones taken from the abbey when it fell into ruin after 1536. The village is small, little more than a hamlet, and is surrounded by ancient farms dotting a rolling landscape of green meadows, with, in spring, an occasional ploughed field exposing its red soil like a bright patch on a well-worn cloak.

From the day of its founding by Cistercian monks in 1150, the abbey and its township often bore the brunt of attacks by the English or the Scots as the borderland continually changed hands. In times of peace the abbey prospered and became the largest supplier of wool in the northern shires.

Edward I stayed there in 1300, and again in 1307 when he made Abbot Robert De Keldsik a member of his council. After Edward's death the Scots returned

BUSY BEES *Honey-bees may fly as far as 3 miles from the hive, gathering pollen and nectar from flowers to make into food. A colony of 50,000 produces up to 100lb of honey in a summer. Abbeystead is famed for bees.*

with a vengeance, and in 1319 Robert Bruce sacked the abbey – even though his father, the Earl of Carrick, had been buried there only 15 years before.

The final blow came in 1536, when Abbot Thomas Carter joined the Pilgrimage of Grace, the ill-fated rebellion against Henry VIII's seizure of Church lands and property. The rebellion was put down with ruthless efficiency, and most of the abbey destroyed, though part of its church's nave survived to become the red-sandstone Church of St Mary, because the locals pointed out that it was the one building that gave them protection against border raids.

It is still the parish church and was restored in 1883 – a strange looking but impressive building with the original nave shorn of its transepts, chancel and tower, which collapsed in 1601. The east and west walls are heavily buttressed and a porch with a new roof protects the original Norman arch of the west door. The porch shelters a stone commemorating Ann Musgrave who was 'murdered with the shot of a pistol' in 1586. A brass plaque on the west wall pays tribute to Joseph Mann from the neighbouring hamlet of Raby. The plaque recalls how his invention of the reaping machine at Holme Cultram in 1820 brought 'lasting benefits to agriculture in all parts of the world'.

A room within the church building, opened by Princess Margaret in 1973, contains the gravestones of Robert Bruce's father, the Lord of Annandale, and of Mathias and Juliana De Keldsik who were probably related to Abbot Robert.

AINSDALE-ON-SEA

Merseyside
4 miles southwest of Southport

So firm are the sands at Ainsdale beach that motorists often use them as a road along which to drive to neighbouring Southport. They have to observe a 10 mph speed limit, which is broken only when official motor races are held on the sands, or when light aircraft take off from them.

Behind the beach, a wilderness of dunes stretches all the way to Hightown to the south and Southport to the north. A road curves through the dunes, following the line of an old railway, and the Royal Birkdale championship golf course lies to the east of the road. More than 1700 acres of the dunes are nature reserves, with varied plant life as well as colonies of the rare natterjack toads and sand lizards.

The national nature reserve has 6 miles of marked paths, including the Fisherman's Path which leads to the shore from the car park near Freshfield Station. Visitors must keep to these routes, as the dune vegetation is fragile. A special nature trail is available to booked school parties in early summer.

Along the 4 miles between Ainsdale and Southport swimmers should stay in the areas marked by red and white flags. These are patrolled by lifeguards, some of whom operate from amphibious vehicles.

AIRA BECK AND AIRA FORCE
Cumbria
1 mile southeast of Dockray

Just beyond the hamlet of Dockray, with its big, good-looking pub, there is a National Trust car park, labelled Gowbarrow. A path leads from this through a steep field to the Aira Beck, a white roaring cataract running down to the dark trench of Ullswater.

Another car park further down the road is the starting point of a path to Aira Force. There, the stream rushes under a little stone bridge and is flung, spitting spray, down a cold, green, 70ft hole lined with ferns and moss. It is easy to imagine that this is one of the most romantic spots in the Lake District.

Legend tells that Aira Force was once the scene of a tragedy of love. Its heroine, Emma, lived in the nearby Lyulph's Tower, and loved a knight called Sir Eglamore. For some reason he left her, and in despair she took to sleepwalking beside Aira Force, the place where they had first met. One night Sir Eglamore came back and found Emma at the waterfall; but when he called her name she awoke suddenly, tripped, and fell to her death in the foaming waters. The grieving knight became a hermit, and lived out his life near the spot where she had died.

A gate from the car park at the foot of Aira Beck is the entry to a field, and from the right of the field a stile leads into the woods and over a footbridge across the beck. The path follows the beck up through the woods – a delightful mixture of oak, ash, alder, willow, beech and the occasional wych elm. Many orchids can be seen, especially purple orchids in late spring and spotted orchids in early summer.

Two bridges span the gorge, one above and one below Aira Force; cross the top bridge and follow the beck upstream on its right-hand side to another beautiful waterfall called High Force. The rock slabs around it seem perfectly made for sitting and contemplating for a while, as the water leaps loud and white towards its dark and silent ending in the lake.

TUMBLING WATERFALL *The sound of rushing water echoes around the remote rocky glen at Aira Force.*

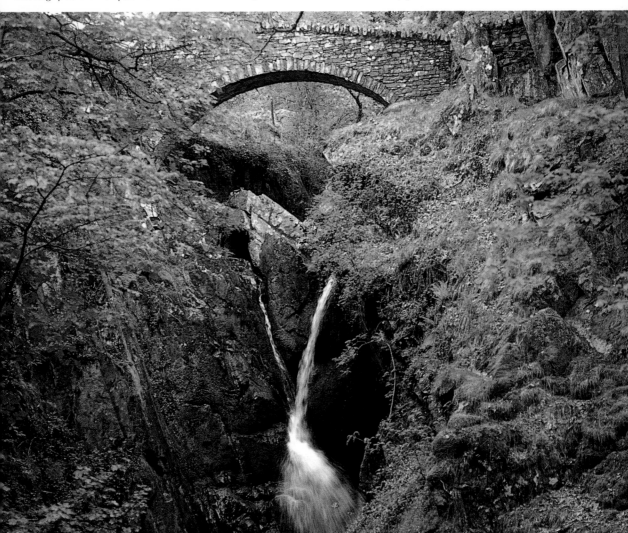

ALDINGHAM

Cumbria
4 miles southeast of Dalton-in-Furness

Over the centuries, Aldingham has lost more and more of its houses to the advancing sea. The parish church of St Cuthbert, which dates back to the 12th century, and the headstones in its little churchyard, today stand just above high-water mark. Behind them are the narrow curving lanes of the more enduring part of the village which was built on the hill overlooking the sea.

ALLONBY

Cumbria
5 miles northeast of Maryport

Allonby Bay faces northwest towards the open sea rather than towards the Scottish shore, so conditions here are safer for bathing than they become further east. Allonby itself is an unassuming but attractive village of cottages which straggle along the Silloth to Maryport coast road. Allonby became popular as a holiday resort about 200 years ago, after a darker and more violent history as a centre for landing smuggled whisky from the opposite coast of the Solway. It still retains the away-from-it-all atmosphere that appealed to those 18th-century smugglers.

Despite a huge expanse of low-tide sand, Allonby is sufficiently remote not to have been commercialised, and is a quiet place even in the middle of August. Horses roam the turf flanking Allonby Bay and wander across the unfenced road south of the village, just as they did when Allonby was considered 'a considerable concourse for bathing in the sea', according to a 19th-century guidebook.

Christ Church, at the southern end of the village, contains a memorial to Joseph Huddart, born in Allonby in 1741 and a surveyor who added to 18th-century knowledge of the coasts and harbours of the Far East. Huddart became wealthy through an invention which grew out of a disaster he witnessed when a cable snapped at sea; he devised a method of ropemaking which ensured that the stresses were divided evenly between the fibres. He set up as a ropemaker in London, and was buried at St Martin-in-the-Fields.

At Crosscanonby, about 2 miles to the south, is the Church of St John the Evangelist, a Norman structure with later additions. It is decorated inside with Saxon and Norman carvings, and 18th-century woodwork.

ALSTON

Cumbria
16 miles northeast of Penrith

At Alston, dry-stone walls border sloping fields, and the surrounding countryside is dotted with woods. Built on a hillside, it commands sweeping views of the South Tyne Valley and the Pennine chain. Claimed to be the highest market town in England – at almost 1000ft – it is also the nearest town to Cross Fell, which at 2930ft is the highest peak in the Pennines.

From Roman times until the early 19th century, Alston was an important mining centre. Silver, lead, copper, iron and other ores were extracted from hills whose economic yield is now only a small amount of anthracite. Side streets lined with stone houses radiate

BIRD'S EYE VIEW *Ambleside is tiny when seen from The Struggle, a steep road up to Kirkstone Pass.*

from the market square. A stone-pillared market house covering an old cross stands in the square. The Friends' Meeting House, nearby, dates from 1732, and near the church is a black-and-white timbered house of 1691. Clarghyll Hall, 2 miles north, was built in 1679.

AMBLESIDE

Cumbria
4 miles northwest of Windermere

A resort at the centre of the Lake District, Ambleside is always crowded with walkers. In season, crowds swirl beneath the jutting boards of hotels, inns, guesthouses, teashops and restaurants, which look like

banners at a medieval tournament. Guides can be hired here, along with rope and tackle, for rock-climbing expeditions.

Even for the less energetic, Ambleside is a pleasant place. It is a serpentine, humpbacked little town built of brown or grey-greenish stone slabs. Bridge House –a doll-sized house perched on a tiny bridge over Stock Ghyll – has been an apple store, a cobbler's and a family home; now it is a National Trust Information Centre. A little upstream is the splendid Old Mill, now a knitwear shop.

Every July the 19th-century Church of St Mary the Virgin observes the custom of rush-bearing, when children parade through the streets carrying rushes and flowers – a tradition handed down from the Middle Ages when rushes were used as carpets.

Among many delightful fellside walks around Ambleside is one to Stock Ghyll Force, a beautiful water-fall set among woods 1 mile to the east. The route is signposted behind the Salutation Inn at the centre of the town. From Waterhead, just south, boat trips can be taken on Lake Windermere, including $1\frac{1}{4}$ hour trips along the full length of the lake to Lakeside.

On the slopes above the lake are the remains of a stone-built 2nd-century Roman fort. Outlines of buildings and part of the defences of the camp – called Galava – can be identified with the help of the display board. The site can be reached by a footpath from Borrans Road, between the A591 and A593.

At Brockhole, about 2 miles south along the shores of Windermere, a white Victorian mansion houses the Lake District National Park Visitor Centre, which is second to none of its kind in this country. Sight and sound exhibitions embrace all aspects of the area. Outside, flowery terraces look over magnificent trees to the lake.

Lakeland scenes that inspired a poet

Craggy fells and peaceful lakes, like Thirlmere, retain the beauty that once inspired William Wordsworth, greatest of the Lakeland poets. He lies buried at Grasmere, which he described as 'the loveliest spot that man hath ever found'. The countryside is little changed since Wordsworth's day – bracken and wild flowers flourish and the hounds of the Blencathra Pack still hunt the fells.

Thirlmere reservoir was once two lakes

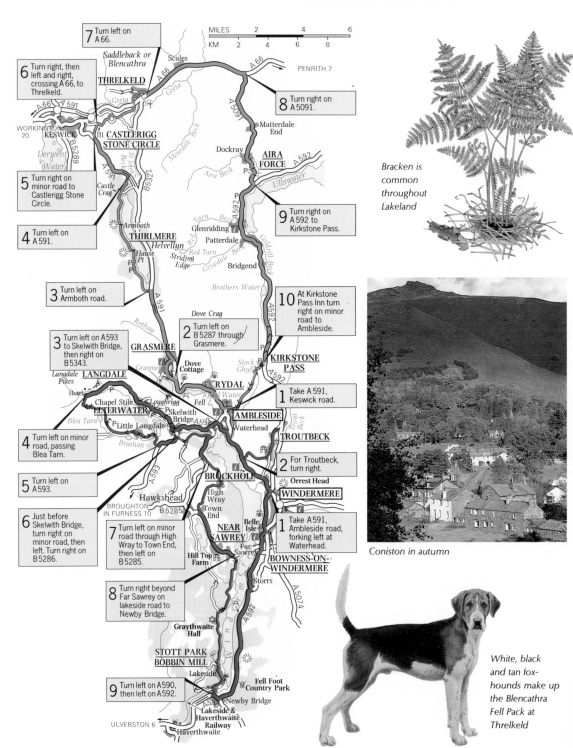

7 Turn left on A66.

6 Turn right, then left and right, crossing A66, to Threlkeld.

8 Turn right on A5091.

5 Turn right on minor road to Castlerigg Stone Circle.

9 Turn right on A592 to Kirkstone Pass.

4 Turn left on A591.

3 Turn left on Armboth road.

10 At Kirkstone Pass Inn turn right on minor road to Ambleside.

2 Turn left on B5287 through Grasmere.

3 Turn left on A593 to Skelwith Bridge, then right on B5343.

1 Take A591, Keswick road.

4 Turn left on minor road, passing Blea Tarn.

2 For Troutbeck, turn right.

5 Turn left on A593.

1 Take A591, Ambleside road, forking left at Waterhead.

6 Just before Skelwith Bridge, turn right on minor road, then left. Turn right on B5286.

7 Turn left on minor road through High Wray to Town End, then left on B5285.

8 Turn right beyond Far Sawrey on lakeside road to Newby Bridge.

9 Turn left on A590, then left on A592.

MILES 2 4 6
KM 2 4 6 8

PENRITH 7

WORKINGTON 20

BROUGHTON-IN-FURNESS 10

ULVERSTON 6

Saddleback or Blencathra
Scales
THRELKELD
Greta
KESWICK
CASTLERIGG STONE CIRCLE
Derwent Water
Castle Crag
Armboth
THIRLMERE
Helvellyn
Hause Pt
Striding Edge
Red Tarn
Matterdale End
Dockray
AIRA FORCE
Ullswater
Glenridding
Patterdale
Bridgend
Brothers Water
Dove Crag
GRASMERE
Dove Cottage
Langdale Pikes
LANGDALE
Hotel
Chapel Stile
ELTERWATER
Blea Tarn
Little Langdale
Brathay
Loughrigg Fell
Skelwith Bridge
RYDAL
Rydal Water
AMBLESIDE
Waterhead
TROUTBECK
Orrest Head
BROCKHOLE
High Wray
Town End
WINDERMERE
Hawkshead
NEAR SAWREY
Far Sawrey
Hill Top Farm
Belle Isle
BOWNESS-ON-WINDERMERE
Storrs
Graythwaite Hall
STOTT PARK BOBBIN MILL
Lakeside
Fell Foot Country Park
Newby Bridge
Lakeside & Haverthwaite Railway
Haverthwaite
KIRKSTONE PASS
Stock Ghyll

Bracken is common throughout Lakeland

Coniston in autumn

White, black and tan fox-hounds make up the Blencathra Fell Pack at Threlkeld

ANDREAS

Isle of Man
4 miles northwest of Ramsey

The sizable and strung-out village of Andreas lies in the midst of what islanders call the Northern Plain – the area of good farmland, and some fen country north of Ramsey. This was an area seized upon long ago by the land-hungry Vikings, and one of the few places on Man where it is possible to forget that one is on an island. There is no sea in sight; and to the south the majestic hills around Snaefell fill the horizon.

The village has some good modern buildings, including a large school; and some good old ones too, like the big white and red farmhouse, which has solid, outside stairs. There are some pleasant smaller houses in the rough, local stone that shows a subtle range of natural colours – soft, charcoal grey, dark green and biscuit, highlighted here and there with a profusion of pink roses tumbling over the top of a wall or roof.

The church is impressive; very large, with a separate tower that has a curiously jagged top. Apparently it had a spire once, which was removed in the 1940s lest it should endanger low-flying aircraft from the wartime airfields nearby. Andreas airfield has long gone, and the spire was never replaced, though the weather vane still lies, forlorn and broken, in the churchyard. This is surrounded by railings culminating in an unusual piece of cemetery furniture – the cast-iron framework of a lantern, complete with steps for the lamplighter to mount.

Inside, the church is a softly lit cavern, with pulpit, gallery and serried ranks of pews in pale wood. In a corner is an important, and well-displayed, collection of early Christian relics. There are Celtic and Viking crosses and other monuments which have been discovered in the parish, some from the excavated Keeil – early Celtic chapel – of Knock y Doonee. One stone depicts the legend of the Norse god Odin being devoured by Fenris-wolf at the ending of the world; the other side of the stone shows a figure carrying a cross and trampling a serpent, symbolising the triumph of Christianity over paganism.

Scenes from Scandinavian mythology appear on other stones too; one shows a hero, Sigurd, roasting the heart of the dragon he has slain. This is an incident in the Icelandic *Völsunga Saga*, and emphasises the island's close connection with the Norse world.

ANGLE TARN

Cumbria
2 miles southeast of Patterdale

Many people consider Angle Tarn the loveliest of all Lakeland tarns, for it has something more than the wildness, isolation and scenic grandeur common to most tarns. Its shoreline is deeply indented, which gives it a very individual beauty, and two small islands standing far out on its trout-filled waters set off the scenery around them perfectly.

Above the tarn rise the peaks named after it – Angletarn Pikes, a summit with two separate peaks, rocky outcrops with a peat bog in the depression between them. The views from the summit are not particularly extensive, but the surrounding countryside is glorious. This is part of the Martindale deer

FISHERMAN'S DELIGHT *Isolated Angle Tarn holds a treasure trove of trout for enthusiastic anglers.*

forest, and herds of red deer can sometimes be seen watering at the tarn. Fell ponies, almost as wild as the deer, also use the tarn as a watering-place, especially at daybreak and twilight.

There are several routes to the tarn, and one of the loveliest is from Dale Head Farm in Bannerdale. The path climbs diagonally past a stone ruin and a sheep-fold before crossing the screes between Heck Crag and Buck Crag. Then, quite suddenly, the tarn comes into view in all its glory. Other ascents start at Patterdale and Hartsop, beginning in wooded lowlands and climbing through boulder-strewn, bracken-covered fells to the craggy heights.

From the tarn a path runs half a mile southeast to Satura Crag, from where there is a splendid view back down Bannerdale.

ANNASIDE
Cumbria
2 miles southwest of Bootle

Because it is some 2 miles from the nearest main road, the long stretch of rock-strewn sand centred on Annaside does not attract the crowds, making the effort of reaching it well worth while on a sunny day.

To reach the shore, leave the main coast road and go through Bootle village. Turn left down a lane which leaves the road after about half a mile and follow it under the railway. The lane winds for just over a mile to a small private bridge over the River Annas, from where footpaths lead to the shore – a 4 mile strip of land sandwiched between the Lakeland hills and the sea, where hundreds of shallow rock pools form at low tide. A walk northwards along the shore leads to the tiny Selker Bay, where the Annas flows to the sea.

APPLEBY-IN-WESTMORLAND
Cumbria
13 miles southeast of Penrith

Appleby lies in the beautiful Eden Valley where it skirts the foot of the Pennines. The town is famous for its lively and colourful horse fair, held every June, and is a popular base for hill-climbing holidays. Boroughgate, its broad main street and market place, has dignified stone buildings of many periods, from Jacobean to Victorian. There are a number of fine Georgian houses, including the Gothic-style White House built in 1756; and on an island in the middle of the road is the late 16th-century Moot (Town) Hall.

The former capital of the old county of Westmorland, Appleby consists of two towns, one on either side of the wide River Eden. Old Appleby is set on a high sandstone bluff, overlooking a ford, and is the site of the 10th-century village of Bongate – where Danish bondsmen used to live. New Appleby, built in the early 12th century by the Normans, is low-lying and fits neatly into a loop of the river.

The town is overlooked by a Norman castle which was restored and much rebuilt in the 17th century. The Norman keep survives and is open to the public from May to September. So are the grounds, which are a Rare Breeds Survival Trust Centre. You can see rare breeds of domestic farm animals and some birds like waterfowl, pheasants, poultry and owls.

One of the castle's 17th-century restorers was the remarkable Lady Anne Clifford, daughter of George Clifford, 3rd Earl of Cumberland, an Elizabethan courtier and seafarer. Lady Anne married twice, to the Earl of Dorset and to the Earl of Pembroke and Montgomery. She was not happy with either of them and outlived them both. Inheriting the large Clifford estates in 1643, during the Civil War, she retired north where she defied Cromwell's express orders and re-built or restored all six of her castles – Appleby, Brough, Brougham, Skipton, Pendragon and Bardon Tower. She lived in each castle in turn, showing great generosity to her friends and dependents, even though she herself lived very simply.

At the Restoration of Charles II, Lady Anne was 70 years old. Nonetheless, she celebrated the event by having 'two stately high scaffolds ... hung with cloth of arras and gold' put up in Appleby. There, she and the mayor and aldermen 'proclaimed, prayed for, and drank the health of the king upon their knees, the aged countess seeming young again to grace the solemnity'.

Appleby owes much to Anne Clifford. She built St Anne's Hospital in Boroughgate in 1651. This stands around a peaceful little courtyard and still provides a home for 13 widows. She also restored St Michael's Church and the parish church of St Lawrence. On her death in 1676 Lady Anne was buried in St Lawrence's in a suitably impressive black marble tomb decorated with heraldic devices.

A stone wall plaque commemorates Richard Yates, a headmaster of Appleby Grammar School in the 18th century. He taught the two elder half-brothers of George Washington (1732–99), first president of the United States of America. George Washington himself was born and brought up in Westmoreland County, Virginia. In 1743 he was due to follow his half-brothers to school in Appleby – but the untimely death of his father kept him at home in America. The old grammar-school building, dating from the 17th century, has been demolished. The three tallest houses in Chapel Street now stand on the site. In 1887 the school was moved to a new site on the road to Penrith. The present school incorporates the headmaster's porch from the old building, dated 1671.

The town is an excellent centre for walking – by the Eden and along the streams of Hoff Beck to the west, Hilton Beck to the east and Trout Beck to the north.

Hilton, 4 miles east, reached by turning off the A66 at Coupland, has a picturesque approach across a common and past fields where horses graze. There is an army firing range near Murton, 1 mile north of Hilton, and walking on the fells is prohibited when a red flag is flying.

RARE ANIMAL *White Park cattle are amongst the unusual breeds on show in Appleby Castle grounds in summer.*

WOODED BANKS *Trees crowd the riverside where the Eden flows serenely through fields near Armathwaite.*

ARKHOLME
Lancashire
4 miles southwest of Kirkby Lonsdale

Beautifully preserved cottages and old stone houses with mullioned windows and colourful gardens line both sides of Arkholme's single street, leading down to the Lune. A prominent grassy dome near the water's edge was the site of a 12th-century fort.

A signposted walk through riverside meadows leads to Loyn Bridge and across the Lune to the village of Hornby and its castle.

ARMATHWAITE
Cumbria
9 miles southeast of Carlisle

The attractive village of Armathwaite is clustered round its bridge over the River Eden. The chapel of Christ and St Mary was restored in the 17th century by Richard Skelton, lord of the manor, after falling into ruin and being used as a cattle shed. His ancestor John Skelton, a poet favoured by Henry VIII, is thought to have been born in the riverside castle, where the surviving tower has been incorporated into a Georgian mansion. Nearby are walks through the Nunnery Woods beside the Eden.

ARNSIDE
Cumbria
13 miles west of Kirkby Lonsdale

Arnside was once a busy port and boat-building centre until more accessible places took its trade and left it to yachtsmen; now the village is an unspoilt little resort on the sandy estuary where the River Kent enters Morecambe Bay. It was created by the coming of the railways in the last century. A spectacular viaduct, one-third of a mile long, connecting it to the

Badgers are known to live in setts near Arnside

north bank of the Kent was built by the Furness Railway Company to complete the railway links between Lancashire and the large district of Furness.

Local limestone was used to build the houses that now rise steeply from the riverside promenade. Small hotels and guesthouses cater for nature lovers exploring the surrounding countryside's rich variety of plants and wildlife, including deer, red squirrels, foxes and badgers, and almost every sea-bird known in Britain. Anglers fish the estuary for eels and flounders in fast currents that can create a strong tidal bore.

A hill called Arnside Knott, a mile south of the village and owned by the National Trust, gives walkers magnificent views although it is only just over 500ft high. It also has rare flowers and fine trees. To the north are many of the rugged, broken peaks of Cumbria's highest mountains, with Shap Fell further round to the northeast. The panorama is completed by the great chain of the Yorkshire Pennines sweeping south towards the Bowland fells, the far-off Lancashire Plain and, just below, Morecambe Bay, noted for the speed with which its tide comes in.

Around Arnside Knott wooded hills, heathland and salt marshes give the district the justifiable distinction of being an official Area of Outstanding Natural Beauty – some of it given over to nature reserves.

HAVEN OF PEACE *An impressive viaduct stretches over the shallow Kent estuary near Arnside (overleaf).*

ASHNESS BRIDGE
Cumbria
On the way to Watendlath, 5 miles south of Keswick

A narrow road, dotted with cattle grids, leads off the B5289 to a tiny humpbacked bridge. A car park just beyond the bridge is the starting point of a short footpath through Ashness Wood to a cliff-edge vantage point known as the Surprise View. Breathtaking panoramas of Derwent Water and Skiddaw are framed by graceful birches and flat-topped pines. The surrounding woodlands are alive with the song of birds in the early morning.

ASKAM IN FURNESS
Cumbria
8 miles west of Ulverston

In the 19th century the little settlement of Askam evolved into a thriving, vibrant mining and iron smelting village. The rock beneath is rich in a high quality iron ore called haematite, and in the past the shoreline was red with run-off from the spoil heaps.

Steel Street and Furnace Place are terraced rows of houses whose names recall the past, but the signs of industry have almost gone, and a long hump of slag jutting out into the sea is now grassed over and supports an impressive growth of wild flowers, including centaury and felwort.

To the east, the sleepy hamlet of Ireleth has altered little with the passing of time except for some new housing. The view is magnificent from the parish church of St Peter over the Duddon estuary, which was beloved of the poet Wordsworth (1770–1850).

Clearly visible in the bay is the small Dunnerholme peninsula, where birdwatchers can observe pintail, wigeon, greylag geese and other wildfowl which winter in the area. A mile to the north of Ireleth an isolated group of white-painted cottages, delightfully and aptly named Paradise, overlooks the estuary.

Just beyond Paradise a left turn follows an attractive hedgerow bordering lush green fields and passing through a complex of ruined barns. The road then becomes a track which leads to the shore and passes the 16th-century Marsh Grange. This venerable old house was the birthplace of Margaret Askew, who left home at the tender age of 17 to marry Judge Fell of Swarthmoor, and after his death married the founder of the Quaker movement, George Fox.

ELEGANT DRAKE *Pintails may be seen near Askam in Furness during winter.*

ASKHAM
Cumbria
4 miles south of Penrith

As attractive as its setting, on the Lake District National Park's eastern rim, Askham lies below rolling fells that sweep gently down towards the River Lowther. The far bank – almost vertical, and thickly wooded – is crowned by the towers and turrets of Lowther Castle, a romantic ruin. From the top of the village there are memorable views over the rooftops to the castle and the distant majesty of the highest Pennine peaks. Tracks and footpaths run westwards over the hills to Pooley Bridge and Ullswater.

Askham is built around two greens, separated by a central crossroads and a tight little knot of buildings which includes the 19th-century village school. The lower green, where geese waddle beneath scattered

trees, is very broad and rises steeply on one side. Many of the cottages date from the 17th century, and one, near the Queen's Head, is an arts centre. The upper green is less spacious, but has impressive views.

The Church of St Peter, standing just above the Lowther a short distance from the village, was built in 1832 by Sir Robert Smirke, the architect of Lowther Castle, on the site of an earlier building. Parish records list vicars since the 12th century. Inside is a chapel dedicated to the Sandford family of Askham Hall, who settled in the village in 1373. The hall, set back behind a wall at the foot of the village, dates from that period, and is the village's oldest building. It was substantially altered at the end of the 17th century, and is not open to the public.

These are also several 17th-century cottages in the village and, nearby at Askham Fell, there is an ancient stone circle and traces of Bronze Age burials.

GREEN AND WHITE *Pretty whitewashed stone cottages decorate a slope near one of Askham's two greens.*

ASTLEY HALL

Lancashire
1 mile northwest of Chorley

Few of the great houses in the north of England can compare with Astley Hall in sheer elegance and beauty, both in the house itself and in its magnificent grounds – acres of green lawns sloping down to a wooded vale and the trickling River Chor.

So lovely is the landscape that it almost distracts the eye from the house. Nothing, however, could completely subdue that splendid façade with its two huge bays rising two storeys high, the tall mullioned windows, the delicate balusters of its rooftop parapet and the arched doorway flanked by two stone lions recumbent on lofty pillars. The oldest parts of the house date from the 16th century, but the imposing front dates from the second half of the 17th century.

Astley Hall has been the home of the Charnock, Brooke and Townley-Parker families. It is now owned by Chorley Borough Council and is open to the public. The rooms contain period furniture, pottery, tapestries and pictures. A shovelboard table in the Long Gallery probably dates from 1666. It is 23½ft long and has 20 legs. In the Cromwell Room is a massive four-poster bed in which the Lord Protector is said to have slept. There is also a glass case in the Great Hall which contains a pair of weathered boots, reputed to have been left behind by Cromwell because they were still wet after he arrived in heavy rain on the night of August 18, 1648.

HALL WITH A VIEW *Astley Hall's windows form a wall of glass looking out onto a lake where swans glide.*

AUGHTON
Lancashire
6 miles northeast of Lancaster

A narrow road lined by strawberry fields and potato fields leads to the pretty village of Aughton. The magnificent tower of St Michael's Church is square at the base, then octagonal, and is surmounted by an octagonal spire. The church rectors are listed from 1246 onwards. Much of the church's splendid medieval architecture remains, although extensive restoration was carried out in 1914. In the bell tower are some 14th-century wooden figures depicting the Stanleys, whose leader became Lord Derby and ruler of the Isle of Man; the three legs of Man are clearly shown on the carved shields carried by the figures.

Opposite the church and close to the Stanley Arms is Aughton Old Hall, not open to the public but easily visible from the road. There are the remains of a 15th-century peel tower in the front garden.

BALLASALLA
Isle of Man
2 miles northeast of Castletown

Historians of the turf might be interested to know, as they pass Ronaldsway Airport on the way out of Castletown, that the first Derby was run not at Epsom, but a couple of hundred yards to the east of them, in 1627. It was inaugurated by the Stanley Earls of Derby, who were also Lords of Man, to encourage local horse breeding. The course is masked by King William's College, a school founded in 1830. William IV donated his name, saying as he did so that he wished he could afford to donate cash as well.

Just north of the airport is the pretty village of Ballasalla. Its musical name derives from the Manx Gaelic words meaning 'village of the willow river', and the old part of the village with its picturesque church, grey cottages and stone barns presents an attractive cluster lining the road down to the ford across the Silver Burn river. About a quarter of a mile upstream is the cobbled Monks' Bridge, built in 1350.

A few hundred yards downstream is the ruined Abbey of St Mary of Rushen. The abbey was founded in 1134 when Olaf I, the fifth in the line of Viking kings who ruled the island from the 11th to the 13th centuries, invited the abbot and monks of Furness Abbey to build another abbey on this spot. Two other Viking kings of Man are buried here – Reginald II, slain in 1250, and Magnus, who died in 1262. The monks improved agriculture and livestock-breeding on the island, but their main achievement was the compilation of *The Chronicle of Man and the Isles*, the earliest written record of the history of the Isle of Man. It was completed in 1374, and is now in the British Library in London.

BALLAUGH
Isle of Man
7 miles west of Ramsey

Ballaugh Bridge is a favourite viewpoint for spectators on the northern part of the Tourist Trophy motorcycle course.

A turning north from the crossroads in the centre of Ballaugh leads, after 1½ miles, to a hamlet called The Cronk, which is notable for its old Church of St Mary de Ballaugh, which dates back to before the 13th century. From The Cronk a winding lane leads to a small car park beside the RAF radar site, on the edge of miles of sandy beach and lonely dunes.

BARBON
Cumbria
3 miles north of Kirkby Lonsdale

A stone sign by an old bridge that carries the A683 northwards towards Sedbergh proclaims 'Main road to Barbon'. It leads to a small village clustered around its church, pub and tiny post office.

The swift-flowing Barbon Beck tumbles straight off Crag Hill, the high fell that dominates the eastern skyline. Then the beck winds through the village and under the old packhorse bridge. Everywhere around the village, stone walls divide a patchwork of fields.

BARDSEA
Cumbria
3 miles south of Ulverston

Standing proudly on a green knoll with the sea lying below it like a silver platter, the pale limestone Church of the Holy Trinity dominates the tranquil village of Bardsea. Although the church dates only from the mid-19th century, its lych gate gives an impression of a more historic past.

The Ship Inn nearby needs no such disguise. Believed once to have been a barn, the Ship sums up the village, which began as a fishing hamlet surrounded by tiny farms and still retains an unhurried air. There is some modern housing, but many of the cottages are converted barns and their limestone walls reflect each and every golden ray of sunlight, and endow the whole village with a warm, bright appearance. A series of short but attractive well-signposted walks lead from the village centre and make Bardsea an ideal place from which to explore the district.

The path signposted Bardsea Green and Well House is a short stroll through timeless rural scenery. Sheep shelter under stone walls hanging with ferns, and wander through woodlands carpeted in season with primroses and bluebells.

Bardsea Green itself is a little group of houses with flower-rich grassland around it. Some depressions in the grassland speak of ancient quarrying for building stone, but one may well have been a cockpit.

A longer stroll leads from Bardsea to Conishead Priory, just under a mile to the north. Built on the site of an earlier leper colony, the priory was established by the Augustinian canons in the 12th century, under the patronage of a Norman nobleman, Gamel de Pennington. They provided a much-needed guide across the treacherous sands of Morecambe Bay to Lancaster. After the Dissolution, in 1539, a fine private mansion was built here, but the guide service continued – provided by the Duchy of Lancaster, as it still is. In 1821 a Colonel Braddyll demolished the earlier mansion and constructed the present ornate but impressive building. It has served since as a rest home for Durham miners and it is now owned by the Tibetan Buddhist Manjushri Institute as a retreat. It is occasionally open to the public. Set among trees in the fine gardens are the original lake and hermitage established by Gamel de Pennington.

About half a mile south of the village – or a 10 minute walk – is the Bardsea Country Park, which has a car park and picnic spaces, marked footpaths and information boards right on the edge of Morecambe Bay. The view across to Morecambe and Heysham is dominated by the bulk of the nuclear reactor at Heysham Power Station.

BARLEY

Lancashire
3 miles northwest of Nelson

The village of Barley, washed by Pendle Water, is the best starting point for the well-signposted and easiest route to Pendle Hill, whose breezy, flat summit is marked by a pile of stones called the Beacon. A visitor centre beside the stream in the village caters for picnickers and walkers, and has become a focal point for visitors to Pendle. Fell races are organised throughout the year, and there are guided walks in summer.

BASHALL EAVES

Lancashire
4 miles west of Clitheroe

The tiny hamlet of Bashall Eaves rests in a cosy fold of green fields, full of sheep and gleaming gold with buttercups in summer. The Red Pump Inn gets its name from the scarlet painted pump on its forecourt.

Beyond the hamlet, along a lane passing between neat hedgerows spangled with roses and honeysuckle, lies Browsholme Hall, home of the Parker family since the 14th century. The present hall dates from 1507, and is open on Saturday afternoons in June, July and August, and at other times by appointment.

The gardens are neat and colourful and the Tudor house, refaced in red sandstone in 1604, has fine furniture, china and some stained glass removed from Whalley Abbey after its dissolution. There is also a gauge once used for measuring dogs to ensure that large animals were not kept by unauthorised owners in a royal forest area where the monarch hunted deer.

BASSENTHWAITE

Cumbria
6 miles north of Keswick

The view from Bassenthwaite village is enchanting, with the fringing hills framing but never overwhelming Bassenthwaite Lake at their feet, where, thanks to a ban on motorboats, silence reigns. The area around once had Roman and Norse settlements. 'Thwaite' is an old Scandinavian word meaning 'clearing'.

Bassenthwaite Lake itself lies 2 miles south of the village. It has the distinction of being the only 'lake' in the Lake District, since all the others are called meres or waters. It is also the northernmost of the lakes and the fourth largest, measuring 4 miles long and half a mile wide. Its shallow waters are the home of the vendace, a white fish found only here and in Derwent Water, which lies to the south.

SWORD AND FISH
Bassenthwaite is said to be the setting described by Lord Tennyson in his Idylls of the King *as the lake into which Sir Bedevere hurled King Arthur's mighty sword Excalibur. True or not, the vendace, a rare white fish, lives here.*

BAYCLIFF
Cumbria
4 miles south of Ulverston

The village of Baycliff has no need to fear the sea, being set at the summit of the low banks which border the west side of Morecambe Bay. Half a mile to the north the attractive public woodlands of Sea Wood lie across the main coast road. Birkrigg Common, 1½ miles northwest of Baycliff, has prehistoric stone circles.

In the nearby village of Great Urswick, on the edge of Urswick Tarn, the 13th-century Church of St Mary contains crosses made by the Angles and Vikings as well as stained-glass windows from Furness Abbey.

BEACON COUNTRY PARK
Lancashire
About 1 mile northeast of Skelmersdale

Straddling a ridge overlooking the fertile South Lancashire Plain, the 304 acre Beacon Country Park is patchworked by grassy meadows sheltered by belts of old oak and newly planted conifers. The visitor centre is the starting point of trails which twist and turn through trees to picnic sites overlooking a golf course.

A mile beyond the centre is the start of a walk to the summit of Ashurst's Beacon. The well-trodden path begins from a large car park just past the Beacon inn. In Tudor times Ashurst's Beacon formed part of an Armada early warning system for Lancashire, stretching from Everton Brow to Lancaster Castle.

From the summit, Blackpool Tower and the Lakeland Hills can be seen to the north of the Mersey, the Welsh mountains to the southwest, the Peaks of Derbyshire to the southeast and the Lancashire Pennines to the northeast.

BEACON FELL
Lancashire
8 miles north of Preston

In the days when national victories or approaching dangers were proclaimed by lighting fires on hilltops, Beacon Fell was an important link in the chain. Its broad dome is clear of vegetation and commands far, all-round views. Indeed, a view indicator on the summit optimistically points to the Welsh mountains some 80 miles away, but the chance of actually seeing them is rare; 60in of rain falls annually on the fell.

For all its impressive views, Beacon Fell is only 873ft high and it is easily climbed. It consists of Bowland shale capped with gritstone, and the line where the two rocks meet is the birthplace of a myriad springs. One of them feeds the pond by the Fell House car park, from which a delightful walk leads around the thickly wooded hillsides. The trees, mainly Sitka spruce, are crowded with the roosts of thousands of starlings. During spring and summer the birds disperse to nest – some as far away as Russia – before returning to their roosts in early autumn. Tawny owls also hunt the forest. In Bull Coppice, southwest of the summit, 5ft high stumps have been left during thinning operations to provide night perches for the birds.

Among the predominant spruces there are stands of sycamore, rowan, wild cherry, oak, alder and beech. The open summit is dressed with purple moor-grass – at its colourful best in July and August – and with ling, bell heather, bilberry, crowberry and mat-grass.

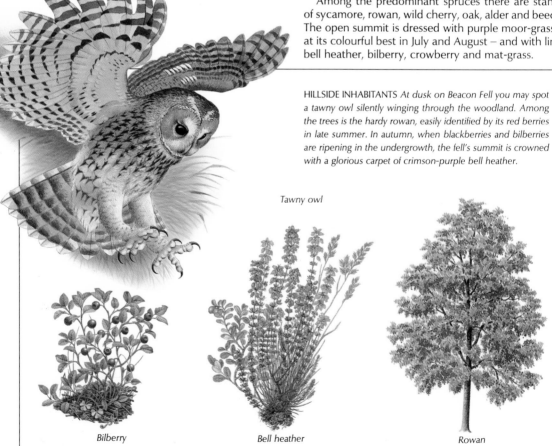

HILLSIDE INHABITANTS *At dusk on Beacon Fell you may spot a tawny owl silently winging through the woodland. Among the trees is the hardy rowan, easily identified by its red berries in late summer. In autumn, when blackberries and bilberries are ripening in the undergrowth, the fell's summit is crowned with a glorious carpet of crimson-purple bell heather.*

Tawny owl

Bilberry

Bell heather

Rowan

BEETHAM

Cumbria
6 miles north of Carnforth

An almost 19th-century atmosphere has returned to Beetham since the M6 motorway drew away the traffic which used to roar along its main street. It has the neat, carefully planned air of an 'estate' village, as it slopes gently up from the banks of the River Bela.

Ashton House, large and elegant, marks the western edge of the village and contrasts with the neat, greystone cottages and cobbled forecourts found elsewhere. The Wheatsheaf Hotel, its bays faced with mock-Tudor timbers, stands next to a combined post office and shop. The post office has a split-level door, studded with iron bolts, which is flanked by Gothic windows, while the first floor has a loading bay complete with a little drawbridge.

The church is much older. Coins dating from Edward the Confessor's reign were found at the base of a pillar during restoration work in the 19th century, although most of the present structure is 12th century. The north wall is unusual in having a stained-glass window in which St Oswald and St Alban flank Charles I, who is described as a martyr. In earlier days, worshippers would walk several miles to the church, many crossing Beetham Fell by way of the 'Fairy Steps' cut into the limestone ridge above the village.

Half a mile to the south, the ruins of Beetham Hall, once a semi-fortified house, can be seen among modern farm buildings.

In the opposite direction, a signposted walk along the river behind the present mill leads to the restored water-driven Heron corn mill, sometimes open to the public. Four pairs of millstones grace the table in the middle of the entrance floor. Grain was stored in sacks on the top floor and fed to hoppers above the millstones. There is also a kiln, with a floor of perforated tiles over a small smokeless fire. Oats were dried there before being crushed.

BLACK AND WHITE *Beetham's old world atmosphere is helped by modern paintwork on The Wheatsheaf Hotel.*

BEWCASTLE

Cumbria

9 miles north of Brampton

The historic village of Bewcastle lies near the site of a Roman fort which was an outpost of Hadrian's Wall. The site covers 6 acres. Four ruined peel towers stand within about 2 miles of the village – at Crew Castle, Woodhead, High Grains and Low Grains.

Bewcastle Cross, in the St Cuthbert's churchyard, is a 1300-year-old cross with Runic inscriptions. The head of the cross is missing, but the surviving shaft is 14ft 6in high. The runes record a dedication to Alcfrith, son of Oswi the Northumbrian king, and the cross is carved with birds, beasts and interlaced patterns.

BIRDOSWALD FORT

Cumbria

1 mile west of Gilsland

After climbing steeply, the road from Lanercost runs right alongside Hadrian's Wall and has fine views southwards over the Irthing Valley. A parking area too small for coaches makes Birdoswald Fort one of the wall's quieter showplaces.

Only a little imagination is needed to visualise Roman soldiers patrolling the walls and guarding the well-preserved eastern gateway. Parts of the walls and towers can also be seen.

Birdoswald – originally known as Camboglanna – was built to guard the Roman bridge carrying the wall over the river at Willowford nearby. It was the largest fortress in the immediate vicinity of Hadrian's wall.

Surrounded by fields, high above the Irthing, the fort covers 5 acres, and was the base for either 1000 foot soldiers or 500 mounted troops. Stones originally quarried, carved and carted by the Romans were used to build the farmhouse which stands by the car park.

BLACK COMBE

Cumbria

2 miles north of Whicham

A soft, sweetly scented cushion of heather covers the 1968ft summit of Black Combe, and on a clear summer day it is possible to lie there for hours admiring the views all around.

This is a mountain made for views, for it stands alone in the extreme southwestern tip of the Lake District, and so commands both land and sea. Snowdon is visible in the far south; the Isle of Man can be seen across the Irish Sea; and to the north the Southern Uplands of Scotland shimmer beyond the Solway Firth. Inland the view swings from the Forest of Bowland right round to the heights of Skiddaw in the distant northeast, with all the majestic summits of Scafell Pikes 15 miles away in front of them. The only sound is the sighing and buffeting of the wind sweeping in from the sea. Birds are the only company – perhaps a kestrel hovering far below in the sun, red grouse starting from the heather or meadow pipits on flickering wings darting from cover to cover.

This most undramatic of mountains has attracted more than its share of folklore, possibly because of the Swinside stone circle on its northeastern flank. The Bronze Age circle, which is 90ft in diameter, is known locally as Sunken Kirk and was once believed to be a supernatural spot. According to legend, Black Combe bees wake from their winter sleep to hum in unison at midnight on Christmas Eve, and cattle kneel in adoration. Tradition also has it that the mountain is possessed by a much less Christian spirit by the name of Hob Thross or Hob Thrust, 'a body all over rough'. People believed he could be summoned to do their bidding in the early hours – so long as he was rewarded with a dish of thick porridge with butter in it.

The easiest ascent of Black Combe is from the little church at Whicham, about a mile from the sea. A path between the church and the school leads to a narrow lane lined with brambles and wild roses, foxgloves and harebells. Beyond a white farmhouse, a track leads over a stile and up a valley on the right. The going is always easy; and after about 2 miles of leisurely zigzagging the path arrives at the summit.

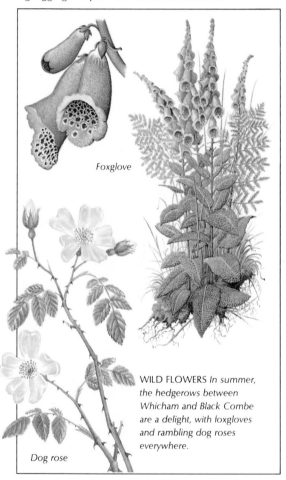

Foxglove

WILD FLOWERS *In summer, the hedgerows between Whicham and Black Combe are a delight, with foxgloves and rambling dog roses everywhere.*

Dog rose

BLACKPOOL

Lancashire

17 miles west of Preston

Brash and cheerful, Blackpool stretches in a long, multicoloured ribbon by the sea, punctuated by three piers and dominated by the steel finger of the Tower. Yet like many other British holiday resorts, Blackpool began as a small and undistinguished fishing village. In 1840 the seafront consisted of a single row of houses; but with the coming of the railway in 1846, the

LANCASHIRE LANDMARK *For almost 100 years Blackpool Tower, the town's best-loved institution, has dominated the coast.*

opening of Central Station and the North Pier in 1863 and the Winter Gardens in 1876, the town's future was established. The number of visitors increased from 3 million at the beginning of the present century to more than 8 million during the 1960s. Today it is estimated that around 6 million different people visit Blackpool each year; but because many people return time and again, the total is about 16 million a year.

Present-day Blackpool is probably best known for its Tower, a landmark which can be seen from Cumbria in the north to the hills of North Wales to the southwest. Built in 1894, it was for many years the highest building in Britain; the 518ft ascent gives a breathtaking view of Blackpool and the surrounding coast, and the Tower also houses a circus, a ballroom, an aquarium and an Educational Heritage Exhibition, as well as bars and restaurants.

Below the Tower is the stretch known as the Golden Mile — in fact more like a quarter of a mile in length. Freak-shows and fortune-tellers have been replaced by amusement centres, discos, bars, restaurants and a waxworks. Each of the three piers has its own theatre, providing live entertainment during the season. The 40 acre Pleasure Beach amusement park offers rides such as the first 360 degree 'loop the loop' roller-coaster in Britain, and tram services run the length of the 7 mile promenade and on into Fleetwood, turning inland to avoid breaks in the promenade. It is possible to walk the whole length of the seafront between Fleetwood in the north and Squires Gate in the south. During the autumn evenings, from September to late October, the whole front is ablaze with more than 375,000 bulbs, laser beams, animated displays and tableaux.

Other attractions include a Zoo Park, ice and roller-skating rinks, a boating lake, a model village and golf courses. On the beach there are donkey rides, boat trips and Punch and Judy shows.

BLACKSTONE EDGE

Greater Manchester
2 miles east of Littleborough

Running along the ridge of Blackstone Edge, on the borders of Greater Manchester and West Yorkshire, is perhaps the most remarkable piece of paved Roman road in the country. It formed a part of the road from the fort at Manchester (Mancunium) to that of Ilkley (Olicana) and, as it climbs on to the crest of the Pennines, the paved way, some 16ft wide, is held in position in the underlying peaty deposits by deeply set kerbs. The oddest feature is the central paved channel in the roadway. The most likely explanation is that it held turf which gave horses a good foothold.

BOLTON-BY-BOWLAND

Lancashire
6 miles northeast of Clitheroe

There are two village greens at Bolton. The smaller, below the church, has the stump of a 13th-century market cross and stocks posts at its centre. It is flanked by the Coach and Horses Inn, and by Rose Cottage — a substantial house built in 1835. Two rows of white-washed cottages run down from the green. One cottage has outside steps leading straight to the upper floor, another has a mounting block for horse riders.

The other green is screened by trees, and lies above

STONE CHARM *Attractive stone cottages are a pleasant feature of the village of Bolton-by-Bowland.*

the 13th-century Church of St Peter and St Paul. A church existed at Bolton in 1190, but the present church was being constructed by Sir Ralph Pudsay when, after the Battle of Hexham on May 15, 1464, Henry VI was given refuge at the now-vanished Bolton Hall. The king took an interest in the church, and is said to have helped design the high tower, which is more typical of churches in Somerset than of those in the North. The tomb of Sir Ralph is in the church, and his three wives and 25 children are also commemorated. Near the feet of the first wife are the Roman characters VI, denoting the number of children she bore. The number under the second wife is II, and under the third an impressive XVII. The boys appear depicted as soldiers or priests and the girls dressed in the costume of the period.

One rector of the church, Richard Dawson, was appointed in 1773 and still in office 53 years later. He seems to have been responsible for installing the church's three-decker pulpit. In the 18th century a parish clerk occupied the bottom deck and assisted the parson in the conduct of the service.

The old church school of 1874 is at the top end of the green, and halfway down the side is the former Court House, with its weather vane in the shape of a fox. The court used to decide rights of dwelling in the Forest of Bowland.

A signposted footpath follows the meanders of Tosside Beck to its junction with the Ribble, and about 2 miles farther on to the historic village of Sawley. The village is overlooked by the ruins of Salley Abbey, a Cistercian house raised in 1147 and ruined in 1536, during the Dissolution of the Monasteries. Many of its stones have been plundered over the centuries and now form part of the walls of local buildings.

BOLTON-LE-SANDS
Lancashire
4 miles north of Lancaster

The whitewashed 17th and 18th-century cottages of Bolton-le-Sands lie behind a busy shopping street overlooking a delightful stretch of the Lancaster Canal. The Packet Boat Hotel, whose name recalls an earlier means of transport, now caters for the many pleasure boats moored nearby.

At the other end of the village the great Perpendicular tower of the parish church of St Michael has been a notable landmark used by generations of seafarers for hundreds of years.

A lane leads over the railway to a picnic area by Morecambe Bay, with fine views of the Kent estuary.

SAND AND SOLITUDE *At low tide, Bolton-le-Sands is perfect for an early morning walk* (overleaf).

BOOT

Cumbria
7 miles northeast of Ravenglass

A pretty white stone oasis in the midst of the dark crags, Boot has two hotels, a miniature art gallery and some old cottages bristling with the largest and latest TV aerials – necessary with the mountains crowding all round. A lane leads down to St Catherine's Church by the chattering Esk river.

From the pub, a path leads to Whillan Beck and to Eskdale Watermill, which has ground corn since the 1570s at least. It is still in working order, although no grinding is done today, and during the summer months puts on an exhibition of milling and of the agricultural life of the district. The present gearing and wheels were probably installed in the 18th century, but the mill is significant for its unusual layout, having two water wheels, each driving directly a pair of millstones.

For a large part of its existence, however, Boot was a mining and quarrying village, producing copper, iron and granite. These called into being the railway that is now the Ravenglass and Eskdale Railway.

Just north of Boot, accessible only by bridlepath, are five stone circles, perched on Eskdale Moor. Each was built about 1500 BC, containing one or more stone cairns. Eskdale Circle has five cairns, each of which covered the cremated remains of a Bronze Age Briton.

About $2\frac{1}{2}$ miles west of Boot is the pretty village of Eskdale Green. Pine trees and rhododendrons flank the road, and there is fine walking alongside the River Esk.

MINIATURE RAILWAY *Immaculate little steam trains pull the passenger coaches of the Ravenglass and Eskdale Railway through glorious Cumbrian scenery on a narrow-gauge track only 15in wide. One of the locomotives, known as Ratty, dates from 1894. From Dalegarth, the inland terminus of the line, a nature trail leads through a gorge to the magnificent Stanley Force waterfall.*

BORROWDALE

Cumbria
5 mile valley between Derwent Water and Seathwaite

Fine walks lead from the steep-sided valley which runs south from Derwent Water to the village of Seathwaite. Sour Milk Gill waterfall pours down the hillside west of Seathwaite to the Slabs, used by climbers as practice slopes. The path southwards leads to the 1600ft Sty Head Pass, where footpaths from Borrowdale, Wasdale, Eskdale and Great Langdale meet.

The route passes the 2949ft Great Gable, one of the highest and best-known mountains of the area, and continues to the hamlet of Wasdale Head. This is a richly satisfying walk, though a challenge in rain.

Near Rosthwaite, $2\frac{1}{2}$ miles northeast of Seathwaite, is the Bowder Stone, a rock weighing almost 2000 tons that has fallen from the crags and appears to be delicately balanced on one edge. A ladder can be climbed to the top. There are splendid walks along the banks of the River Derwent, whose lovely green pools mirror birch trees. Beside the river is the 900ft Castle Crag, the summit of which – reached by a fairly easy walk – provides a superb view of Derwent Water.

BORWICK

Lancashire
2 miles northeast of Carnforth

The small, leafy hamlet of Borwick, is dominated by its magnificent Tudor hall. The earliest building is the partly ivy-clad, 14th-century defensive peel tower which occupies four storeys. The delightful baronial

hall was built in the late 16th century after peace had been made between England and Scotland and the need for a defensive house had passed.

The 9 acres of grounds include woodlands and formal gardens. Borwick Hall is now a residential training centre, but it is open to the public for three weeks in mid-summer.

BOWNESS-ON-SOLWAY

Cumbria
4 miles north of Kirkbride

Sandstone cottages line the narrow streets of Bowness-on-Solway, where Roman soldiers guarded the western end of Hadrian's Wall until about AD 400, when the legions abandoned Britain. The fortress encouraged a civilian settlement to develop along what is now the road to Kirkbride. Bowness-on-Solway was the end of the wall which, at this point, was only a turf rampart but forts and towers ran down the coast for another 40 miles.

Today little remains in Bowness as a reminder of the great barrier, but one link with a later episode in Bowness's violent past has survived. Stealing church bells was a popular activity among the raiders who crossed the Solway in the 17th century, and one party of Scots who stole the bells of St Michael's Church managed to get halfway back across the estuary before they were overtaken and had to abandon them. The bells now in the church porch at Bowness were seized from villages on the other side of the Solway in retaliation. The narrow, winding streets of Bowness today slumber in rural peace.

MAJESTIC FELLS *Clumps of woodland relieve the stark scree slopes above this Borrowdale farm.*

Half a mile west of the village, the coast road crosses a bridge by a tree-tangled, stone-faced embankment. It is all that remains of a huge railway viaduct, opened in 1869, which crossed the Solway Firth to Scotland.

Storm-driven ice up to 10ft thick caused much damage during the exceptionally severe winter of 1875, but the line remained open until 1924. Ten years later the viaduct was demolished.

BOWSCALE TARN

Cumbria
3 miles northwest of Mungrisdale

The surface of Bowscale Tarn is like a black mirror reflecting the bleak, scree-laden cliffs of Tarn Crags. It seems to concentrate in one place all the loneliness of the landscapes around it. Only the occasional croak of a carrion crow, echoing off the rocks, disturbs the deep quiet.

It was this silent and empty wilderness, known as 'Back o' Skidda', that often echoed to the clamour that 'waked men from their beds and the fox from his lair in the morning', as John Peel partook of his favourite pastime. Born at Caldbeck in 1776, John Peel spent most of his 78 years hunting the fox on foot or pony – heedless of the demands of his 13 children.

The climb to the tarn starts low down in the valley of the River Caldew and leads up through rough moorland to the great dam of Ice Age litter which forms a barrier, holding back the tarn's dark waters.

The path begins just beyond a row of cottages where the road turns sharply through the hamlet of Bowscale. There a gate leads on to the open fellside and the path climbs steeply to the west for a few yards before levelling out.

Across the valley, the slopes of Carrock Fell sweep down in a cascade of scree, and at the foot of the scree a road runs up to the valley head where a mine producing wolfram – tungsten ore – was working until 1985. Geologically the fell is exceptionally complex, and 23 minerals have been found there.

The path crosses Drycombe Beck, then winds round the next bluff before climbing diagonally up the moraine dam to Bowscale Tarn. The land is littered with boulders, many of them scratched or smoothed by the glacier which deposited them at the end of the last Ice Age. Everywhere Skiddaw Slate breaks through, the rock from which the whole of this area is formed. And then, over the brow of the dam, lies the tarn – black, menacing and seemingly devoid of life.

BRAITHWAITE

Cumbria
About 2 miles west of Keswick

Just beyond the Royal Oak a road to the left sign-posted 'Coledale' offers splendid views over the village of Braithwaite, above which looms the frowning 2593ft mass of Grisedale Pike. Well-marked walks lead 6 miles over the fells to Crummock Water and Buttermere.

BRAMHALL

Greater Manchester
3 miles south of Stockport

Started in the 14th century and extended in the 1590s, Bramall Hall is one of the finest timber-framed 'magpie' houses in England.

There is a splendid spiral staircase leading to the Elizabethan drawing room, and among the original furnishings are a 16ft long high table held together by wooden pegs, a rare Flemish travelling bed, a Jacobean four-poster and several fine portraits dating back to the late 16th century.

A tapestry in the master bedroom is the work of Dame Dorothy Davenport – one of the owners in the 1590s. It took her 36 years to complete. The house was restored in the 1880s and is usually open to the public.

BRAMPTON

Cumbria
9 miles northeast of Carlisle

Wooded hills on the western flank of the Pennines shelter this small, ancient town where slate-roofed buildings of mellow brick and sandstone look down on cobbled streets. Brampton's most eye-catching feature is the octagonal Moot Hall, built by Lord Carlisle in 1817, with a jaunty clock tower-cum-belfry, external staircases and iron stocks smoothed by the legs of countless petty criminals. Now an information centre, it stands in Market Place, where Wednesday's stalls and chatting, bargain-hunting shoppers are reminders that markets have been held there ever since Henry III granted the town's first charter in 1252.

Around the corner, in High Cross Street, a shoe shop now occupies the house that was Bonnie Prince Charlie's headquarters before he and his Jacobite army marched southwards in November 1745. It was there that the Mayor of Carlisle handed over the keys to the city after its garrison surrendered to the rebels.

The church was built in 1874 by the Earl of Carlisle: the ruins of the original Norman church, built on the site of a Roman fort, are a mile west. A quarry near the River Gelt, about 2 miles southwest, still bears inscriptions scratched by Roman workmen.

The route out of Brampton passes The Mote, a steep hill where shaded footpaths explore the site of a long-vanished medieval castle.

BRIGFLATTS

Cumbria
1 mile west of Sedbergh

Close to the banks of the River Rawthey in the tiny hamlet of Brigflatts is the second oldest Friends' Meeting House in England. The oldest, built in 1670, is in Hertford. The plain stone building, surrounded by a small garden, was built in 1675 by the early followers of George Fox, founder of the Society of Friends – the Quakers – who came to the district to preach their gospel in the mid-17th century.

Inside the meeting house the simple oak panelling and benches create an atmosphere of enduring peace which must have comforted those who, because of persecution, had been forced to worship secretly in farm buildings or on the nearby fells. The heavily studded door is always open to visitors.

BRINDLE

Lancashire
6 miles southwest of Blackburn

Surrounded by a patchwork of rolling farmland, Brindle remains as peaceful today as it has been through many centuries. To the west the land falls away to reveal the Lancashire Plain, and to the east the horizon is framed by high Pennine moorland.

It is hard to believe that the village, clustered around its old parish church of St James, is but a few miles from several industrial towns. Even a small development of modern homes, hardly in keeping with the rest of the village's sturdy gritstone cottages, scarcely intrudes upon its quiet rural charm.

There has been a church here for at least 800 years, and the present one dates back to the 16th century – a fine stone building enhanced by magnificent stained-glass windows. Two of its six bells are as old as the building itself and, until recently, the locally made tower clock had kept time for the villagers for almost 300 years. Now the original clock is on loan to the Liverpool City Museum and a new clock with a smart white dial looks down from Brindle's church tower. The church is also renowned for its collection of fonts, having no fewer than five.

Next to the church is the whitewashed Cavendish Arms pub – once the manor house. In the 16th century, Sir Thomas Gerard, in whose patronage the church lay, incurred the anger of Elizabeth I for supporting the Roman Catholic Mary, Queen of Scots. To help pay the fine to secure his release from the Tower of London, the manor of Brindle – with suitable exaggeration as to its size and value – was sold to William Cavendish, an ancestor of the Dukes of Devonshire, and the Cavendish family remained associated with the village until the present century.

Farther along the main street an old pound where stray cattle were once held is now marked as a site of interest – evidence of Brindle's agricultural past.

These days, the village has an air of quiet prosperity, but a reminder of harder times can be found at the site of the old workhouse a mile or so along the descriptively named Top o'th Hill Lane. A master of the workhouse and some who were forced to seek its shelter lie buried in the village graveyard.

BROUGH
Cumbria
8 miles southeast of Appleby-in-Westmorland

Brough Castle, frowning over the village from a beetle brow, once belonged to a bloodstained baron fittingly known as The Butcher. He was John, 9th Baron Clifford (1435–61), known also as Bloody Clifford, an unyielding Lancastrian and ruthless persecutor of Yorkists in the Wars of the Roses. He was killed – an arrow through

CASTLE REMAINS *A cow peacefully patrols ruined Brough Castle, which survives on the site of a Roman fort.*

his throat, it is said – just before the Battle of Towton, near Tadcaster, and his castle was taken by the Yorkist Warwick the Kingmaker. But Bloody Clifford lives still, savage as ever, in Shakespeare's *Henry VI*.

His son Henry, 'The Shepherd Lord', eventually got back the castle and large family estates and Brough Castle became his favourite home. Sadly, though, it was burnt down two years before his death in 1523. It remained a ruin for 138 years until his descendant Lady Anne Clifford repaired it. But the castle was destroyed by another fire in 1666.

Today, visitors with a head for heights can climb the battlements and enjoy glorious views across the Vale of Eden and the Stainmoor Gap to the craggy escarpments of the Northern Pennines. The ruin stands where the Romans built a fort, Verterae, which they garrisoned for 300 years. The Brough Stone, now in the Fitzwilliam Museum, Cambridge, is a sad memorial to a 16-year-old Roman soldier, and practically all that remains of Verterae – the stones of the fort were used by William Rufus to build the castle soon after 1092. The foundations of Rufus's keep and parts of the walled bailey have survived. The fine round tower was built by Anne Clifford.

Brough (pronounced 'Bruff') is in two parts, separated by the main Barnard Castle to Appleby road. Beneath the castle is Church Brough, with the medieval St Michael's Church, whose masonry contains stones from the Roman Fort, more stone houses and a tree-shaded green that has a maypole where a market cross once stood. Another cross now tops a clock tower built in 1911 in the other part of the village, which is called Market Brough.

Market Brough grew around a 14th-century bridge over Swindale Beck, at the junction with a major road from Kendal. A charter for a weekly market and annual fair was granted in 1331, and a fair is still held on September 30, each year. Great prosperity came in the 18th and 19th centuries, with up to 60 stagecoaches a day halting at the village, on their way from London to Carlisle and on to Glasgow, or from York to Lancaster. The coaches, passengers, coachmen and horses had their needs attended to by no fewer than 17 inns at Brough and nearby Stainmoor. They employed a small army of stableboys and ostlers, housekeepers and cooks, serving girls and tapsters – not to

MOUNTAIN MARKET *Steep streets lined with grey houses spring to life on market day in Broughton in Furness.*

mention smiths, wheelwrights and harness-repairers.

Only two or three inns remain, among them the Castle Hotel at Market Brough, where the stables and outbuildings have survived. However, many of the others have been put to different uses – the White Swan, built in 1770, is now the post office.

BROUGHTON IN FURNESS
Cumbria
8 miles northwest of Ulverston

The quiet of this town overlooking the Duddon estuary is shattered on Tuesday – market day. This is a particularly busy day at summer's end, when loud bleating and floating clouds of straw herald the arrival of sheep brought down off the fells to be auctioned.

At any time, Broughton is a place to test one's fitness. It is built on slopes and stairs. Its largest shop is the Mountain Centre, where a notice exhorts people to canoe, sail, cycle, walk and climb. Equipment for all these pursuits – including no fewer than 12 different kinds of canoe – is on sale.

The square, overhung by chestnut trees, has a set of stocks in full working order, a slate table on which fish were once displayed for sale, and a graceful obelisk commemorating the Golden Jubilee of George III in 1810. A yellow Georgian building with a small belfry houses the Jack Hadwin collection of vintage motorcycles.

The heart of the town is a 14th-century peel tower built by the Broughton family, who held the manor from Saxon times until the 1480s. An 18th-century house has been built around it – not open to the public but visible from footpaths in the grounds. The Church of St Mary Magdalene, dating partly from Norman times, has been much restored.

Only minutes from the scene is the road to Ulpha and the high passes. Four miles north, the steep S-bend, turning off northwest at the Traveller's Rest Inn, leads to a wonderful high mountain plateau with walks over Birker Fell and Ulpha Fell and views northwards of the highest Lakeland peak, Scafell Pike.

Up and away on two mountain passes

Among high Lakeland crags is Hardknott Pass, with its spectacular view of a vast Roman fort. Below Wrynose Pass, Coniston offers its secluded beauty.

Shiny conkers drop from horse chestnut trees to the floor of Grizedale Forest in the autumn months

Roe deer, with distinctive white rumps, live wild in Cumbrian forests

Roman remains at Hardknott Castle

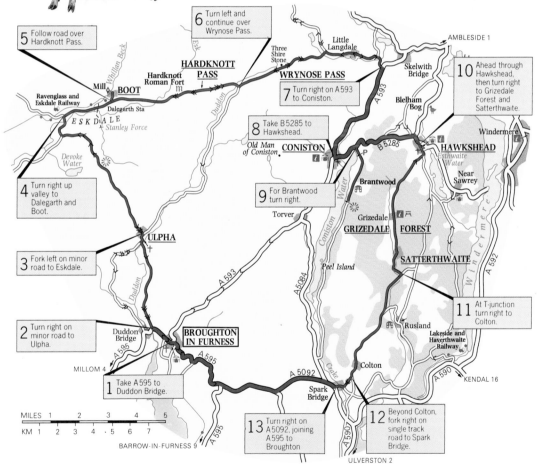

5 Follow road over Hardknott Pass.

6 Turn left and continue over Wrynose Pass.

10 Ahead through Hawkshead, then turn right to Grizedale Forest and Satterthwaite.

7 Turn right on A593 to Coniston.

8 Take B5285 to Hawkshead.

4 Turn right up valley to Dalegarth and Boot.

9 For Brantwood turn right.

3 Fork left on minor road to Eskdale.

11 At T-junction turn right to Colton.

2 Turn right on minor road to Ulpha.

1 Take A595 to Duddon Bridge.

13 Turn right on A5092, joining A595 to Broughton

12 Beyond Colton, fork right on single track road to Spark Bridge.

AMBLESIDE 1

HARDKNOTT PASS

Hardknott Roman Fort

WRYNOSE PASS

Three Shire Stone

Little Langdale

Skelwith Bridge

Blelham Bog

Windermere

BOOT
Mill

Ravenglass and Eskdale Railway

Dalegarth Sta

ESKDALE

Stanley Force

Devoke Water

Old Man of Coniston CONISTON

HAWKSHEAD

Esthwaite Water

Near Sawrey

Brantwood

Grizedale

GRIZEDALE FOREST

SATTERTHWAITE

ULPHA

Torver

Coniston Water

Peel Island

Duddon Bridge

BROUGHTON IN FURNESS

Rusland

Lakeside and Haverthwaite Railway

MILLOM 4

Colton

Windermere

KENDAL 16

Spark Bridge

BARROW-IN-FURNESS 9

ULVERSTON 2

MILES 1 2 3 4 5

KM 1 2 3 4 5 6 7

Coniston Water lies hidden behind trees and fields

The Old Man of Coniston looms above Coniston village

BURGH BY SANDS

Cumbria
5 miles northwest of Carlisle

A lofty sandstone pillar, rising in splendid isolation from the sheep-grazed saltings of Burgh Marsh, marks the spot where Edward I, 'Hammer of the Scots', died in 1307. The pillar is signposted from the village centre.

Edward I died, aged 68, as he was marching northwards to do battle with an army raised by Robert Bruce. Sickness had prevented him covering more than 2 miles a day since leaving Carlisle. St Michael's Church, where the dead king was taken, still watches over Burgh by Sands, a peaceful little village of warm sandstone and old weathered brickwork, built over the site of a Roman fort. St Michael's is built with stones from the Roman defences, and stands in the middle of the site. It, too, had a defensive role to play, as a refuge from Scottish raiders, and the 14th-century tower has no outside doorway. The only entrance is through a heavily bolted iron gate from the nave while the tower windows are small slits.

Near the church, the thatched roof of 17th-century Lamonby Farm catches the eye; the farm may be visited on application to the owner.

West of Burgh – pronounced 'Bruff' – cattle wander across a long, straight road which is liable to tidal flooding. It follows the line of the old Roman vallum, the southern ditch of Hadrian's Wall. Springy turf and fine views across the Solway Firth make this a delightful place for strolls and picnics, but walkers must be careful when exploring the sandbanks. As a character in Sir Walter Scott's *Redgauntlet* was warned, the tide races in faster than a galloping horse.

BURNMOOR TARN

Cumbria
2 miles north of Boot

From Eskdale Green to Boot is only a couple of miles along the flat road beside the River Esk; but a delightful 6 mile valley walk connects the two villages, climbing up Miterdale from Eskdale Green, turning round the windswept waters of Burnmoor Tarn, and dropping down again to Boot beside the Whillan Beck.

The first part of the walk northeast up Miterdale leads through Forestry Commission plantations, with many broad-leaved trees mixed in with the usual conifers, a wide variety of wayside and woodland flowers, and the River Mite always close at hand. After about a mile, at Low Place, the forest ends and a footbridge leads across the river. On the east side of the valley the fell is bare and stony, with some prehistoric stone circles and cairns up on Low Longrigg. There are impressive views northwards of the backs of Illgill Head and Whin Rigg, the fells which, on their northwest sides, form Wast Water's Screes.

The path climbs steadily northeast towards the isolated depression between Tongue Moor and Eskdale Moor, passing a lovely small amphitheatre on the right, with cliffs, waterfalls and a delightful greensward. Soon afterwards it reaches the graceful Burnmoor Tarn, where the view to the northeast is particularly impressive. The ridge ahead is Scafell and, beyond Slight Side, the southernmost summit, the well-named Crinkle Crags can be seen in the distance.

The path southwest down to Boot starts from the northeastern corner of the tarn, where a complicated maze of tiny streams marks the point where Whillan

Beck flows out of the tarn and Hardrigg Gill flows into it. The path is dry and follows the course of Whillan Beck a few hundred yards above it on the fellside. This is the old 'corpse road' from Wasdale.

Bodies had to be brought to the Church of St Catherine, at Boot, because there was no consecrated ground in Wasdale. In the deep winter snows this was a hard journey for a funeral procession, and sometimes ponies took fright, bolting across the fells with their burdens. It was said that one pony was never recaptured, and lone travellers claimed to have met a ghostly coffin-bearing pony on the moor.

BURTON-IN-KENDAL

Cumbria
7 miles west of Kirkby Lonsdale

The old village of Burton-in-Kendal lies quiet and unseen to the east of the busy M6 motorway. A jumble of cottages and fine old houses – some whitewashed, others pebbledashed and many rough-dressed in the silver-grey local limestone – blends with the rolling sheep-farming country around. Sheltering the village from east winds are the wooded slopes of Dalton Crags, while to the north, Farleton Fell raises a high shoulder of bare rocky scree, indicating that this is the beginning of the southern Lake District.

Maybe it was this feeling of being about to leave gentle countryside for the rugged mountains ahead that made Burton the important staging post it used to be – a tradition echoed by its small motorway service station. Both remaining pubs, the Royal Hotel and the King's Arms, almost opposite each other near the market square, were coaching inns, and stone mounting steps still stand outside the King's Arms.

Another relic of an earlier form of transport is a disused section of the Lancaster Canal. A lane beyond Deerslet Farm, south of the village, leads to a flight of locks, now gateless and abandoned, that have become cascades of clear water – a delight to angler and walker alike. Sea-going ships also figure in Burton's history: a long-since silted-up inlet provided a safe anchorage only two miles or so away. Beams and joists used in many of the village's old cottages were fashioned from the timbers of laid-up ships, and display tell-tale wooden dowelling and other unmistakable signs of the shipwright's craft.

Trading in corn was the village's principal occupation, and the tall Georgian houses around the market square underline the importance of its market, established in 1661. Recesses in the base of the 18th-century market cross show where leg irons were once fitted to hold law-breakers. Despite the imposing buildings here and on Main Street, it is the nooks and crannies, like the old stabling yards, that give Burton its atmosphere. So, too, do the quaint street names – Boon Walk, Cocking Yard, Neddy Hill, Tanpits Lane. Several houses have projecting upper floors.

Worshippers have attended the parish church of St James since at least 1180, and parts of a Saxon cross found in the churchyard suggest an even earlier date. The church, which was restored in the last century, stands before the dramatic backdrop of the lofty, scree-covered slopes of Hutton Roof Crags.

BREATHTAKING VILLAGE *Pretty Burton-in-Kendal is not disturbed for long by tourists heading for the lakes.*

BUTTERMERE

Cumbria
13 miles southwest of Keswick

In 1802 the hamlet of Buttermere found national notoriety with the story of Mary Robinson, 18-year-old daughter of the landlord of the Fish Hotel and known locally as the Beauty of Buttermere. Her charms attracted a man calling himself the Hon. Augustus Hope, new in the district and impressing local gentry with his extravagant ways. He even franked letters with his own name – in those days a privilege granted only to the high and mighty.

When he asked for her hand in marriage, immediate permission was given, and they were married on October 2, 1802. But after a short honeymoon Hope was arrested. He was a confidence trickster with one other wife and a trail of defrauded victims behind him. But he was not charged with bigamy. His crime was defrauding the Post Office – and franking letters without authority was a capital offence.

At his trial in Carlisle the jury baulked at hanging a man for fiddling the Post Office, but were shocked at the fate of poor Mary and her predecessor. So the Hon. Augustus Hope – born plain John Hatfield – went to the gallows on September 3, 1803.

The case caught the imagination of the Lakeland writers Wordsworth, Coleridge, Southey and De Quincey, and several plays based on the story appeared on the London stage. And Mary? Far from wringing her hands in anguish, she cashed in by staying on at the inn, where tourists flocked to see the Beauty of Buttermere.

Paths lead from Buttermere to two of Cumbria's most beautiful lakes, mighty tumbling waterfalls, woodlands rich in wildlife, and rolling fields sprinkled with grazing sheep and hedged with hawthorn.

Much of this can be seen from the tiny parish church of St James, reached from the hamlet by a short, steep climb and overlooking farm buildings and Buttermere Lake. For almost 700 years Buttermere hamlet was part of the immense parish of Brigham, and an ordained priest for each was thought too

SWEET HAWTHORN
White flowers in spring are followed by cheerful red haws in autumn.

expensive. So Buttermere and similar chapels were served by non-ordained men called readers.

One of these readers, Robert 'Wonderful' Walker, of Seathwaite, who served Buttermere until 1736, lived to be 93 and died in 1803. Despite a low stipend Walker left £2000 in his will, a tribute to his frugality and an iron constitution which enabled him to augment his income by writing letters for the illiterate, ploughing fields, spinning cloth, and availing himself of four ancient customs. These customs were known as clog-shoes, harden-sark, whittle-gate and goose-gate, and gave a reader the right to claim from the parish shoes, clothing, food and board – and grazing for his goose.

Opposite the Bridge Hotel is Ghyll Wood, full of flowers in spring and summer. The Fish Hotel is at the centre of the hamlet and a path to its left leads to Buttermere Lake and the waterfall of Scale Force, while that to the right follows a leafy path to Crummock Water, a beautiful 2½ mile long lake which lies to the northwest.

It is possible to walk right round Buttermere Lake – through pine trees, bracken, and at one point through a tunnel in a cliff. The eastern road approach to Buttermere is over the fierce-looking 1176ft Honister Pass, which has 1-in-4 gradients. At its western end a footpath through Warnscale Bottom follows a spec-

LAKELAND BEAUTY *A lake hemmed in by mountains and a maiden wronged in love brought fame to Buttermere.*

tacular route between the 1900ft Hay Stacks and the axe-edged 2126ft Fleetwith Pike.

Both lakes are overlooked by towering hills, but High Stile, High Crag and Red Pike – down which tumbles the foaming Sour Milk Gill – seem less austere than the towering Mellbreak, brooding over Crummock Water. Fishing permits for Buttermere can be obtained from Gatesgarth Farm. Fishing and boating permits for Crummock Water can be obtained from Rannerdale Farm.

C

CALDBECK
Cumbria
11 miles southwest of Carlisle

An elaborate headstone carved with hunting horns stands near the door to Caldbeck's church, marking the grave of John Peel who died in 1854 after falling from his horse. A local man, born in 1776, he fathered 13 children after eloping to Gretna Green with Mary White. Peel is immortalised in the song *D'ye ken John Peel*. The words were written by his regular drinking companion and friend John Woodcock Graves, who worked in a mill making the grey cloth mentioned in one of the verses. A sandstone shelter opposite the churchyard gate is dedicated to Peel and Graves, but there is no mention of William Metcalfe, the Carlisle Cathedral organist who set the song to music.

Although Peel's grave is the main attraction, Caldbeck is a captivating little village in its own right, with fine views southwards to the Lake District's serried peaks. The attractive church, restored in 1932, dates from the 12th century. It is dedicated to St Kentigern, who is said to have preached at Caldbeck on his way from Scotland to Wales in AD 553. The churchyard is overlooked by a handsome 18th-century rectory with Gothic windows, and there are 18th-century cottages in the middle of the village, known as Midtown. A picturesque stone footbridge arches over the Caldbeck, behind the church, and leads to Friar Row, a group of stone cottages tiled with Cumberland slate and built about 1800.

HUNTSMAN'S GRAVE
John Peel is buried at Caldbeck. He loved hunting, often following the hounds on foot in traditional Lakeland style.

CALDER BRIDGE
Cumbria
4 miles southeast of Egremont

The little village of Calder Bridge sits in the midst of the oddest contrast on this coast. Less than a mile up the swift-flowing Calder river to the east is Calder Abbey, founded by the Cistercians in 1134, badly knocked about by the Scots four years later, and reoccupied by monks from Furness until the Dissolution in 1536. The ruins, which include the church and the chapter house, are serene, but too shaky to walk among; they can be seen, however, from the road.

Then to the west, on the edge of the sea, are the domes and towers of Calder Hall nuclear power station and the nuclear fuel reprocessing plant, a part of the Sellafield complex. An exhibition, open daily, shows the development of nuclear power in Britain and the work of British Nuclear Fuels.

CALF OF MAN
Isle of Man
Southwest of the Isle of Man

The road from Port St Mary reaches the southwestern tip of the Isle of Man at a car park on a grassy slope overlooking the treacherous, rock-strewn passage of Calf Sound. To the left is the massive cliff of Spanish Head; a footpath leads to its summit, from which there

are fine sea views. Straight ahead are the islets of Kitterland, and behind them the now uninhabited island of the Calf of Man. This is owned by the Manx National Trust, and is a nature reserve for large colonies of guillemots, razorbills, kittiwakes and puffins. There are also smaller groups of hooded crows and choughs.

Boat trips can be made to the Calf of Man from Port Erin or Port St Mary when the weather is settled. In storms, these waters can be treacherous: the white stone cross on the edge of the cliffs commemorates the bravery of local lifeboatmen in the rescue of the crew of the French schooner *Jeanne St Charles* in 1858.

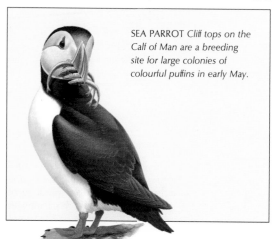

SEA PARROT *Cliff tops on the Calf of Man are a breeding site for large colonies of colourful puffins in early May.*

FORMER HUNTING GROUND *Green fields and inviting fells entice walkers to John Peel's haunts near Caldbeck.*

CARLISLE
Cumbria
70 miles north of Lancaster

Its position near the border with Scotland made Carlisle a strategically important city from early times, and this long history is reflected in the ancient remains that mingle with its modern industrial development.

There was probably a settlement on the grassy bluff above the River Eden's confluence with the Caldew in prehistoric times. In AD 78 the Roman leader Agricola chose it as the site of a fort on the fortified east-west road called the Stanegate. However, this defensive line began to be replaced in 122 by the more formidable Hadrian's Wall. Stretches of the wall can still be seen east of the city. Agricola's fort on the Stanegate was superseded by the town of Luguvalium, and now lies buried beneath the city centre.

From Norman times Carlisle continually changed hands between England and Scotland, a struggle that finally ended only in 1745, when English troops drove out Bonnie Prince Charlie's men.

Walking is the best way to explore the city. Paternoster Row, paved with cobbles, is overlooked by the red-sandstone cathedral, the second smallest in England — only Oxford Cathedral is smaller. It began in

Ports with a past on Solway Firth

Sweeping sands and marshes border Cumbria's northern coast in a little-explored corner of England. Here every village has memories of distant wars with Scotland, just across the waters of the Solway Firth.

Thistly sea holly has round flowers

Neat little cottages line Maryport's harbour

Pink thrift thrives in salt-marshes

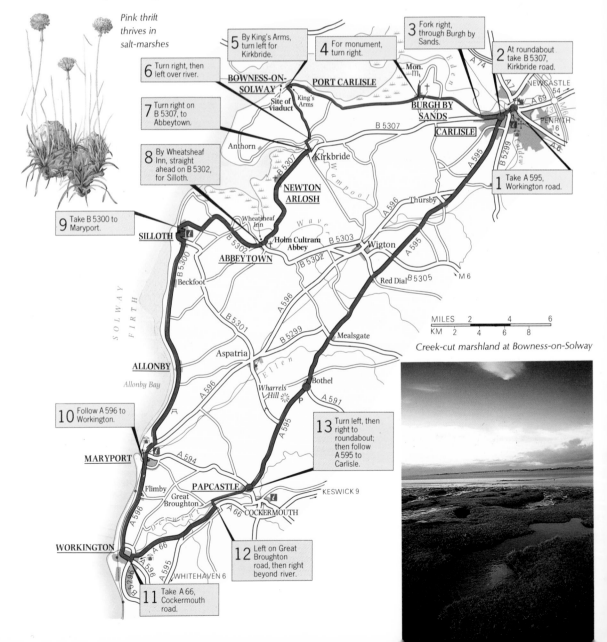

5 By King's Arms, turn left for Kirkbride.

4 For monument, turn right.

3 Fork right, through Burgh by Sands.

2 At roundabout, take B 5307, Kirkbride road.

6 Turn right, then left over river.

7 Turn right on B 5307, to Abbeytown.

8 By Wheatsheaf Inn, straight ahead on B 5302, for Silloth.

9 Take B 5300 to Maryport.

10 Follow A 596 to Workington.

13 Turn left, then right to roundabout; then follow A 595 to Carlisle.

12 Left on Great Broughton road, then right beyond river.

11 Take A 66, Cockermouth road.

1 Take A 595, Workington road.

BOWNESS-ON-SOLWAY
PORT CARLISLE
BURGH BY SANDS
CARLISLE
NEWCASTLE 54
PENRITH 16
Mon.
Site of viaduct
King's Arms
Anthorn
Kirkbride
NEWTON ARLOSH
Thursby
Wheatsheaf Inn
Holm Cultram Abbey
Wigton
SILLOTH
ABBEYTOWN
Red Dial
M 6
Beckfoot
Mealsgate
ALLONBY
Aspatria
Allonby Bay
Bothel
Wharrels Hill
MARYPORT
Flimby
Great Broughton
PAPCASTLE
KESWICK 9
COCKERMOUTH
WORKINGTON
WHITEHAVEN 6

B 5307 B 5303 B 5302 B 5301 B 5299 B 5305 B 5300

Creek-cut marshland at Bowness-on-Solway

MILES 2 4 6
KM 2 4 6 8

1123 as a Norman priory church, in 1133 its eastern end was made a cathedral, while its nave served as the parish church of St Mary. It was rebuilt after fire had damaged it in 1292. The Early English choir is dominated by the beautiful east window, one of the finest in the country, with 14th-century stone tracery.

Much of the nave was destroyed during the Civil War, but it continued to be used as a church until 1870. In 1797 the novelist Sir Walter Scott was married there. The cathedral became a memorial chapel for the Border Regiment in 1949.

Carlisle Castle was founded by William Rufus in 1092, and strengthened in the following century by David I of Scotland. The chief remains today, within the still-intact outer walls, are the 12th-century keep, the 14th-century main gate and part of Queen Mary's Tower, named after Mary, Queen of Scots, who was held prisoner there in 1568. The castle is now the headquarters of the King's Own Border Regiment.

In the central market place stands the Guildhall, a wooden-framed building with overhanging upper floors, probably dating from the 14th century. Also in the market place, in front of the 18th-century Old Town Hall, is Carlisle Cross, erected in 1682. From the steps of the cross, in August every year, the opening of the 600-year-old Carlisle Great Fair is proclaimed.

The main surviving part of the medieval city wall is on the west side of the city. It includes the Sallyport, a secret gateway out of the city. Nearby stands the recently restored medieval tithe barn.

After centuries as a garrison town, Carlisle began to prosper as a textile centre from the end of the 18th century. This prosperity led to the development of fine roads of Georgian and Victorian houses, such as Abbey Street and English Street, which runs down to the red-sandstone battlemented Citadel.

Carlisle Museum and Art Gallery is mainly housed in Tullie House, a graceful Jacobean mansion built in 1689. The museum includes a fine Roman collection and is also a national study centre for the whole Hadrian's Wall defensive system.

BORDER FORTRESS *Carlisle Castle survived seven centuries of conflict between Scotland and England.*

CARNFORTH

Lancashire
6 miles north of Lancaster

The town of Carnforth was once a busy industrial town with a steelworks which processed the Cumbrian iron ore. This closed in 1931, but Carnforth remained important as a railway junction; the Furness

Railway line diverges at Carnforth from the main London to Glasgow railway line to run along the Cumbrian coast to Carlisle, giving fine views of the coast and Morecambe Bay.

At Steamtown, signposted from the town centre, steam engines are housed in Carnforth's old steam engine shed. They include the *Flying Scotsman*, which in 1928 made the first non-stop run from King's Cross to Edinburgh. The engines are on view daily, and are used for regular mainline excursions. There are also locomotives in various stages of repair, and model and miniature railways.

CARTMEL

Cumbria
13 miles southwest of Kendal

Cut off from the bustle of 'mainland' England, Cartmel stands on a stubby peninsula which juts out into the huge tidal waste of Morecambe Bay. It is one of the gems of northwest England, richly endowed with a character that has taken centuries to develop.

Cartmel's greatest treasure is the Priory Church of St Mary and St Michael, which has all the grandeur and atmosphere of a cathedral. It dates from the end of the 12th century when William Marshall, Baron of Cartmel and later the 2nd Earl of Pembroke, founded an Augustinian priory in the village. This was dissolved by Henry VIII and most of the priory buildings were destroyed, but St Mary and St Michael was spared – after the roof had been stripped of its lead – to serve as the parish church. The door in the southwest corner of the priory is called Cromwell's door. Holes in it are said to be bullet holes made by indignant villagers firing at Cromwell's soldiers who had stabled their horses in the nave.

The church has a wealth of carved oak, an east window with 15th-century stained glass, carved misericords on the choir stalls, and the 14th-century tomb of the 1st Lord Harrington and his wife. The church's towering belfry is a local landmark.

Opposite the churchyard entrance is a building which dates from the start of the 18th century and has arched windows, framed by weathered red sandstone. Westwards, down the street, stone shops and cottages, many painted white or pale grey over the roughcast finish, lead to a little bridge across the shallow River Eea.

At the centre of the village is a square with tiny, cobbled forecourts, an old market cross and, in one corner, a house whose upper floor, supported by pillars, projects over the pavement. The lofty gatehouse, now owned by the National Trust, is all that remains of the priory buildings. The rest were demolished and served as a convenient material for Cartmel's 16th-century builders. An archway under the 14th-century gatehouse leads into Cavendish Street, where another collection of attractive buildings includes a tiny, bow-windowed cottage. More cottages of charm and character face the street that swings northwards from the square and runs out into open country past Cartmel Racecourse, where meetings are held on five days a year.

On the opposite side of the village, a milestone with old-fashioned 'human' fingers gives 'over the sands' distances to Lancaster and Ulverston. It is a reminder of the days when travellers risked crossing the tidal estuaries rather than make lengthy detours.

STONE ENIGMA *Mystery surrounds the Castlerigg Circle, erected 3500 years ago for a long-forgotten purpose.*

CASTLERIGG STONE CIRCLE

Cumbria
1 mile east of Keswick

The poet John Keats described Castlerigg Circle, a 3500-year-old Bronze Age monument, as 'a dismal cirque of Druid stone upon a forlorn moor'. The site is today a neat, sheep-nibbled green field guarded by a National Trust sign.

None of the 38 stones are much more than 6ft tall, and it has none of the awesomeness of Stonehenge or Avebury or the mighty stone circle of Orkney, though its greatest diameter is over 100ft. Nevertheless, standing there on its hillock and gazing outwards to the ring of surrounding mountains, it is obvious that the circle was sited by someone with a magnificent sense of drama, and it remains a noble tribute to gods or goddesses unknown.

CASTLETOWN

Isle of Man
10 miles southwest of Douglas

The little stone town that was once the Manx capital lies at the southern, flatter end of the island – the old racetrack end, where the first Derby was run in 1627, long before the Epsom race acquired the name. The Stanley Earls of Derby were 'kings' and lords of Man for centuries – although in 1764 a descendant sold the title to the British Crown for £70,000. Today the races that attract visitors are the motorcycle Tourist Trophy in June and the Manx Grand Prix in September.

It is also the airport end, so for many people Castletown is their first introduction to this enchanting island. There is no doubt that the visitor from the mainland is 'abroad'; street names given twice – in English and in Manx, a Gaelic language now almost extinct – palm trees mixed with fuchsias and valerian in the gardens, MAN number plates on motor vehicles, different (and handsomely designed) coins, stamps and banknotes, policemen in white helmets.

There are other differences too. There are the houses of rough limestone, with doors and window frames painted in bright pastel colours – primrose, violet, pale green. People stand in their open doorways watching the world go by and chatting with neigh-

bours in the pleasant Manx accent, which is Irish with a dash of North Country, or maybe the other way round. And, perhaps the nicest change of all, the feeling that there is no need to hurry for anything.

Castletown was the island's capital until 1874 when the House of Keys – the Lower House of the Manx parliament, the Tynwald, the oldest continuous parliament in the world – was moved to Douglas. But it still has a Parliament Square that contains the dignified building that was the House meeting place. It is now the Commissioner's Offices, or Town Hall.

Behind it is the deep chasm of the harbour, full of largish, enviable yachts. There, too, is the Nautical Museum, whose star is the schooner-rigged yacht *Peggy*, built in 1791 for the Quayles, a prominent and influential local family. She is housed in a three-storey boathouse built at the same time; in fact, when her sailing days were done, she was bricked up inside it and virtually forgotten until rediscovered in 1935. The room above the boathouse was designed by the Quayles as a replica of the stern cabin of a warship of Nelson's period – and theirs. Among the other exhibits are models and memorabilia of Manx fishing boats, of the Karran fleet of deep-sea merchantmen whose home port was Castletown, and of the Peel schooner *Vixen* that took emigrants to Australia.

The true heart of the town is Market Square, or Kerrin y Vargee. Here are the banks and some pretty 18th-century houses, one of which was the home of Captain Quilliam RN, Nelson's Flag Lieutenant at Trafalgar. Here, too, is a tall, sandstone column to the memory of Colonel Cornelius Smelt, an early 18th-century Lieutenant-Governor of the island. The column also thriftily commemorates the site of the old Market Crosse – and where Margaret Inequane and her son were burnt at the stake for witchcraft in 1617.

Filling the rear of the square is the battlemented and rather gloomy parish church. Behind it, and the car park, is the low, whitewashed Chapel of St Mary. The chapel dates in part from the 13th century and was for many years the grammar school.

The most splendid confirmation of Castletown's capital status is Castle Rushen, which overlooks the square and, indeed, all the rest of the town. Its unblemished limestone walls defy its great age – the earliest parts were built about 1150, although little remains that dates from before 1370. It was the palace of the Norse Kings of Mann and, later, a meeting place of the House of Keys, a prison, lunatic asylum, barracks and court house, which it still is.

Deep beneath its appalling dungeons, giants are said to lie in an enchanted sleep; and among some evocative exhibits is ironmongery employed in hangings, gibbetings and mere imprisonment. There are, too, some fine models depicting Charlotte, widow of James, 7th Earl of Derby and Lord of Man, surrendering the castle to the Commonwealth commander during the Civil War; the preparation of boiling oil; and other lively moments in the building's history. A notice reads: 'When the King of Mann lived here, those who dropped litter had their hands chopped off. Please use the baskets; he may be watching you.'

Several fine walks from Castletown lead to hills that are sometimes shrouded in mist; in Manx legend the mist is the protective cloak of Mannanan, an ancient sea god, hiding the island from would-be attackers.

HARBOUR GUARDS *Castle Rushen's ancient walls and a flock of swans defend Castletown against invaders.*

CAUTLEY SPOUT
Cumbria
1 mile north of Cautley

An impressive waterfall on the wild Cumbrian moorlands north of Sedbergh, Cautley Spout descends
600ft over the naked rock of Cautley Crag. Just
beyond the Cross Keys Inn – its doorway is dated
1732, and teas are served under ancient beams – a
footpath leads to the Spout.

CHAPEL STILE
Cumbria
4 miles west of Ambleside

There is a mountaineering atmosphere about Chapel
Stile. This hamlet has the last petrol pump and the last
shop before entering the Langdale Valley – which has
a magnetic attraction for Lakeland climbers.

The Langdale Pikes mark the head of Langdale,
2½ miles west, and the Old Dungeon Ghyll Hotel is
an excellent vantage point for watching helmeted
climbers scaling rock faces. Behind the New Dungeon Ghyll Hotel, an easy but spectacular walk by the
side of the Dungeon Ghyll waterfalls leads to Stickle
Tarn. Over this circular mountain lake towers the
precipitous 2288ft Pavey Ark, an impressive and
memorable sight.

From Stickle Tarn the footpath continues west to
the main part of the Langdale Pikes, crowned by the
magnificent 2323ft Pike of Stickle and the 2403ft
Harrison Stickle. Both these peaks can be covered
quite easily during a single day's walking.

CHEADLE AND GATLEY
Greater Manchester
3 miles west of Stockport

Cheadle and Cheadle Hulme are linked with Gatley in
a mainly residential district of Greater Manchester.

Most of Cheadle's older buildings date from the
19th century, when merchants and industrialists
moved there from Manchester, Salford and Stockport.
The red-brick, Gothic Town Hall, started in 1847, was
originally built as a merchant's house.

The Church of St Mary was rebuilt between 1530
and 1558, but has some earlier tombs, including one
surmounted by the alabaster figures of two knights
which dates from the 15th century. There are several
fine timber-framed mansions in the area, including
Bramall Hall, 1 mile southeast of Cheadle Hulme.

CHIPPING
Lancashire
4 miles north of Longridge

In old English, the word *chipping* means 'market', and
until local industry began to flourish in the 17th
century the village of Chipping was simply that – the
market which served this region of Lancashire. Later,
like the stone-built Gloucestershire villages it so closely resembles, it became a thriving centre for the wool
trade: many of its buildings date from the 17th
century, when trade was at its most buoyant. Sheep
grew fat on the Bowland fells, which rise steeply to the
north of the village. And their fleeces were processed

WATERSIDE CHARM *A rushing stream flows past the old water
mill in the timeless village of Chipping.*

by local weavers, who sold the cloth to towns such as
Preston and Blackburn. At the same period, flax-
spinning was another source of local prosperity.

At the southern end of Windy Street, a carved
stone on what was Chipping's first village school –
now a youth club – commemorates the village's most
notable benefactor, a dyer and dealer in cloth called
John Brabin. He died in 1683, having drawn up a will a
year earlier leaving money for the relief of the poor
and for the building of a village school. His name, and
the date 1684, also appear on the gable end of the
neighbouring terrace of stone-built almshouses, which
were paid for with his money. Another inscription, at
22 Talbot Street, marks the house where Brabin lived,
now a post office and crafts centre.

Windy Street's cobbled pavements pass some of
Chipping's most attractive houses. These include numbers 17 and 19, which stand at right angles to the road
overlooking tiny gardens. Like many other houses in
the village, they have quaint, stone-mullioned
windows. A delightful little courtyard, overlooked by a
house with diamond-paned windows, is tucked away
near the shop on the corner of Talbot Street and
Windy Street.

Talbot Street itself runs down to a bridge over
Chipping Brook: from the bridge there are pleasant
views downstream, with an old mill in the foreground
complete with undershot water wheel, and the long

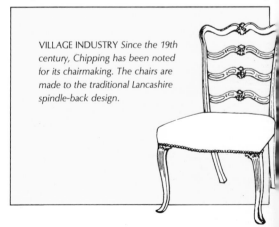

VILLAGE INDUSTRY *Since the 19th
century, Chipping has been noted
for its chairmaking. The chairs are
made to the traditional Lancashire
spindle-back design.*

wooded crest of Longridge Fell in the distance. Just below the mill, which has been converted into a restaurant, a footbridge crosses the brook.

Chipping's roots delve back far beyond the Norman Conquest. The first church was built in 597, and the area around the village was given full parish status around 1040, shortly before the start of Edward the Confessor's reign. In the early 14th century, when the area was laid waste by marauding Scots, the inhabitants were described as 'few, untractable and wild'; but Chipping recovered to become a prosperous community attracting trade from neighbouring villages, hamlets and farms. Until the middle of this century, its markets and fairs remained highlights of the local calendar.

One fair was always held on St Bartholomew's Day, August 24, in honour of the village church's patron saint. The church itself has a tower built about 1450, while the rest of it was rebuilt in 1506 and heavily restored in 1873, by which time the roof was badly dilapidated and even the lead in the windows had decayed. A brass plate near the altar commemorates Marie and Anne Parkinson, the wives of Robert Parkinson, who died in 1611 and 1623 respectively.

CHORLEY
Lancashire
10 miles northwest of Bolton

Cotton weaving, calico printing and engineering are the industries of the busy town of Chorley. Henry Tate, the sugar magnate and founder of the Tate Gallery in London, was born here in 1819.

The 14th-century parish church of St Lawrence recalls Chorley's pre-industrial past as a trading centre for the surrounding farmland. So too does Astley Hall, an Elizabethan mansion set in parkland beside a lake.

On the east, the town is overlooked by Healey Nab, which can be reached by ancient pathways defined by boulder walls. From the top, 682ft high, the stark moors and deep valleys of Anglezarke and White Coppice can be seen to the east. This is ideal countryside to explore on foot. Rivington Pike, 4 miles southeast, is a popular viewpoint with a stone tower at its 1191ft summit.

Eccleston, 4 miles west of Chorley, is worth visiting for its 14th-century Church of St Mary, which has later additions, including a late Perpendicular south aisle. It was restored in the 18th and 19th centuries, when some of the wall monuments were added. There are also an altar tomb with the 15th-century brass of a priest, and an octagonal 15th-century font.

CLAIFE HEIGHTS
Cumbria
2 miles north of Near Sawrey

Strange stories are told of the Windermere ferry, where an unbroken succession of ferrymen have plied their trade for a thousand years or more. On a stormy night in the 16th century one of them heard a cry from the Claife shore. He set out to collect the passenger and returned, apparently alone, but he was dumb with fear and died soon after. According to local legend he had brought back a phantom passenger, the Crier of Claife, who was eventually exorcised by a priest and put to rest in an old quarry known now as Crier of

Claife Quarry. On a fine day, such hauntings seem impossible in this lovely place. The gently rolling countryside of Claife, lying between Esthwaite Water and the enclosing curve of Windermere, provided an appropriate background for the stories of Beatrix Potter. Six of her books are set at Hill Top Farm at Near Sawrey.

One of the most interesting of the walks on Claife Heights begins just below Hill Top Farm. Take the path north from opposite the Tower Bank Arms in Near Sawrey. The countryside all around is typical of the southern lakes — partly woods where roe deer roam and partly fertile grazing land with occasional outcrops of shale. The path climbs upwards through some very large rock outcrops and soon reaches Moss Eccles Tarn. Here ducks and the occasional diver and grebe dabble on the water, while coots and moorhens dodge among the reeds. Larches, copper beeches and huge rhododendrons fringe the banks of the tarn. Further on lies Wise Een Tarn, wrapped like a silver boomerang around a dark mass of conifers.

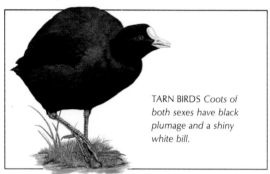

TARN BIRDS *Coots of both sexes have black plumage and a shiny white bill.*

CLITHEROE
Lancashire
10 miles northeast of Blackburn

Clitheroe, an ancient market town, lies between two lofty landmarks: the ruins of a small Norman castle on a tall, limestone spur, and a mostly 19th-century church. The town grew around the foot of the castle, started by Roger de Poitou, the first Norman Lord of Clitheroe, but mostly built by the de Lacy family who lived here until 1311. Then the castle went to the Earls and Dukes of Lancaster, passing to the Crown when Henry IV, whose father was Duke of Lancaster, came to the throne in 1399. The keep, measuring less than 36ft square, is one of the smallest in England, and the entire fortress took up no more than an acre.

During the Civil War, Clitheroe Castle was briefly captured from the Roundhead townsfolk by the Royalists. When the Roundheads eventually won they destroyed it so that 'it might neither be a charge to the Commonwealth to keep it, nor a danger to have it kept against them'. Only the keep survived, and in 1920 the ruins and grounds were taken over by the local authority and opened to the public.

Perched on a hill facing the ruins, the original parish church of St Mary Magdalene was built about the same time as the castle, in the early 12th century. But of that building only part of the east window and the west tower remain. Most of the church dates from the late 1820s and its spire with flying buttresses was added in 1844. In 1981 it was restored after a bad fire.

Inside, two of Clitheroe's most renowned sons are commemorated. There is a brass memorial to the

Reverend Dr John Webster (1610–82), headmaster of Clitheroe's Royal Grammar School. He wrote *The Displaying of Supposed Witchcraft*, a celebrated book when it was published in 1677, in which he attacked those who dabbled in the occult. At this time locals believed that the district was overrun with witches. The second memorial is to the Reverend Thomas Wilson, another headmaster of the Royal Grammar School, who compiled a dictionary of archaeology in the 18th century and dedicated it to another lexicographer, Dr Samuel Johnson. The Alleys Chapel also has two fine 15th-century alabaster effigies of a local landowner, Sir Thomas Radcliffe, and his wife.

Clitheroe's two landmarks are joined by Castle Street and Church Street, with the Market Place in between. Most of the 18th and 19th-century buildings are made of sandstone and limestone.

Until the 1850s Clitheroe's water came from medieval wells – some have now dried up, but water still flows from Heald Well in Wellgate and Stocks Well in Parson Lane. At the other end of the town, nestling just below the castle, is the Rose Garden. It contains an ornate turret taken from the Palace of Westminster and presented to the town in the 1930s by the local Member of Parliament, Sir William Brass – later Baron Chattisham of Clitheroe.

Clitheroe has long been associated with the occult. As Dr Webster recorded in his book, Pendle Hill, whose 1831ft summit rises 4 miles to the east, was notorious in the 17th century for the impoverished and homeless so-called witches who congregated there. In August 1612, ten of these women – including a half-blind, 80-year-old beggar-woman named Old Chattox – were hanged at Lancaster as witches. It was also on Pendle Hill that George Fox had a vision in 1652, which led him to preach and form the Society of Friends. Today the hill is better known for its spectacular views westward to the Forest of Bowland, the flat Fylde Pain and the Irish Sea beyond.

The River Ribble is said to be haunted by an evil spirit, named Jennie Greenteeth, who claims a life every seven years. Local children are still warned not to play too near the water, or Jennie will pull them in. They associate the sprite with green water plants.

COCKERMOUTH
Cumbria
8 miles east of Workington

On April 7, 1770, the poet William Wordsworth was born in a handsome, foursquare Georgian house in Cockermouth's tree-lined Main Street. Dorothy, his sister, was born here the following year, and with their three brothers they grew up in the house until 1783. Wordsworth House, as it is now called, belongs to the National Trust and is open to the public from Easter to October, except on Thursdays. The family's morning room, dining room and drawing room can be seen, as well as treasures that include Wordsworth's bureau-bookcase and his early 19th-century grandfather clock.

When the Wordsworths lived here, the house was owned by Sir James Lowther of Lowther Castle. Wordsworth's father, John, was Sir James's agent and lived here rent-free. Not surprisingly, the poet later declared himself 'much favoured' in his birthplace, and the River Derwent, which runs along the bottom of the garden, was for him the 'fairest of all rivers'.

Cockermouth stands where the Derwent and Cocker rivers meet between two hills. On one of the hills stands a castle dating mostly from the 14th century. An earlier castle is believed to have been built in 1134 by a Scottish noble, Waltheof, son of the Earl of Dunbar. At that time much of Cumbria frequently changed hands as England and Scotland disputed for it. The fortress is now mostly in ruins, and is not normally open to the public. The town below is a maze of old streets, alleyways and yards, which come to life on Mondays, when the market is held.

The sheep and cattle market occupies premises on South Street, where the fast-talking patter of the auctioneer echoes out from the auction sheds. Inside, tiers of brown-painted seats rise from a central ring, from which dalesmen make their bids.

WORDSWORTH'S BIRTHPLACE
The pride of Cockermouth is this Georgian house where the poet William Wordsworth was born in 1770.

The rest of the market is in the Market Place, on the other side of the Cocker, where there is an old bell which is still rung during the summer months to start the proceedings. In the market, general produce and clothing are bought and sold.

Above the Market Place in Kirkgate is the 19th-century Church of All Saints. Its stained-glass east window is a memorial to Wordsworth, and his father's tomb is in the churchyard. Near the church is a hall which stands on the site of the old grammar school, where for a while the poet was educated. Another famous pupil was Fletcher Christian, ringleader of the mutiny on the *Bounty*, who was born in Moorland Close, a farmhouse 2 miles away, in 1764.

The Derwent is famous for its fine and tasty trout, and among the many who have fished it was the American entertainer Bing Crosby (1904–77). He stayed, appropriately enough, at the Trout Hotel in Main Street, where there is a signed photograph of him displayed at the bar.

River trout are distinguished by red-spotted backs.

COCKERSAND ABBEY
Lancashire
6 miles southwest of Lancaster

Some scattered ruins on the top of a headland projecting into the Lune estuary are all that remain of Cockersand Abbey, once one of the wealthiest religious houses in the northwest. The abbey was built in 1190, and its buildings covered at their greatest extent more than an acre. The surviving fragments show the outline of the cloisters and of the chapter house which, built in 1230, was used 600 years later as the burial chapel for the Daltons, who owned the land.

Close to the chapter house is a stretch of beach with a small lighthouse and the walls of a fish-trap, built by the monks of Cockersand Abbey to catch salmon from the river estuary as the tide fell. Over the centuries, stone and other materials have been taken from the ruins and incorporated in other buildings. Crook Farm, 2 miles north, has several windows and doorways which apparently came from the abbey.

In the nearby village of Cockerham, the church of St Michael has a 17th-century tower, but the rest of the church was built in 1910. The churchyard has many old gravestones, including that of a vicar who, at the time of the Great Plague, buried 11 of his parishioners in a single month before dying himself.

To the southwest of Cockerham lie Cockerham Marsh and Pilling Marsh. It is not safe to walk across the marshes, but from the ruins of Cockersand Abbey a footpath skirts the eastern edge of Cockerham Marsh before joining the main road. From the path there are views of the channels leading to the sea and the estuary, and of the sea-birds which nest there.

CONISTON
Cumbria
6 miles southwest of Ambleside

Old slate quarries and copper mines have not diminished the majesty of the Old Man of Coniston. Its summit, 2627ft above sea level and almost 2500ft above Coniston Water, completely dominates this village where buildings of dark local stone mingle with others whose walls gleam with whitewash. One of the most handsome architectural features of Coniston is a whitewashed, seven-doorway terrace, right beneath the Old Man and overlooking the Church Beck's boulder-strewn waters. The terrace, which is known as The Forge, is about 150 years old.

Nearby, in the main street, a museum commemorates the life and work of John Ruskin, the Victorian writer, critic and social reformer, who had a profound influence upon the general artistic taste of his time. Ruskin lived at Brantwood, a sprawling white house on the far side of Coniston Water, from 1871 until his death in 1900. Spurning the chance of a grave in Westminster Abbey, he chose to be buried at Coniston and lies beneath a splendidly carved cross in the northeast corner of the churchyard.

Brantwood was a power house of the Victorian art world, and this is reflected in its astonishing collection of paintings, furniture and memorabilia. A special joy is a mass of drawings by J. M. W. Turner, who was Ruskin's particular favourite.

Another evocation of Coniston's yesterdays is the National Trust's flagship – in fact, the sole member of its fleet. This is Steam Yacht *Gondola*, first launched on Coniston Water in 1859. The elegant craft carries passengers on lake trips through most of the year. One of the features she passes at the southern end of the lake is Peel Island. In *Swallows and Amazons*, Arthur Ransome transported it to Windermere and called it Wild Cat Island.

It could be said that Coniston Water is the most satisfactory of the lakes, at least by Victorian standards of the picturesque. It neatly divides complementary kinds of scenery, so that the village looks across to tiered forest rising from the lake shore.

Coniston Water has been used for several water-speed record-breaking attempts, it being more placid than Windermere. A slab of inscribed slate on the village green commemorates Donald Campbell, who died trying to break the world water-speed record in 1967. His jet-powered *Bluebird* went out of control at more than 300 mph, and his body was never found.

The village is a fine centre for walkers. Paths lead to the summit of the Old Man, but less energetic explorers can stroll beside the lake or wander through the Grizedale Forest on its eastern shore. Two miles northeast of Coniston is the half-mile long, tree-lined lake many people consider the prettiest of all in the Lake District, Tarn Hows. It was originally three smaller lakes, but a dam that was built about 50 years ago joined them together.

CORBY CASTLE
Cumbria
4 miles east of Carlisle

Rising from the east bank of the River Eden, Corby Castle overlooks Wetheral, on the opposite bank of the river. The castle, with its bulky, 13th-century keep, was originally a defensive tower which was expanded in the 17th and early 19th centuries. The castle's terraced gardens are open to the public in the summer.

RIVER OF PLENTY *For centuries, medieval salmon traps in the River Eden provided fish for Corby Castle.*

CREGNEISH

Isle of Man

1 mile west of Port St Mary

There has probably been less alteration to Cregneish in the last 200 years than to any other village on the Isle of Man. For this reason, part of it has been taken over by the Manx Museum as a folk museum.

Set in a dip on high ground in the extreme southwest of the island, it overlooks the Calf of Man, a mile-square islet and bird sanctuary, separated from Man by the treacherous waters of Calf Sound. The village is probably a survival of an ancient Celtic settlement. For centuries, a community of less than 50 people gained a living from the thin acid soil. Six families farmed 300 acres of arable land, while others worked as fishermen or labourers.

Many of the dwellings in Cregneish are traditional Manx cottages, their thatched roofs held in place by ropes and nets fastened to stone pegs at the top of the gables and under the eaves.

The folk museum centres on a typical fisherman-crofter's dwelling known as Harry Kelly's Cottage, after the owner, who died in 1934. The cottage, which is more than 150 years old, has the traditional Manx *chiollagh* – open hearth and chimney – and furnishings. Other buildings are a crofter's farmstead, a smithy and a weaver's workshop with a hand-loom on which demonstrations are given in the summer. There is also a small, thatched building fitted up as a joiner's workshop. It contains woodworking tools, including a treadle lathe.

In the field adjoining the museum buildings, two or three of the strange-looking, Manx four-horned Loghtan sheep can often be seen grazing. The intimate little church in the centre of the village was built in 1878.

About 1 mile to the north of the village stands the Meayll Circle, the burial ground of a Stone Age culture which flourished there between 4000 and 2000 BC. The circle consists of six pairs of chambers, each with a flagged floor. When they were first investigated during the 1890s, the chambers held the remains of 26 burial urns, but originally there must have been many more.

CROSBY

Merseyside

6 miles north of Liverpool

The original Crosby was the hamlet of Little Crosby, $1\frac{1}{2}$ miles inland, which has changed little over the years; the Georgian Crosby Hall stands beside the old smithy and a group of 17th-century cottages. The name of the village comes from two Norse words meaning 'the place of the crosses' and one of these survives – a wayside cross used to mark a resting place beside an old 'church way', along which coffins were carried to the burial grounds.

Modern Crosby, which retains a sense of period charm, began in the district called Waterloo, at the edge of the sea. It was there that wealthy Liverpool merchants, anxious to escape the bustle of the city for the peace and fresh air of the seaside, built their houses. The area still has a strong Regency flavour, with terraces and crescents of late Georgian houses, wrought-iron balconies and verandas. Later settlers expanded Crosby inland, to make it a Victorian suburb of Liverpool.

The deep Crosby Channel runs parallel to the shore and less than a mile from the beach, and the district called Waterloo makes an ideal viewpoint for watching the busy river traffic. The sandy beach is safe for bathing, but small-boat sailors need to beware of the busy shipping lanes. The beachside Marina is a large enclosed stretch of water where beginners can learn to sail in safe surroundings.

CROSBY

Isle of Man

6 miles southeast of Peel

To savour Crosby's amenities calls for a certain crispness of reaction on the part of the motorist; the village stands astride the Peel to Douglas road and, pushed along by the traffic, it is quite easy to go right through it while making up one's mind to stop. Once off the highway, however, this is a pleasant little place of

CREGNEISH CROFTER *Harry Kelly, a fluent Manx speaker, kept sheep and hens, and caught fish from his boat.*

TRADITIONAL SHOWPLACE *The dresser in Kelly's cottage displays chinaware and ornaments from England, and wooden bowls and horn beakers made by local craftsmen.*

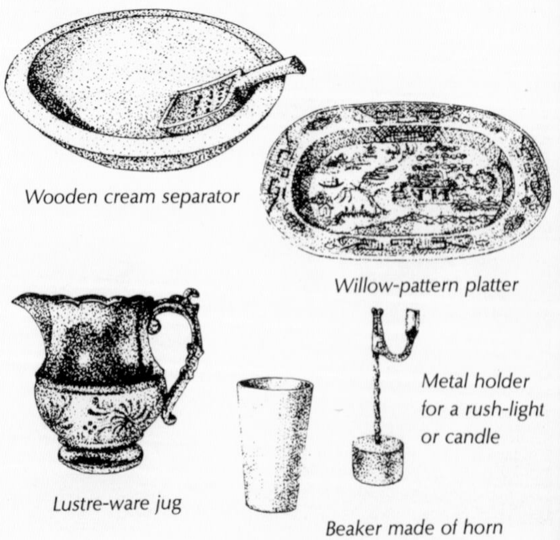
Wooden cream separator
Willow-pattern platter
Metal holder for a rush-light or candle
Lustre-ware jug
Beaker made of horn

houses and farms old and newish, climbing up the wooded slopes of Mount Rule to the east, and up again to the parish church of St Runius Marown on its hill to the south.

St Runius was one of the early bishops of the island, and he may well lie beneath the overgrown, wind-bent grass of the churchyard, together with two of his successors. His chapel is a paragon of the early medieval Church of Man – small, simple, but stoutly built (of rough local stones) and meant to last.

Its doorway is like the entrance to a cave, and from it a rope runs up the outside of the wall to the bell in its tiny belfry. The building was restored in the 1950s by volunteers who, with few resources, managed to nurture the spirit of the place. There are some curtains on and about the altar, and some pieces of polished brass and flower vases about the battered box pews. They accord well with the simplicity of the ancient Norse and Celtic monuments in the walls.

A little to the west of Crosby is another chapel, dedicated to the Scottish St Trinian. Four-horned Manx sheep nibble the turf about the building, which is roofless, and always has been, since a local goblin called a buggane will not allow one to be put on. Indeed, whenever anyone tried to, the buggane would rise up through the ground and scatter beams and stones in all directions.

Only one man, a tailor, ever dared challenge it. When the next roof was put on, he volunteered to sit in the chapel 'for as long as it took to sew a pair of breeches', in the hope that this might persuade the creature to desist. And when the buggane arrived, it was disconcerted, but only for a moment. 'Don't you see my big teeth and long claws?' it howled. 'I see 'em,' replied the tailor calmly, and went on stitching without showing any signs of fear.

The buggane stamped until the walls shook, and tore at the roof. The tailor made his last stitch and dived through the window as the rafters crashed behind him. He raced off, pursued by the buggane, and leapt over the wall into St Trinian's churchyard. Seeing its prey escaping, the buggane snatched off its head and hurled it after him. But as the head touched holy ground it turned to stone and broke into a thousand pieces. No one has seen the buggane since. But, not surprisingly, neither has anyone tried to put another roof on St Trinian's.

CROSBY RAVENSWORTH
Cumbria
7 miles southwest of Appleby-in-Westmorland

Prehistoric man built burial mounds and settlements on the bare, low fells around Crosby Ravensworth, a neat village on the delightful Lyvennet Beck. Sheep farming and a consequent absence of the plough have preserved them. Ewe Close, a settlement a mile or so to the southwest, is one of the most important in northern England – a complex system of walls enclosing an area of nearly 18 acres. Among the remains of circular huts within it is one measuring 50ft across.

The fertile valley has attracted settlers ever since. The Vikings came – Ravensworth derives from the Danish word meaning 'raven-black' – and Saxons built a wooden church here. It was replaced by the Normans with a stone church, destroyed in turn by the Scots in the 12th century. Near the main doorway of the present Church of St Lawrence is the shaft of a medieval cross. The 7th-century missionary and first Bishop of York, St Paulinus, is said to have worshipped here with his followers. The church itself stands like a cathedral in miniature beside the beck, encircled by ancient trees and, though much rebuilt in the 19th century, retaining still a fine 13th-century doorway.

Footbridges span the beck – some narrow and made of wood, others arches of old stone – and standing on its bank amid beautiful grounds is the fine, towered Flass House, with a stepped porch.

Just over a mile north, at Maulds Meaburn in the remote Lyvennet Valley, is Meaburn Hall. Built in the late 16th century, it was home to the 1st Earl of Lonsdale, who had the body of his mistress embalmed and placed in a glass-lidded coffin which he kept in a cupboard. The father of Joseph Addison, creator of Sir Roger de Coverley, was born here in 1672.

CROSTON

Lancashire
6 miles west of Chorley

Deep banks and high walls hold back the River Yarrow, which twists and turns through Croston. The village lies in a vale, and its Old English name means 'Town of the Cross'. This name may commemorate a 7th-century wayside cross used by the Celtic missionaries who brought Christianity to much of northern England. But there is no Celtic cross in existence: the present village cross was placed there in 1950.

In the centre of Croston stands the late-Gothic Church of St Michael. It is reached by a narrow lane flanked by terraced brick houses, and has a fine stained-glass window over the studded north door. On one side of the church is a small cloister, on the other, the school – founded in 1372 by John of Gaunt, Duke of Lancaster. The duke virtually ruled England in the last years of his father, Edward III, and in the first years of the reign of the boy king, Richard II.

The school was endowed by James Hyett, the vicar of Croston, in 1660. Two years later, however, his living was taken away from him because he refused, as a Puritan, to conform to the Act of Uniformity, whose demands included the use of the revised Anglican prayer book. He died in 1663 and was buried 'without ceremony or book', but is remembered by a stone plaque on the school wall.

The main road through Croston passes beside the strengthened Town Bridge. A short way from the village are the chapel and remains of Croston Hall. The Hall was the home of the de Trafford family from the Middle Ages until the early 1960s – when the last of the de Traffords died and it was demolished.

SPANNING TIME *Croston's humpback bridge has been carrying traffic over the River Yarrow since 1682.*

CRUMMOCK WATER

Cumbria
8 miles south of Cockermouth

Several lay-bys offer spectacular views across Crummock Water, formed by the River Cocker and once joined to Buttermere. The 1½ mile long lake is now separated from the larger lake by a three-quarter-mile strip of low-lying fields. There is a car park just beyond Rannerdale, and two at Lanthwaite from which paths yield views over the lake.

CURRAGHS WILDLIFE PARK

Isle of Man
1 mile northeast of Ballaugh

Occupying some 26 acres of old, lush marshland in the Ballaugh Curraghs, this wildlife park has acquired a collection of birds and beasts from all over the world – llamas, monkeys, ornamental pheasants, parakeets and many others. Few, however, have an odder appearance than the native Loghtan sheep of Man with its long brown wool and, in the case of the rams, four long, curly horns sprouting from behind their ears. The park is open daily in summer.

Near the park are several of the classic features of Man's Tourist Trophy racecourse. They include Ballaugh Bridge with its humpback, and the three-fold Quarry Bends followed by the Sulby Straight, where the bikes start to make up for lost time.

DACRE

Cumbria
5 miles southwest of Penrith

A clear stream trickles down the cheek of the hills above Ullswater; its name is Dacre Beck, and Dacre is derived from the Welsh word *daigr*, 'a tear'. But there is nothing sorrowful about the village, which lies in a fold of the hills in unspoilt isolation, though the presence of Dacre Castle shows that it was not always peaceful. The fortress was built in the 14th century, one of a chain of peel towers in and around the Eden Valley, which all too often was attacked by Scots raiding across the border.

Villagers could seek refuge in the towers, and Dacre Castle must have given formidable protection with its 66ft high walls and impressive battlements. Its present state, little changed from those times, is a testament to its impregnability. The castle is now a private residence, open by written appointment only.

Across the beck stands St Andrew's Church, which has stood on its hillside since before 1296, when its earliest recorded vicar vacated the living. It is almost certain that an Anglo-Saxon monastery stood on the site, and it was probably here that Athelstan, King of England, Constantine, King of Scotland and Eugenius of Cumberland, met to verify the 'Peace of Dacre' in AD 926. At the meeting Constantine and Eugenius swore allegiance to Athelstan and were baptised into Christianity. The early medieval historian William of Malmesbury recorded this historic meeting, but no historian or archaeologist has been able to explain why there is a carved stone bear in each corner of the churchyard.

The church shelters the mutilated effigy of a knight, clad in chain mail and a surcoat, who is thought to have been a crusader. A more recent link with campaigns in far-off lands is the memorial to Charles James Salmond, a Bengal Cavalry officer killed during the Indian Mutiny of 1857.

About a mile east of Dacre is Dalemain, home of the Hasell family since 1679. It has a Georgian façade but the earliest part of the house is a peel tower which dates from Norman times. It is open to the public daily, except Fridays and Saturdays, in summer.

DALBY

Isle of Man
4 miles south of Peel

At sunset on a clear day the Mountains of Mourne, some 40 miles away across the Irish Sea, can easily be seen from Dalby. The name of the village derives from the Norse *dal-byr*, 'the croft in the glen'.

St James's Chapel is described by the poet and architectural enthusiast, Sir John Betjeman (1906–84) in his book *English Parish Churches*, as 'pinnacled without and unrestored within'. Its eccentricity lies in the fact that it was both a chapel and a school. It is built in two tiers on a hillside, and two sets of immense sliding doors separated the chapel from the old school rooms, and the school rooms from each other. It is now the village hall.

At Niarbyl Bay, a small rocky cove where the rare red-legged chough breeds, there are traditional Manx thatched cottages just above the tideline.

MASTERS OF FLIGHT
*Choughs wheel and soar over
Niarbyl Bay's cliffs, searching
in small flocks for worms, beetles,
ants, caterpillars and shellfish.*

FOUR BEARS OF DACRE *No one knows why there are stone bears in the churchyard, even their age is a secret.*

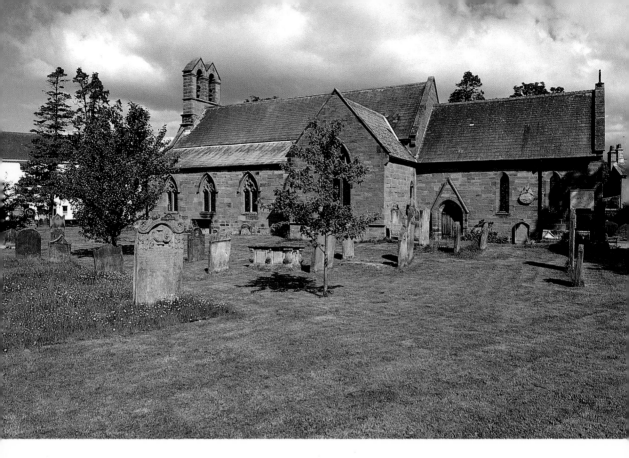

ANGELIC CHURCHYARD *Beautiful walks skirt Dalston's 13th-century Church of St Michael and All Angels.*

DALSTON
Cumbria
4 miles southwest of Carlisle

Attractive cottages, many of them with colour-washed walls, sweep round Dalston's sandstone church. Dedicated to St Michael and All Angels, it dates from the early 13th century, but was restored in 1890. A 17th-century Bishop of Carlisle is buried in the grounds, which lead to a stretch of the River Caldew.

Just over a mile to the northeast of the village is Dalston Hall, now a hotel, which is thought to have been built about 1500. However, its front dates mostly from 1899. Standing beside it is a battlemented peel tower, complete with turret.

DALTON-IN-FURNESS
Cumbria
3 miles south of Askam

Two roads down the Furness Peninsula — one from Duddon Bridge and the other from Ulverston — meet at Dalton-in-Furness. The whole area is honeycombed with old iron-ore quarries and mine workings. The splendour of St Mary's Church, with its large nave and imposing west tower, bears witness to the past prosperity of the village. This was the birthplace in 1734 of the fashionable portrait painter George Romney, son of a local cabinet-maker. He died at Kendal in 1802 and was buried in Dalton churchyard.

The ruins of nearby Dalton Castle, which include a 17th-century peel tower, have been restored by the National Trust, and there is a small museum on the site containing 16th and 17th-century armour.

On the edge of the Duddon estuary, 3 miles west of Dalton, are the sand dunes of Sandscale Haws, where miles of open sands are exposed at low tide. Bathing is safe only at high water, when the incoming sea holds back the dangerously fast river currents.

DENT
Cumbria
4 miles southeast of Sedbergh

Although in Cumbria, Dent lies within the Yorkshire Dales National Park. It stands slightly above the sparkling River Dee and is watched over by a cluster of steep, sheep-grazed hills — Barbon High Fell, Middleton Fell, Rise Hill and Whernside, at 2414ft the highest point in the park.

The narrow streets that twist and turn through the compact heart of Dent are surfaced with cobbles which, in the absence of pavements, spread right across from doorstep to doorstep. Sturdy cottages of grey stone sit snugly beneath thick-slabbed roofs built to defy the upland weather's most ferocious moods. Natural stone is dominant, but many cottages are colour-washed and have bright doors and window-frames. The Sun Inn is an attractive black-and-white building, and has an old mounting block outside as a reminder of the days when horsepower meant four legs and a saddle. However, the railway station at Dent, now open only on special days, has the distinction of being the highest main line station in England.

A huge piece of rough-hewn Shap granite stands in the centre of the village as a memorial to Adam Sedgwick. Born at Dent in 1785, he became a pioneer geologist and a Fellow of Trinity College, Cambridge, in whose chapel he is buried. Behind the monument, which also serves as a drinking trough, a path flanked by neat railings leads across the spacious churchyard to St Andrew's Church. It stands on 11th-century foundations, but was rebuilt in 1417 and has been restored three times since then.

DERBYHAVEN

Isle of Man
1 mile east of Castletown

The deep, curving bay of Derbyhaven faces eastwards, separated from the larger Castletown Bay by the rocky headland of Langness. Two viewpoints show the island's coastal scenery at its best: one is by the Dreswick Point lighthouse, and the other is at the northeastern end of the headland, by the old fort on St Michael's Island.

At Hango Hill, on the road to Castletown, the ruins of an old summerhouse stand on top of a mound facing the sea. The mound became an execution site during the Civil War, when the leader of the local rebels who sympathised with the Parliamentary cause was shot there on the orders of the Stanleys, the Royalist owners of the island.

The name of Derbyhaven is associated with the classic horse race. In 1627 the Earl of Derby, who then owned the island, organised a horse race along the greensward on the western side of the bay, in an attempt to encourage local horse breeders. The race was called 'The Derby', but it was a later Lord Derby whose name was given to the race run at Epsom for the first time in 1780.

DHOON GLEN

Isle of Man
2 miles northeast of Laxey

One of the most spectacular glens on the Isle of Man, Dhoon Glen is formed by a fast-running stream which cuts its way down through the cliffs to fall into the sea at Dhoon Bay. The path down to the shore crosses the fern-clad glen by a series of rustic bridges, passing two steep waterfalls, each of which drops 60ft or more. For those who find the climb back too steep, there is a less pretty but easier path on the south side of the glen.

DODD WOOD

Cumbria
2½ miles north of Keswick

The large car park at the edge of Dodd Wood looks down over the long stretch of Bassenthwaite Lake. Near the car park are the remains of an old sawmill, and walks lead through the haunts of roe deer and red squirrels, which visitors are quite likely to spot.

By the lakeside is the 17th-century Mirehouse, the home in the 19th century of James Spedding, biographer of Francis Bacon. The house contains portraits and manuscripts of Francis Bacon and some of Spedding's literary friends, including Lord Tennyson who was a frequent visitor. The house is open to the public on some days in summer, and a lakeside walk from the house is open daily.

DOLPHINHOLME

Lancashire
6 miles southeast of Lancaster

At Dolphinholme the swiftly flowing Damas Gill joins the Wyre, which at one time provided water to power a now vanished textile mill. Beside the bridge is a restored gas lamp, installed in the early 19th century.

Pine martens have been sighted in Dodd Wood.

The village is a pleasant mixture of the old and the new, with late 18th-century cottages by the bridge and more recent houses sprinkled about. The late 19th-century St Mark's Church is low-lying with a stumpy central tower. Just to the southeast of Dolphinholme is Wyreside Hall, built in the early 1800s of a dignified, dark grey stone.

DOUGLAS

Isle of Man
19 miles south of Point of Ayre

From out at sea, Douglas – the capital of the Isle of Man and its most popular holiday resort – looks like a long line of white cliffs, which on closer viewing resolve themselves into the hotels that back the promenades for 2 miles between Douglas Head and Onchan Head.

Despite this, Douglas has a cosily old-fashioned air, like that of a seaside resort of the days before the Costa del Sol was dreamt of. The spacious sea-front promenade is level with the clean, white sand; police in white helmets direct the traffic and horse-drawn trams trundle gently along. The service began in 1876 and uses 50 horses. That splendid piece of restored Victoriana, the Gaiety Theatre, also belongs to the same bygone era.

The excellent Manx Museum tells the story of the island during the days of the Norse occupation – and has natural history, archaeological and folklife collections besides. On Prospect Hill stands the House of Keys, the Lower House of the Manx parliament, the Tynwald, whose Scandinavian origins are earlier than those of Westminster.

The Tourist Trophy motorcycle race begins and ends at Nobles Park in Douglas in the early part of June each year. The T.T. is world famous, but in fact is only one of several road races held on the island during the season.

According to legend, the famous tailless cat of the Isle of Man was originally a cross between a cat and a hare. Today cats are bred at the Manx Cattery, close by the T.T. grandstand. Douglas has long been the island's commercial centre, based on its busy harbour, now also a haven for pleasure craft. The bustling town was made the island's capital in 1869.

Near the harbour is the terminus of the Isle of Man Steam Railway, a 3ft gauge steam-hauled line which runs to Port Erin on the island's southwest coast in summer. The railway was opened in 1874 and originally had branches from Douglas to Peel and from Peel to Ramsey. Of the original 16 locomotives, five remain to pull red-and-cream carriages at a leisurely pace along the 15 mile route.

EVENING REFLECTIONS *Douglas Bay's fort is a reminder that visitors have not always been welcome* (overleaf).

A Viking trail on the Isle of Man

Secluded beaches fringe an island of green hills, rugged glens and wild moors. The small fishing towns and villages have changed little over the years. There is even a reminder of the Isle of Man's lead-mining days in the giant water wheel at Laxey.

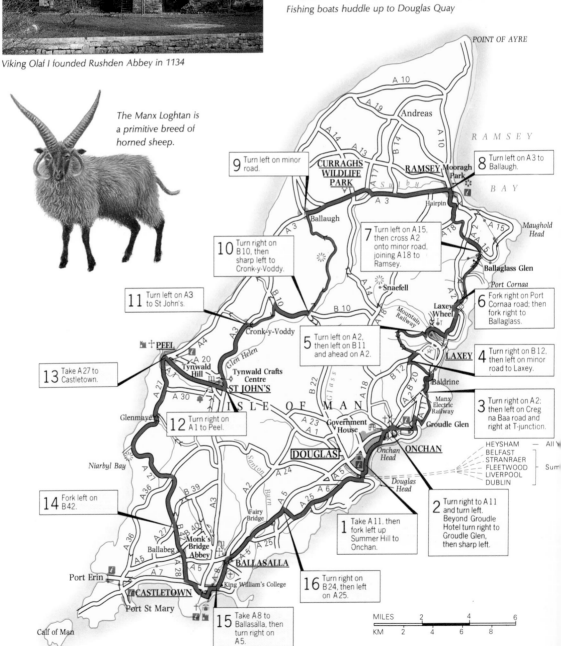

Fishing boats huddle up to Douglas Quay

Viking Olaf I founded Rushden Abbey in 1134

The Manx Loghtan is a primitive breed of horned sheep.

9 Turn left on minor road.

8 Turn left on A3 to Ballaugh.

7 Turn left on A15, then cross A2 onto minor road, joining A18 to Ramsey.

10 Turn right on B10, then sharp left to Cronk-y-Voddy.

6 Fork right on Port Cornaa road; then fork right to Ballaglass.

11 Turn left on A3 to St John's.

5 Turn left on A2, then left on B11 and ahead on A2.

4 Turn right on B12, then left on minor road to Laxey.

13 Take A27 to Castletown.

3 Turn right on A2; then left on Creg na Baa road and right at T-junction.

12 Turn right on A1 to Peel.

2 Turn right to A11 and turn left. Beyond Groudle Hotel turn right to Groudle Glen, then sharp left.

14 Fork left on B42.

1 Take A11, then fork left up Summer Hill to Onchan.

16 Turn right on B24, then left on A25.

15 Take A8 to Ballasalla, then turn right on A5.

MILES 2 4 6
KM 2 4 6 8

DOWNHAM

Lancashire
3 miles northeast of Clitheroe

For centuries, most of Downham has been in the hands of a single family, the Asshetons. Thanks to them, the village has retained its unity of atmosphere and style over the centuries. The first Asshetons built Downham Hall in the 13th century, but it was not until the early 1800s that the family really made their mark. In 20 years of almost continuous building, two William Asshetons, father and son, gave Downham its vicarage and school. They added a Regency façade to the hall, and improved the largely medieval Church of St Leonard. The hall is not open to the public.

The village sits on the slope of Pendle Hill, beside the old Roman road linking the forts at York and nearby Ribchester. One of the legionaries died beside the road, and was buried near where he fell. His gravestone is said to protrude from the base of a wall surrounding Downham Hall, just left of the gates.

The church (with the stocks opposite), Downham Hall and the inn, the Assheton Arms, are around the village green at the top end of the village. Below them, stone cottages are grouped around another green.

DRUMBURGH

Cumbria
4 miles west of Burgh by Sands

The small village of Drumburgh marks the site of the next Roman fort to Bowness eastwards along Hadrian's Wall. The fort itself has gone, but the road through the village still twists around the line of its outer walls, and to the east of the village the low sea-wall follows the line of the original turf rampart.

Nearby, Drumburgh Castle Farm was built on the ruins of an old fortified tower-house established by Thomas, Lord Dacre early in the 16th century. The end wall was built of Roman stones from the fort.

DUFTON

Cumbria
3 miles north of Appleby-in-Westmorland

Squat sandstone houses are set round a spacious green in Dufton, an ideal starting-point for exploring some fascinating countryside. From just north of the village, a track leads to the summit of the 2930ft Cross Fell, 6 miles away, while a narrow road leads off towards Knock village and Great Dun Fell. This road ceases to be public at a point about $1\frac{1}{2}$ miles beyond Knock, and from that point the 2780ft peak can be reached only on foot along a bridle path or the Pennine Way.

At Great Rundale – a wild and lovely valley stretching east from Knock – there are old mine workings where amateur geologists may find glassy barytes crystals (used in paint manufacture) as large as a man's fist and extremely heavy. Knock village has red cottages and narrow roads between high sandstone walls. In summer, the surrounding fields are full of flowers; in autumn, the hedgerows are covered with nuts and rosehips, tinted gold.

DUNSOP BRIDGE

Lancashire
8 miles northwest of Clitheroe

Between a bridge at one end and the 18th-century Thorneyholme Hall, now a hotel, at the other, is the tranquil hamlet of Dunsop Bridge. Children paddle in the safe, clear waters of the River Dunsop – which, a short way to the east of the village, merges with the River Hodder, rushing down from the Trough of Bowland. Just beyond the junction, the Hodder feeds a trout farm, whose waters seethe with fish being fattened for the table and to stock local rivers.

STEPS TO THE PAST *The heavily studded upper door of Drumburgh Castle Farm dates from 1518.*

EASEDALE TARN

Cumbria
2 miles northwest of Chapel Stile

The poet Thomas De Quincey said that Easedale in relation to Grasmere was 'a chapel within a cathedral'. Walled round by cliff-like mountainsides, the valley preserves this sense of seclusion. De Quincey also noticed the pathos of the miniature settlement, cut off from the world and dwarfed beneath bleak and unfriendly fells. Even on fine days the dark mountain shadows seem to fall ominously across the tiny green fields, and there is a sinister violence about the stream that rushes past them, aptly named Sour Milk Gill because of the curdling whiteness of its churned water. A mile further up the valley, it issues from Easedale Tarn, rated – by De Quincey again – as 'the most gloomily sublime' of Lake District tarns.

The 2 mile walk to Easedale Tarn, very steep and wet in places, is dominated at first by the immense mass of Helm Crag to the north, with its fantastic rock formation known as The Lion and the Lamb.

The walk starts from Easedale Lane in Grasmere. Follow the lane across Goody Bridge then, ignoring the turn on the right, cross Easedale Beck by the next bridge. For the rest of the walk the beck remains on the right.

Large boulders litter the valley, the so-called sheep rocks of the Ice Ages, whose shapes, when seen from a distance, resemble those of sheep sleeping on the hillside. Glaciers smoothed the backs of the rocks, and carved out their downhill faces.

The stony path climbs steeply upwards until, suddenly, the tarn lies ahead with Tarn Crag towering some 900ft above the water. The best time to see it is in the morning or early afternoon, when the sun is still catching its sheer, gleaming precipices.

EASTHAM FERRY

Merseyside
2 miles southeast of Bebington

The first ferry between Eastham and Liverpool was Job's Ferry, run by a brotherhood of local monks, but regular ferry-boats plied between here and Liverpool, carrying passengers and freight from Chester and Shrewsbury, from the early 1800s until 1929. Since then, the commercial bustle has been replaced by an oasis of calm represented by the Eastham Country Park, overlooking the River Mersey.

EGREMONT

Cumbria
5 miles south of Whitehaven

The mellow ruins of a Norman castle stand high above Egremont, on a grassy hill that overlooks the lovely valley of the River Ehen to the south, and the village's market place and wide, tree-lined main street to the north. There has been a market at Egremont since 1267, and every Friday the street is thronged with shoppers from all over the district, bargain-hunting among the colourful stalls.

The main street is virtually the whole of Egremont. Its two-storey, flat-fronted houses open their front doors straight onto the pavement. Windows and doors are surrounded by massive stone blocks, and probably the walls are stone too, except that they have long disappeared under cheerful coats of blue, yellow, green or cream. Lowes Court, on the wide main street, is an art centre featuring the work of local painters.

The castle was built between 1130 and 1140 by William de Meschines where a Danish fortification once stood. The most complete part still standing is a Norman arch that once guarded the drawbridge entrance. Nearby is the stump of a market cross, which may date from the early 13th century. It stands close to an unusual four-sided sundial. Through the arch lies the grassed centre of the castle, now set with trees, and beyond the ruined walls are views across the village, the valley and the meandering Ehen.

Rising above a screen of trees is the red-sandstone tower of the parish church of St Mary and St Michael, built in the early 1880s and a superb example of Victorian Gothic architecture. Inside, slender pillars support the roof and nave arches, with the capitals at the top carved in foliage designs; there are almost 100 such carvings and no two are alike.

The village is rich in ancient legends, including that of the Horn of Egremont. In the Middle Ages this great horn hung in the castle and could be blown only by the rightful lord.

It is said that in the 13th century Hubert de Lucy arranged to have the rightful lord, his brother Eustace, murdered while on a crusade, so that he could claim the castle for himself. But the plot misfired and Eustace returned to blow the horn and thereby establish his rightful claim. Hearing the horn, Hubert fled and entered a monastery. The horn and the legend are recalled in the name of a local pub and in a poem by William Wordsworth.

In September each year, legend becomes fact when Egremont celebrates its Crab Fair. The fair dates from the 13th century, when crab apples were distributed to bystanders. Now Worcester apples are thrown from a lorry as it drives down the main street and the day proceeds with traditional sports such as wrestling and hound trailing, in which specially bred hounds, similar to foxhounds, follow an arduous trail over hills and across the River Ehen in a kind of fox hunt without a fox. But the highlight of the celebrations is the World Championship Gurning Contest – a beauty competition with a difference. Each 'gurner' places his or her head through a horse collar and tries to pull an ugly face. The face judged to be the ugliest is the winner.

Just outside the village of Beckermet, 3 miles south, is Yeorton Hall, once the home of Hugh Gaitskell, the former Labour Party leader. From the village, a pleasant 1 mile walk leads southwest to Braystones, where there is a sandy beach and safe bathing.

ELTERWATER
Cumbria
3 miles west of Ambleside

An open expanse of bracken-clad turf above the village is a wonderful viewpoint, looking over Elterwater's clustered rooftops to the craggy Langdale Pikes which rise to almost 2500ft beyond. The grandeur of the mountains is emphasised by the fact that Elterwater is only 206ft above sea level.

Flanked by tree-clad slopes, the village is built of attractive, grey-green stone and has as its focal point a small triangular green overlooked by the whitewashed Britannia inn. Nearby, a bridge spans Great Langdale Beck as it splashes down over mossy boulders. Bridge End, on the far bank, is an old cottage with a periodic carpet of moss over its slate roof. The curious little first-floor galleries on some cottages are spinning galleries on which women used to weave and spin the local wool, making the best of natural light. At Barnhowe, spinning lessons can be arranged at short notice.

Elterwater was once a centre for charcoal burning. Charcoal made from juniper wood was particularly suitable for making gunpowder, which became an important Lake District industry in the 18th century. The gunpowder works at Elterwater did not close until the late 1920s. Today, slate quarrying is a flourishing local industry and much of the slate is exported.

Great Langdale Beck flows into Elter Water, one of the area's smallest lakes, a few hundred yards below the village. A lovely walk, much of it through National Trust woodlands, leads southwards for a mile or so to Skelwith Bridge, where there is an impressive waterfall.

UNDERCOVER *Slate rooftops overlook colourful flower gardens in the sheltered village of Elterwater.*

ENNERDALE
Cumbria
About 11 miles south of Cockermouth

Seven miles of fell, forest and water combine to make Ennerdale one of the wildest and most attractive valleys in the Lake District. It is the only one not accessible by car – the motor road stops by Bowness Knott, half a mile from the north bank of Ennerdale Water. But there are excellent footpaths north, south and west of the lake shores, with views of the 811ft Angler's Crag rock that towers to the north of the lake.

Three miles east of the lake is the 2927ft Pillar mountain. Its famous crag, mentioned in Wordsworth's *The Brothers*, presents a challenge to climbers.

FINSTHWAITE

Cumbria
8 miles northeast of Ulverston

One of the Lake District National Park's smallest villages, Finsthwaite nestles among low, wooded hills in a beautiful landscape near the southern end of Windermere. It is reached along narrow lanes, or by a walk of just under 2 miles which starts from Newby Bridge and skirts the grounds of Finsthwaite House. Another footpath runs on from the village into the heart of Grizedale Forest, where deer roam and buzzards wheel above the trees. Immediately north of the village, space is provided for motorists to park their cars and take a short, woodland walk to High Dam pool, in the lee of Finsthwaite Heights.

Finsthwaite itself is an attractive little cluster of typical Lakeland farms and cottages. Whitewashed walls contrast pleasantly with the bare, rough-hewn stones of their neighbours.

The buildings lie in a bowl which slopes gently down to the village church and the school, built in the 19th century and now used as a community centre.

The church, crowned by a squat steeple, has a timber-framed porch and, within, a fine coloured ceiling. The building dates from the 18th and 19th centuries. On Finsthwaite Heights a tower commemorates the 'Officers, seamen and marines of the Royal Navy whose matchless conduct and irresistible valour defeated the fleets of France ... and promoted and protected liberty and commerce, 1799'.

FLOOKBURGH

Cumbria
2 miles south of Cartmel

A thriving fishing fleet operates from Flookburgh, and its catches of flukes (the local name for flounders) gave the village its name. It is also an important centre for the local shrimping industry.

Flookburgh was originally granted a borough charter in the reign of Edward I, and the original charter can be seen in the parish church, which has a weather vane in the form of a fluke, or flatfish, crowning its massive west tower.

FORMBY

Merseyside
11 miles north of Liverpool

More than a mile of high sand dunes separate the town of Formby from its beach. Two lanes lead to beachside car parks from which there are splendid walks with views of the ships entering and leaving the Mersey, backed by the distant mountains of Wales.

Much of the coastline is managed by the National Trust. A bumpy road slicing through an avenue of Scots pines leads from the National Trust warden's hut to a large car park beside the sand dunes. Formby Point, 2 miles west of Formby, and Ainsdale National Nature Reserve are linked by a footpath from Freshfield station and form one of the most extensive dune

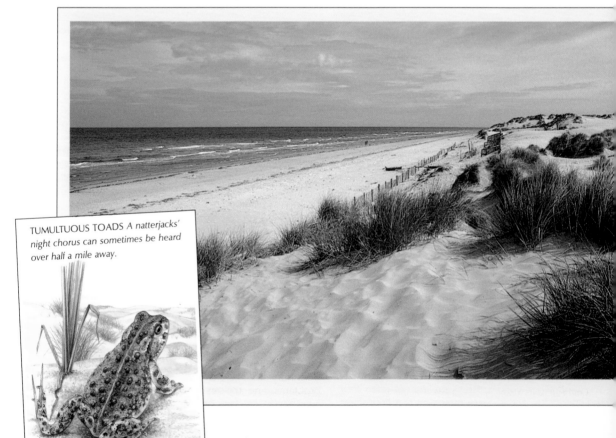

TUMULTUOUS TOADS *A natterjacks' night chorus can sometimes be heard over half a mile away.*

systems in Britain. There is a red squirrel reserve here and this is also one of the last remaining strongholds of the natterjack toad, which breeds in the shallow pools.

Formby's sandy beach is one of the finest on the northwest coast, although bathing is only safe close inshore, because of strong currents further out at sea and the speed with which the incoming tide can cut off whole areas of beach with little or no warning. To the south, near the point where the little River Alt flows into the sea by Hightown, the dunes are used as firing ranges. Volunteer lifeguards patrol from Formby Point south to the Alt.

FOXDALE
Isle of Man
6 miles southeast of Peel

As any Manx naturalist will confirm, there are no foxes on the Isle of Man, nor have there been in human memory; perhaps St Patrick banished them, together with the snakes. The name of the village is actually derived from the Norse *Fos*, meaning a 'waterfall' or 'rapid'. The fall still exists in Lower Foxdale, close to where the little River Neb runs under a bridge half-buried in flowering plants and creepers, then continues down rocky steps through a wooden glen. The fall is no Niagara in summer, but in winter it has been known to push banks aside and wash cars away.

Close by the bridge is the very attractive Mill House, its walls agleam with white paint and hung with flower baskets filled with petunias. A little uphill is a terrace of hardly less handsome brownstone cottages. There is a gap between Lower Foxdale and Foxdale itself, and this too is pretty, with white and brown houses perched high above the road, and surrounded by walled gardens filled with flowering shrubs. The villages lie in a bowl of towering, wooded hills, whose lower slopes are a smoothly rounded pattern of pastel-coloured fields, neatly divided by hedgerows.

This peaceful idyll is by no means ancient. During the 18th and 19th centuries, mines around Foxdale produced large quantities of lead and a fair amount of silver – so much so that a railway was opened in 1886 to carry the minerals to St John's. But the last mine petered out in 1911 and the railway, too, closed – in the 1930s – leaving only the trackway and the fading scars of the mines on the hills to the east above the village. As for the miners, they took their skills – and their Manx names – to Australia, the United States and the goldfields of South Africa.

FRECKLETON
Lancashire
2 miles south of Kirkham

A large straggling village on the road which runs along the north bank of the River Ribble, Freckleton has a small brick church built in 1837 which has box pews and a lovely Jacobean pulpit which came from Kirkham church. The pulpit's eight sides are embellished with miniature, minutely detailed faces and the inscription: 'Cry aloud, spare not: lift up thy voice like a trumpet'.

On the marshland near the edge of the River Ribble a force of Roundheads under the command of Colonel Booth defeated the Royalists in the Battle of Preston in 1648, taking 1000 prisoners.

FRIAR'S CRAG
Cumbria
On the eastern shore of Derwent Water

A large car park is the usual home during the summer months of the mobile Century Theatre, which presents varied productions. From the theatre an easy stroll leads to Friar's Crag, from which there is one of Lakeland's most magnificent views. A monument to John Ruskin, who recorded his 'intense joy' at the view from the crag, looks out over Derwent Water, with a backdrop of hills including the humpbacked Cat Bells.

The viewpoint, owned by the National Trust, is often crowded in summer. However, for winter visitors the views of snow-kissed mountains turned pink by the light of the setting sun are memorable.

FURNESS ABBEY
Cumbria
2 miles northeast of Barrow-in-Furness

Furness Abbey was founded in 1123, but the present buildings belong almost entirely to the period after it became a Cistercian house in 1147. A great deal of the abbey survives, including the east end of the church and the transepts up to roof level, and the east side of the cloister with the adjoining 13th-century chapter house. The surviving parts of other monastic buildings make it possible to appreciate the size of the abbey. The dormitory was over 200ft long, the infirmary 126ft, and the refectory nearly 150ft (at Fountains Abbey in Yorkshire the refectory is about 100ft long and the dormitory about 110ft). The abbey's great size created problems, and the refectory in particular seems to have been made smaller, possibly in 1500.

SAND FLOWERS *A rich variety of rare plants grows on the sand dunes in Ainsdale Nature Reserve. Round-leaved wintergreen, dune helleborine and grass-of-Parnassus live around the shallow salty pools. On the drier dunes there is an array of colourful plants, including evening primrose, which has a delicate fragrance and numerous medicinal properties.*

Common wintergreen   *Evening primrose*

GARRIGILL

Cumbria
4 miles southeast of Alston

A homely village, Garrigill is bypassed by the holiday routes, at the foot of the Pennines. Stone houses, one shop, a small church of 1790 and a handsome Congregational chapel of 1757 are set around a spacious green near the South Tyne river. A lane parallel with the river leads south and becomes a track, part of the Pennine Way, climbing through wild moorland to the summit of Cross Fell – which, at 2930ft, is the highest point along the walk.

GISBURN

Lancashire
7 miles northeast of Clitheroe

On Thursdays Gisburn's pubs are open all day and its narrow street echoes to the sound of cattle, sheep and the patter of the auctioneer. The village has long been a market centre, and a focal point for travellers between Lancashire and Yorkshire.

Gisburne Park, formerly the family seat of Lord Ribblesdale, is now a hospital and not open to the public, but it is ringed by footpaths and its grounds are often visited by a wild herd of sika deer.

At Todber, 1 mile south, is a steam museum, and steamrollers and tractors are often heard and seen clanking and puffing along the road between Gisburn and the museum. Todber has a caravan site and a large playground for children.

GLASSON

Cumbria
1 mile southeast of Port Carlisle

The Lancaster Canal meets the sea at Glasson's docks, whose cheerful bustle makes a happy contrast with the commercial decay of many other harbours on this coast. The harbour was built in 1783, and its docks were among the earliest in England to have lock-gates which could keep the water level constant as the tide outside rose and fell.

The original West Indies trade through Lancaster died early in the last century. Glasson is now an important boating centre, while its nearness to the M6 has revived the coastal trade, and small trading vessels are now using the dock again.

GLEN MAYE

Isle of Man
3 miles south of Peel

The coast road running south from Peel leads into the steep, narrow valley of Glen Maye. In front of the Waterfall Hotel there is a large car park, from which a path leads down the glen and past a magnificent waterfall and a fast-flowing stream. A lane from the

hotel runs parallel to the glen and leads to a small park near to the point where the stream reaches a pebbly beach through steep, overhanging cliffs. The meeting place of the path and the lane is the starting point of another footpath which runs for 3 miles over Contrary Head, with marvellous views all the way.

GLEN MOOAR

Isle of Man
1 mile southwest of Kirk Michael

A narrow lane off the coast road leads to a small car park in Glen Mooar above the waterfall of *Spooyt Vane* – Manx for 'White Spout'. Above the west bank of the stream are the remains of a Christian chapel dating back some 1000 years, with a hermit's cell called in Manx *Cabbal Pheric*, or 'Patrick's Chapel'.

GOSFORTH

Cumbria
2 miles northeast of Seascale

The western gateway to the Lake District National Park, Gosforth is an attractive place of sturdy stone-and-slate houses that might have been built at any time in the last 300 years. A clue is provided by the library, over whose door a plaque reads: 1628 JOHN ET MARGARAT SHEARWEN. There is an excellent crafts shop and a temptingly scented home bakery.

The chief treasures of Gosforth, however, are the church and its remarkable collection of Norse and early Christian monuments, many of which were discovered in the foundations during 19th-century renovations. Finest of all is the tall, slender cross in the churchyard whose carvings of wolves, snakes and dragons, mingled with Christian motifs, are said to depict the old Norse saga *Volispa*, which deals with the triumph of Christianity over paganism.

GRANGE-IN-BORROWDALE

Cumbria
4 miles south of Keswick

At the point where Borrowdale opens out to meet the southern shore of Derwent Water, the village of Grange – once the grain store for Cistercian monks at Furness Abbey – lies in a landscape of soaring splendour. Grange itself is barely 250ft above sea level, but scree-covered slopes patchworked with turf and bracken tower immediately behind the village. There are craggy peaks more than 2000ft high little more than 1 mile away.

The clear, pebble-bedded River Derwent is spanned by a graceful but narrow bridge which links Grange to the Keswick road.

Until the road was built, probably in the 18th century, the small, scattered villages of Borrowdale could be reached only on foot or horseback. The bridge is overlooked by a little Methodist chapel built

from local green stone at the end of the 19th century. Beyond it, cottages and a farm are grouped round an open space which forms the centre of the village. It is a pleasant blend of natural stone and whitewash. Stone slabs set on end form a fence in front of the Chapel of the Holy Trinity, built in 1860 beside the road between Grange and Braithwaite.

Just beyond the village on the Rosthwaite road is Quay Foot Quarry car park, from which a signposted footpath leads through woods to the Bowder Stone. This 2000 ton rock was probably left perched on its narrow base by the melting of a huge glacier. Steps lead to its summit, from which there are magnificent views into Borrowdale.

GRANGE-OVER-SANDS
Cumbria
9 miles north of Morecambe

All the amenities of a modern holiday resort are found at Grange in the surroundings of a genteel Victorian watering place. The town takes its name from the grange, or granary, once built there by the Augustinian monks of Cartmel Priory which stood $1\frac{1}{2}$ miles

OVERLOOKED VILLAGE *Grange-in-Borrowdale lies nearly 2000ft below the summit of Castle Crag Mountain.*

inland. Grange grew in the 16th and 17th centuries on the thriving coastal trade in coal, and its modern role as a holiday resort was assured when it was joined to the main Furness Railway line in 1857.

Grange's position, facing southeast and therefore sheltered from westerly winds, makes it a gardener's paradise, and its ornamental gardens are renowned. A mile-long promenade curves around the shore of Morecambe Bay, fringed by rare trees and shrubs. Bathing is best confined to the public swimming pool, because of currents off the beach and the rapid approach of the incoming tide.

Hampsfield Fell, behind the town, is crowned by the Hospice, a shelter for travellers built by Thomas Remmington, Vicar of Cartmel between 1835 and 1854. An indication on the 700ft hilltop identifies the peaks which make up the spectacular view.

At Lindale-in-Cartmel, about 2 miles north, is an iron monument to the 18th-century ironmaster John Wilkinson, who spent his youth in the district and went on to cast the pieces for the world's first iron bridge – at Ironbridge, Shropshire.

GRASMERE

Cumbria

3 miles northwest of Ambleside

William Wordsworth spent 14 of his most creative years in Grasmere, living at Dove Cottage, Allan Bank and The Rectory. Buildings of rough-hewn local stone nestle in a great natural amphitheatre, with the 2003ft high summit of Heron Pike dominating the view eastwards.

The village and its valley are seen at their best from the surrounding hills, but motorists can enjoy fine views from the Keswick road as it sweeps down from the north. On the left is the Swan Hotel in which Sir Walter Scott is said to have had breakfast when staying with the frugal Wordsworth. Swan Hill, opposite the hotel, runs gently down towards the centre of Grasmere after crossing the River Rothay. Several hotels are clustered in the heart of Grasmere before the main road reaches St Oswald's Church, on the banks of the Rothay. The small building by the lych gate was the village school from 1660 until 1854. Since then it has been notable for 'Sarah Nelson's Original Celebrated Grasmere Gingerbread', which is baked on the premises to a traditional village recipe. Wordsworth knew the church well and described it in his epic poem, *The Excursion*.

Every year, on the Saturday nearest to August 5, St Oswald's Day, a colourful 'rush-bearing' procession wends its way through Grasmere to the church. The ancient ceremony, kept alive only in Grasmere and a few other North of England villages, dates from the time when church floors were of bare earth and had rushes scattered over them for warmth and cleanliness. Grasmere's church was paved with flagstones in the 19th century, but children still take symbolic gifts made of rushes and flowers to the church. The rush-bearers are given pieces of gingerbread stamped with St Oswald's name.

One of eight yews planted by Wordsworth in 1819 stands near his grave, in the southeast corner of the

LAKESIDE BEAUTY *Wooded slopes sweep down from the village to Grasmere's tranquil lake.*

FAMILY NEST *Three of Wordsworth's children were born in Dove Cottage, where he lived for nine years.*

churchyard. The poet is buried with his wife, Mary, who died in 1859. In the same corner are the graves of Dorothy Wordsworth, William's devoted sister, and three of the poet's children, Dora, Catherine and Thomas, who died at The Rectory in 1812.

Beyond the church, Stock Lane skirts fields leading to Grasmere lake before reaching Town End — a delightful 'mini suburb' of stone, slate-roofed cottages with superb westward views. Dove Cottage is in a small lane just off the road. William and Dorothy moved there in December 1799, paying an annual rent of £8. Three years later the poet married Mary Hutchinson, and three of their children — John, Dora and Thomas — were born at Dove Cottage during the following four years. In 1808 the Wordsworths moved to Allan Bank, and the cottage became the home of their friend Thomas De Quincey, author of *The Confessions of an English Opium Eater*. The Wordsworth Museum, 25yds from Dove Cottage, contains many of Wordsworth's personal possessions, and there is also a reconstruction of a typical farmhouse kitchen. The museum is open for most of the year.

Allan Bank, where the Wordsworths lived until 1811, is private and not open to visitors. The poet and his family next spent two years in The Rectory, opposite St Oswald's Church, before moving to Rydal Mount – on the road between Grasmere and Ambleside – where Wordsworth lived until his death in 1850.

Grasmere Sports – England's equivalent to the Highland Games – are held on a Thursday in late August, and regularly attract up to 12,000 spectators. The main events include traditional wrestling, races to the summit of Butter Crag and back, and hound-trailing in which dogs race over the surrounding hills following a scent laid earlier in the day.

GREAT SALKELD
Cumbria
5 miles northeast of Penrith

Red-sandstone buildings, typical of Cumbria's Eden Valley, flank the road for almost half a mile before forming a cluster around Great Salkeld's ancient, part-Norman church. Monks are said to have rested there with St Cuthbert's coffin after fleeing from Viking raiders in the 9th century.

The church is dedicated to St Cuthbert and has a sturdy, ivy-clad tower, built in the 14th century to serve as a refuge when raiders swept over the border from Scotland. The south doorway, sheltered by a porch, is a fine example of Norman work with heavy, dogtooth carving and numerous heads. A sword and several pieces of armour hang on the west wall. They were found in 1644, after a Civil War skirmish.

Great Salkeld is a village where attractive cottages and farmhouses blend with sandstone barns. Several buildings have external staircases of stone. The Highland Drove, a whitewashed, late 18th-century pub near the church, recalls the days when Highland cattlemen drove their herds south to English markets.

GREYSTOKE
Cumbria
5 miles west of Penrith

Hills sweep up to almost 1200ft above Greystoke, and on the edge of a vast, wooded park stands a castle. Seen from the road the castle is an impressive sight, but little of its medieval origins remain and the present battlemented, Elizabethan-style building was built in the 19th century by the Howard family. It is privately owned and not open to the public.

A stone gateway at the entrance to Greystoke Castle overlooks the tiny village green. The Boot and Shoe Inn, on the opposite side, dates from the 19th century, and behind it are attractive 17th-century cottages with cobbled forecourts and dates carved above their doors. Most of the other buildings in the village are of the clean-cut stonework typical of the 19th century. Among them is the village school, built in 1838.

Greystoke's church, St Andrew's, is larger than most parish churches in Lakeland. It was built in the 13th century, at about the same time as the original castle. Traces of that period survive, though the building was considerably altered in the 15th century. The east window has medieval stained glass showing incidents in the life of St Andrew. There were once six chantry chapels in use, but today only one remains, dedicated to those who died in the Second World War.

To the east of the village are three farmhouses, built in the 18th century by the 11th Duke of Norfolk to 'enhance' the landscape. They are follies; Fort Putnam and Bunkers Hill are shaped like forts and Spire House resembles a church. Two nearby cairns, Blencow Bank and Leadon Howe, mark Bronze Age burial sites.

GRIZEDALE FOREST
Cumbria
Between Coniston Water and Windermere

About 8700 acres of integrated forest and farmland make up Grizedale Forest, which is run by the Forestry Commission. The introduction to the area is a glorious drive through rolling wooded hills, with meadows running up from the edge of the road to the tree line.

Car parks and picnic sites are numerous, and at the heart of the forest is the Visitor and Wildlife Centre. It stands near the site of Grizedale Hall, which was a Second World War prison camp for German officers. The hall was demolished in 1956, but the outbuildings remain to provide a nucleus for the visitor centre, a forest shop, a theatre and other facilities.

Throughout the summer there is an exhibition on the natural history, archaeology and industries of the forest. Concerts, lectures and film shows are held in the theatre.

A number of waymarked trails begin at the Centre. They range from the mile-long Millwood Forest Trail to the $9\frac{1}{2}$ mile Silurian Way, and provide opportunities to observe the forest's plants and animals – including red squirrels and the roe and red deer whose ancestors roamed these hills long before man came. There are observation hides in the forest, including one overlooking a tarn where wildfowl can be seen.

GROUDLE GLEN
Isle of Man
3 miles northeast of Douglas

Trains on the Manx Electric Railway stop at Groudle Glen, one of the island's best-known glens. Paths with bridges descend a narrow valley through groves of beech, larch and pine and past rocky cliffs and rushing rapids to a small stony beach.

GUTTERBY SPA
Cumbria
2 miles northwest of Silecroft

The difficulty involved in reaching the stretch of wild, open beach known as Gutterby Spa often leaves it deserted even on the hottest summer day. The approach track, narrow and badly surfaced, turns off the Whiteheaven to Broughton in Furness coast road and winds for more than a mile down to the beach. The journey is amply rewarded by the empty beach and the splendour of the view, with the mountains inland dominated by the 1970ft Black Combe.

The beach of sand and shingle is backed by high cliffs – but nowhere is there any sign of the mineral spring which it was once hoped would turn Gutterby into a spa resort.

HADRIAN'S WALL

Cumbria, Northumberland and Tyne and Wear
Extending between Bowness-on-Solway and Wallsend

As a barrier against infiltration by barbarians from Scotland and as a base against attack by them, a great wall was built by order of the Roman Emperor Hadrian in the years AD 122–30. It ran for 73 miles, from the mouth of the River Tyne in the east to the Solway Firth in the west, taking advantage of every natural point of strength and, at its highest, following ground 1230ft above sea level.

Built of stone and 20ft high in its eastern part, and of turf and 12ft high in its western sector, it had 17 large forts about 5 miles apart, and a line of smaller forts each a Roman mile apart. Between each pair of these 'milecastles' were built two signal towers 20ft square. On the northern side of the wall ran a continuous protective ditch, averaging 27ft in width and 9ft in depth. On the southern side was the *vallum*, a flat-bottomed ditch about 20ft wide and 10ft deep, with earthworks on either side; it ran straight from point to point like a Roman road and therefore often deviated from the course of the wall. This ditch seems to have served as the civil boundary. A road, now known as the Military Way, was built later between wall and *vallum* and was about 20ft wide. The wall was abandoned in AD 197 and a century later was rebuilt and regarrisoned. It was finally abandoned in AD 383.

The first important survey of the wall was made by William Camden, scholar and historian, who first published his *Britannia* in 1586. Archaeological research has continued from his day to the present. The wall suffered much destruction after the Jacobite rebellion of 1745, the stones being used to build a new road from Newcastle to Carlisle; and even in the Second World War 300yds of it were quarried for military use. The museum in Carlisle has an excellent collection from the wall, including votive stones and altars dedicated to many different deities – Jupiter, Fortune, Germanic gods, the Mother Goddesses, and the soldiers' god, Mithras. There are also other museums along the wall, notably in Northumberland at Housesteads, Chesters, Corbridge and Vindolanda.

AN ENGINEERING MIRACLE *Hadrian's Wall, most remarkable of all Roman frontier works, took just over 7 years to build.*

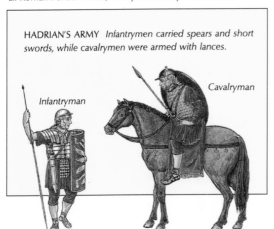

HADRIAN'S ARMY *Infantrymen carried spears and short swords, while cavalrymen were armed with lances.*

Infantryman

Cavalryman

HALLIN FELL

Cumbria

½ mile northwest of Howtown

It is not always the highest peaks that provide the finest views. Hallin Fell is not much more than 1260ft above sea level, and yet a superb Lakeland panorama is visible from its neatly built summit cairn. The mountain is tucked into the inside of Ullswater's 'elbow', and commands views down both stretches of the lake. Across the water are the craggy splendours of Gowbarrow Park. To the northwest lies the Skiddaw massif. The great ridge of Helvellyn dominates the southwest. To the south are the beautiful valleys of Boardale, Bannerdale and Rampsgill, flat-bottomed and U-shaped in perfect Lakeland style. The valley bottoms are stone-walled, carefully tended, green and lush; but beyond the walls bracken sweeps over the fell, a dark blanket broken only by the darker outlines of naked crags. The path to the summit of Hallin Fell starts from opposite Martindale church. It is said that the fell can be climbed comfortably from the church in bare feet, so velvety is the turf.

Hallin Fell is also a good starting point for a fine walk of about 5 miles along the lake shore, from the hamlet of Howtown, at the foot of the fell, to Patterdale; in parts it is woodland walking at its finest, through oak, beech and sycamore with the shining waters of the lake visible through the trees. The stretch of juniper scrub on Birk Fell is the most extensive in the Lakes. It is possible to return to Howtown by lake steamer from Patterdale between Easter and September.

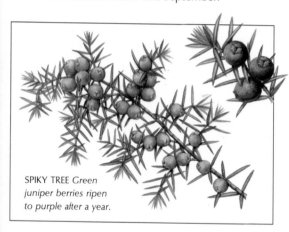

SPIKY TREE *Green juniper berries ripen to purple after a year.*

HALTON

Lancashire

3 miles northeast of Lancaster

An iron bridge just wide enough for a car spans the tree-lined banks of the River Lune at Halton. A mile upstream is the Crook of Lune, a beautiful wooded valley. Norman kings chose the village as the chief centre for their 22 Lonsdale Townships and built a castle high above the river; no trace of it remains but its site, a grassy mound marked by a flagpole, is a fine viewpoint.

The village is a delightful mix of cottages and imposing houses, all of them built in local stone. St Wilfrid's Church has a dominating 15th-century tower, and an 11th-century carved cross in the churchyard. The Boat House, opposite, is built on the site of an old ferry-stage by the river.

UNUSUAL ENTRANCE *St Wilfrid's in Halton has a rare half-timbered porch underneath its 15th-century tower.*

A parking area by the southern end of the bridge is a convenient starting point for walks beside a stretch of river which is popular with anglers and oarsmen, and noted for the fine quality of its trout and salmon. Farther upstream the river is more turbulent, and canoeists can often be seen exercising their strength and skills in the torrents cascading over the weirs.

Aughton, a picturesque village on a hillside, lies 3 miles northeast of Halton. The thriller writer E. C. Lorac (1894–1958) lived here and often referred to the Lune Valley, notably in *Stillwater* and *Crook o' Lune*.

The road continues through the hidden hamlet of Gressingham, then crosses the Lune over a narrow bridge to Hornby, whose castle keep can be seen for miles. The keep was erected by Sir Edward Stanley, who became Lord Monteagle after the Battle of Flodden Field in 1513. His coat of arms decorates the church tower in thanksgiving for his safe return from the battlefield.

HARDKNOTT PASS

Cumbria

Between the Duddon and Esk river valleys

A battery of notices at the bottom of Hardknott Pass warn that the pass is a single-track road, unsuitable in winter conditions, has severe gradients (maximum 30% – 1-in-3), is unsuitable for caravans and requires extreme caution. Often an RAF Mountain Rescue truck stands by.

Though the gradients are fierce, the road is adventurous rather than terrifying. In any case, it is a challenge that should be met, for Hardknott Pass contains one of the great sights of England. This is Hardknott Castle, a vast stone fort that the Romans called Mediobogdum and set high in the fells to command Eskdale and the road to the east.

Despite its size – it covers some 3 acres – the fort is remarkably easy to miss when coming from the west. The road passes it by without acknowledgment or sign, and the only clue is a small car park cut into the bank on the left about half a mile back from the summit. The fort lies just behind the car park.

Eased into a wild, sloping plateau, the outer wall – partly rebuilt – stands 10ft high and even after 1800 years the foundations of the commandant's house, and the granaries, are perfectly clear. So are those of the bath-house outside the wall, though the wooden barracks in which the troops lived have long vanished.

The garrison was not drawn from imperial legions, who were seldom posted to such distant stations, but from auxiliaries recruited in the provinces. The regiment at Hardknott was the 4th Cohort of Dalmatians from what is now Yugoslavia. What they thought of the Cumbrian winter winds after their sunny homeland might easily be imagined – though they could be drilled into warmth on the parade ground east of the fort. This ground was hammered out, with enormous labour, from the boulder-strewn mountainside; military priorities change little with the centuries. What gives the scene its particular attraction is how very little it can have altered since Roman days. There are the same sounds of wind and water, the same crags standing over the pass. The toy-like farms and fields away down in Eskdale are tidier now, probably, than they were then. But the hard glint of the sea at the far end, and the mountain clouds touched by pillars of light, are unchanging.

HAVERIGG

Cumbria
1 mile southwest of Millom

The 12 mile long sweep of beach which stretches from the estuary of the River Esk at Ravenglass to the estuary of the River Duddon ends at Haverigg in a long expanse of low-tide sand, backed by broad sand dunes. On the eastern side of the little village are the remains of old ironstone mines and quarries, some of which have been flooded to create the Hodbarrow Hollow lake.

The beach is ideal for picnics and sunbathing, and swimming is safe enough close to the shore when the tide is rising. Further out in the estuary, strong currents have scoured deep channels, making conditions treacherous. Footpaths along the edge of the dunes give views across the estuary to Barrow and the coast of the Isle of Walney.

HAWESWATER AND HARTER FELL

Cumbria
4 miles west and 7 miles southwest of Shap

Haweswater is the most isolated of all the lakes, accessible by road only from Shap in the east or Askham in the north. It was originally only 2½ miles long, but a dam, completed in 1940, turned the lake into a 4½ mile long reservoir – supplying Manchester with water, and submerging the village of Mardale, which used to be at its head. The ruins of Mardale's Holy Trinity Church, demolished in 1936, can be seen through the waters. Local legend says that the church bells can still be heard when the waters are whipped by strong winds.

The fearsome crags of Harter Fell, at the southern tip of the lake, are impressive on their own; but they become doubly so when seen in combination with Haweswater and the jewel-like beauty of Small Water. Every approach to the fell celebrates the marriage between rock and water. Climb up the Gatescarth Pass from Longsleddale, with the infant River Sprint tumbling beside the grass-verged track and the enormous masses of Goat Scar and Buckbarrow Crag towering over it, and from the top of the col there is a

breathtaking view over Haweswater. In a series of gigantic steps the north face of Harter Fell plunges 1800ft to the head of the lake. Continue northwest from the pass along the crag top, and Small Water lies like a sparkling teardrop far below.

A path drops diagonally down Small Water's corrie walls, and continues to the valley of the Small Water Beck. On its way to Haweswater, the stream tumbles down waterfalls, gurgles in deep pools and potholes, and races down long waterslides. From crevices in the rock, rowan trees grow at giddy angles, while the tremendous scatter of drumlins – hummocks of

WATERY GRAVE *Under the shimmering surface of Haweswater lies Mardale – from time to time the ruined church can still be seen.*

rubble left by melting Ice Age glaciers — makes the landscape wild and strange.

Another approach to Harter Fell is from Bampton by the lakeside road on the southeastern shore of Haweswater. Beyond the village of Bampton, the rolling countryside, woods and gentle fells are reminiscent of the Yorkshire Dales; but once through the woods at the northeastern end of the lake, the valley shows its proper face. The crags of Whelter, Bason, Lad and Laythwaite wall in the northwestern shore; the great masses of Harter Fell and High Street close in the head of the valley.

Two paths lead on from the car park at the end of the road. The one to the left goes to the Gatescarth Pass, a mile away; the one straight ahead climbs some 700ft to Small Water. Beyond Small Water the path strikes up the formidable corrie slope at the western end; and the backward views from here are superb. But for many it will be enough just to sit on one of the slabs of rock which surround this lovely lake, and to gaze up at the mighty bulk of Harter Fell above it.

SEVERE BEAUTY *Harter Fell's craggy heights rise to 2500ft and are often capped with snow in the summer.*

VILLAGE SCHOOL *Although Hawkshead School has been rebuilt since Wordsworth's day, it retains its charm.*

CUMBRIAN DREAM *With no cars, overhanging gables and cobbles, Hawkshead is almost too good to be true.*

HAWKSHEAD
Cumbria
4 miles south of Ambleside

It is easy to understand how Hawkshead inspired the young William Wordsworth to write some of his earliest poems. The village is a place of great charm and character, and has a timeless atmosphere. It is set halfway between Windermere and Coniston Water, with the wooded hills of Grizedale Forest rolling southwards. Esthwaite Water – on the southern edge of the village – is one of the region's smaller lakes.

Wordsworth was born in Cockermouth in 1770, but went to the grammar school in Hawkshead at the age of eight, following his mother's death. He spent much of his time there, lodging in the village until going to Cambridge in 1787. He used to stay at Anne Tyson's Cottage, where Vicarage Lane meets what is now named Wordsworth Street. It is one of several cottages with flights of outdoor steps.

The rebuilt school still stands, and inside are the original desks, including one on which Wordsworth carved his name. Other features include chimneys like upturned tubs, and an old sundial set in the wall above the door. The school is open to the public from Easter until October. It was founded in 1585 by Edwin Sandys, a local man who became Archbishop of York. In the Church of St Michael and All Angels, set on a grassy hillock above the school, is the chapel he dedicated to his parents, William and Margaret. A church has stood on the site since 1150, but the present building dates mainly from the 16th century.

Several buildings in Hawkshead, together with land

overlooking Esthwaite Water, were given to the National Trust by Beatrix Potter, the author of children's books, who lived 2 miles away in the village of Near Sawrey. Probably the oldest building in the village is the Courthouse, now a museum. It is the gatehouse of a long-vanished manor that belonged to Furness Abbey.

700-YEAR-OLD FIREPLACE *Pot-hangers swing from an adjustable fire-crane in Hawkshead Courthouse.*

HEALEY DELL

Lancashire
1 mile south of Whitworth

A tree-lined valley rich in flowers, Healey Dell forms a nature reserve beneath an aqueduct towering 105ft above the River Spodden. The 200ft long, eight-arched viaduct was built around 1880 to carry the railway from Rochdale to Bacup. It now forms part of a nature trail beginning close to the main Bacup road, and provides spectacular views. The railway closed in the 1960s, but the ruins of the old station at Broadley can still be found amid tangled vegetation. Below, the Spodden tumbles through the narrow, winding dell.

HERDHILL SCAR

Cumbria
About 1 mile west of Bowness-on-Solway

The small headland of Herdhill Scar projecting out into the Solway Firth from the Cumbrian coast is all that remains of the embankment and approach to a railway viaduct which once ran for more than a mile across the firth to the Scottish shore. The viaduct was opened during the railway building boom of 1869 to provide a direct link between the iron-ore mines of Cumbria and the smelting furnaces of Lanarkshire, bypassing the main line through Carlisle and Gretna.

The viaduct never carried heavy traffic, and was vulnerable to wind and weather. In the winter of 1875, water penetrated into the hollow centres of the bridge pillars and froze, expanding and cracking the supports. Six years later drifting ice floes were blown against the bridge supports, tearing open gaps in two places.

Amazingly, the viaduct was repaired, and trains continued running across it until the 1920s; the viaduct was not demolished until 1935. Until then the mile-long walk across the estuary was popular in good weather, especially among thirsty Scots wanting to enjoy a drink at an English pub on a Sunday evening.

HESKETH BANK

Lancashire
2 miles north of Tarleton

The village of Hesketh Bank lies on the Ribble estuary where it is joined by the River Douglas. The road through Hesketh Bank turns sharply to the southwest, and for about 4 miles runs along the edge of salt marshes stretching into the distance and merging with the mud and sand flats of the estuary. The whole area looks wild and forbidding, but has a haunting beauty when the sun bathes it in a shimmering haze.

HESKET NEWMARKET

Cumbria
8 miles southeast of Wigton

If you approach Hesket Newmarket from Hutton-in-the-Forest, there are spectacular views of the slopes and summits of Blencathra, Carrock Fell and Caldbeck Fells to the south and west before the road drops into the River Caldew's valley – the Lake District National Park's boundary – and you reach the tiny village.

Hesket Newmarket used to have a flourishing market where sheep and cattle were sold. A small, open-sided 18th-century building with a cobbled floor and slate roof was then the focal point for the village and the surrounding countryside. Known as the market cross, it still stands on the long, sloping village green.

HEST BANK

Lancashire
4 miles north of Lancaster

A residential suburb of Lancaster, Hest Bank lies at the start of an ancient low-tide route across the open sands of Morecambe Bay to Kents Bank, near Grange-over-Sands. At one time the route ran all the way to Bardsea, near Ulverston. Nowadays there are regular organised walks along the 11 mile route to Kents Bank, under the control of an experienced guide – an essential precaution in an area where the incoming tide can quickly advance with little warning. The walk should not be attempted without a guide.

HEYSHAM

Lancashire
3 miles southwest of Morecambe

Modern Heysham is centred on the freight harbour from which ferries also carry cars and day trippers to the Isle of Man. The huge square block of Heysham's nuclear power station can be seen from as far away as Barrow, on the opposite side of Morecambe Bay.

Old Heysham, to the north, is a village of twisting narrow streets dating back to the 7th century. On the cliff above the village is the ruined chapel of St Patrick, only 28ft long by 9ft across, the sole surviving example of a Saxon single-cell chapel in England, having no partitions or porches. A few yards away are several ancient graves cut into the rock, shaped for the head and body with a socket to hold a wooden cross. When these graves were made, perhaps 1200 years ago, they would have been covered by stone slabs. St Peter's Church, set among the trees on the headland, has a Saxon doorway and west window.

HILBRE ISLANDS
Merseyside
1 mile off Hilbre Point at the northwest tip of the Wirral Peninsula

Hilbre Island and Little Hilbre Island are surrounded by a scattering of other rocks and islets, including Little Eye, on the fringe of the wide sandbank which stretches out from the Wirral shore at low water. This part of the estuary is a refuge for many different kinds of water birds – curlews, redshanks, ring-tailed plovers, knots, bar-tailed godwits, oystercatchers, dunlins and sanderlings are all here. Seals may occasionally be seen, and Hilbre Island is a nature reserve.

It is possible to visit the islands on foot: apply for a permit from the Department of Leisure Services and Tourism and follow the route shown on the map beside the lake entrance in Dee Lane. The walk takes 1 hour, and walkers should remember that the tide surrounds the islands 3 hours before high water until about 3 hours afterwards. There are no shops, tourist facilities or even fresh drinking water on the islands, and little shelter against bad weather.

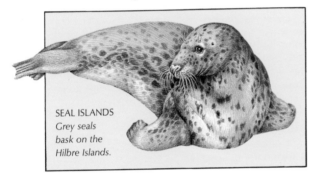

SEAL ISLANDS
Grey seals bask on the Hilbre Islands.

HINDBURNDALE
Lancashire
2–5 miles northeast of Lancaster

The River Hindburn begins as a cluster of little moorland streams rising high on the Bowland fells. The streams drain the moor top, but only after rain storms are they any more than thin trickles, running down small gullies lightly grooved into the sparse soil. Neither the streams nor their surroundings give any hint of the loveliness that lies downriver.

By Lower Thrushgill Farm, where the gullies have merged into a steep, well-developed valley and the streams have become a river, the first trees lean over the waters or sprinkle shadow on the hillsides. From the double bridges below Helks Bank Farm, a network of footpaths runs down the valley – some close to the river, some higher up the valley side – towards the village of Wray. Which path to take is a matter of on-the-spot choice. It is easy to improvise a circular walk which leads round through Lowgill – where traces of a Roman road can be seen – and back to the bridges.

But perhaps the most attractive part of Hindburndale lies even further down the valley. The road that climbs steeply out of Wray from the bridge leads up on to the flank of fellside which swells between the valleys of the Hindburn and Roeburn, and then drops down again past Park House towards the Hindburn. Here, sunlight beams through a thick canopy of oak, ash, beech and sycamore, and sparkles on the water. And the water is in full voice, rushing noisily over rapids and tumbling down small waterfalls.

SIR LOIN *James I was so impressed with his loin of beef at Hoghton Tower in 1617 that he knighted it!*

HOGHTON TOWER
Lancashire
5 miles west of Blackburn

A long, rhododendron-lined drive leads to Hoghton Tower, a fine 16th-century house perched on a hill above the River Darwen. It has always been the home of the de Hoghtons and still belongs to the family. The house is only open occasionally at weekends.

The finest room is the magnificent banqueting hall where, in 1617, James I is reputed to have dubbed a loin of prime Lancashire beef 'Sir Loin' in jest, thus adding to the butcher's list of prime cuts. The great carved oak table at which he sat is still in the hall.

The house, which was restored in the late 19th century, is built around two courtyards. The first of these is entered from the drive through a gatehouse tower which leads in turn to a terrace with fine 18th-century iron gates, and an Old English rose garden. Inside the building is a collection of antique dolls and dolls' houses, some fine 17th-century panelling and pictures of local interest.

HOLKER HALL

Cumbria
2 miles southwest of Cartmel

A magnificent deer park surrounds the stately home of the Cavendish family, close to the village of Cark. Extensively rebuilt last century after a fire, Holker Hall is an impressive mixture of 17th-century, Georgian and Victorian architecture, and is open in the summer except on Saturdays. The Victorian wing houses the library and other rooms containing fine furniture, porcelain and paintings. Over 22 acres of formal and woodland gardens are colourful in spring and summer with rhododendrons, azaleas and magnolias.

A replica of Sir Malcolm Campbell's *Bluebird* is among a collection of more than 70 vintage cars and motorcycles in the Lakeland Motor Museum, converted from Holker Hall's old stables. There are also a Craft and Countryside Museum and a Lakeland Industries Museum, as well as a baby animal farm. Events held in the grounds include hot-air balloon races, horse-team driving and old car rallies.

VINTAGE SPLENDOUR *Holker Hall's Lakeland Motor Museum has motoring memorabilia and a 1920's garage on show.*

HOLLINGWORTH LAKE

Greater Manchester
1 mile south of Littleborough

Built to provide a reliable flow of water for the Rochdale Canal, Hollingworth Lake is now under the shadow of the bridge carrying the M62. Sometimes there are boats for hire, and a ferry shuttles visitors to a wooded island with play and picnic areas and a comfortable tearoom. A visitor centre near the Fisherman's Inn provides leaflets describing the nature trails which follow the rich hedgerows and reed beds.

HOLME WOOD
Cumbria
8 miles south of Cockermouth

Seen from the road along the northeastern shore of Loweswater, across the lake's gently rippling surface, Holme Wood is a beautiful decoration, a mile-long strip of mixed woodland running from the water's edge up to the 900ft contour. But the real beauty of the wood is in its heart, where there are mature, broad-leaved trees.

A walk is the best way to savour this beauty. Go to the southeast end of the lake and walk through Watergate Farm and along the shoreline. Ford the Holme Beck and turn up along the stream, past the sparkling Holme Force waterfall. Return through the woods to the shore, where you can look across the water to the slopes of Darling Fell. At the northern end of the lake, climb to the terrace on the 900ft contour and return round the top of the wood. The scene is a perfect blend of woodland, water and hills.

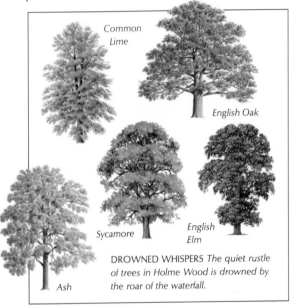

Common Lime

English Oak

Sycamore

English Elm

Ash

DROWNED WHISPERS *The quiet rustle of trees in Holme Wood is drowned by the roar of the waterfall.*

HOLMROOK
Cumbria
3 miles east of Seascale

A pretty village by a good fishing river, the Irt, Holmrook has wonderful views of Muncaster Fell. There are easy walks on bracken-covered land. Boulders in the area are stained red where sheep have rubbed dye from their coats.

Irton Church, 1 mile northeast, is built on a site where an early crusader was buried. There are striking views through the church windows of the Wasdale peaks to the northeast.

HORNBY
Lancashire
8 miles northeast of Lancaster

Gargoyles on the battlements of Hornby Castle grimace down on the village, which is divided by the River Wenning. Below the castle, Hornby's main street leads down from the 19th-century Church of St Margaret to the three-arched stone bridge across the Wenning. The street is bordered by Georgian houses and cottages, and the Royal Oak Inn bears the names of its original owners, William and Emma Gelderd, together with the date 1781.

On the other side of the bridge, the street broadens and runs between terraces of stone cottages and shops – some of which have bottle-glass windows. At the far end the street divides, one branch climbing past the old village school and the other running into the valley towards Lancaster. At the fork there is a Victorian drinking fountain, with a badge showing a cat with a rat in its jaw above a castle tower.

Hornby Castle, situated on a high hill, was built by the Normans, and the gargoyles were added by Sir Edward Stanley who commanded a contingent of Lancashire men-at-arms at the Battle of Flodden in 1513. Henry VIII created Stanley Lord Monteagle in

COMMANDING POSITION *Normans built Hornby Castle high above the Wenning, which flows through the village.*

gratitude for the part he played in the English victory over the Scots. In turn, the nobleman built the imposing Eagle Tower over the castle's central keep. He then erected the eight-sided tower at the west end of St Margaret's Church, with a Latin inscription which, translated, reads: 'Edward Stanley, Soldier, Lord Monteagle, caused me to be made.'

Later, the castle passed into the hands of the notorious forger and gambler Colonel Charteris. The colonel was cashiered from the army for cheating at cards and, in 1713, he bought the castle with his ill-gotten winnings. It is not open to the public.

Hornby contains two churches. As well as St Margaret's, there is the small Roman Catholic Church of St Mary which was built around 1820 by its priest, the historian Dr John Lingard.

HOYLAKE
Merseyside
7 miles west of Birkenhead

Best known as a golfing centre, Hoylake's name came from the Hoyle Lake, which was a broad, deep stretch of water sheltered from the open sea by sandbanks. Ancient coins found on the shore show that Hoylake was settled in Roman times. When the Dee changed its course in the 18th century, with catastrophic effects on the harbours further up the estuary, the sand filled up the Hoyle Lake, creating the broad sandbank which stretches northwards from the promenade at low water, providing a beach more than 2 miles across.

Swimmers need to beware of sudden deep channels and pools in the otherwise flat sand, and bathing is dangerous near the harbour, where sailing boats tie up to moorings which dry out at low water.

HUMPHREY HEAD
Cumbria
2 miles southeast of Flookburgh

Most of the Morecambe Bay coast is low-lying, but the cliffs at Humphrey Head, between the estuaries of the Rivers Kent and Leven, rise to 172ft, giving wide views over the sands to the Lancashire coast to the south. A hole in the face of the cliff known as Grand Arch gives a rocky climb to the top of the headland.

At the foot of the cliffs is St Agnes Well, whose waters were supposed to cure a variety of ailments including gout, ague and worms. The well brought a steady stream of pilgrims during the Middle Ages and, later, traders who sold phials of the water in the markets of Morecambe.

Nearby the 14th-century Wraysholme Tower, an old fortified farmhouse, was once the home of John Harrington, who was said to have killed on Humphrey Head the last wolf seen in England.

HURST GREEN
Lancashire
3 miles northwest of Whalley

The neat little village grouped around the Shireburn Arms has changed little since the early 1800s, when enterprising local people, learning of the new road-building techniques of John Loudon McAdam, made

FAMOUS AUTHORS *Sir Arthur Conan Doyle (left), creator of Sherlock Holmes, and J. R. R. Tolkien, who wrote the Hobbit books, were both pupils at Stonyhurst.*

the undulating road into Hurst Green one of the first in Britain to be 'macadamised'.

Just past a group of ornate almshouses a tree-lined road leads towards the mansion of Stonyhurst, built around 1600 for the Shireburn family. Since 1794 it has been a Roman Catholic boarding school for boys.

The splendid Tudor building is approached over a long grassy causeway between two lakes where wild-fowl breed. Additions over the centuries include a magnificent chapel and an observatory in classical style. A road runs alongside the buildings, and the school is open to the public occasionally during the summer. Clearly signposted footpaths run from the village through ancient woodlands straddling the banks of the River Hodder, one of England's best salmon runs. The river features in the poems of Gerard Manley Hopkins, who taught at Stonyhurst during the mid-19th century.

HUTTON-IN-THE-FOREST
Cumbria
5 miles northwest of Penrith

A drive through wooded parkland suddenly reveals the battlemented sandstone towers of Hutton-in-the-Forest. The mansion has been inhabited for more than 600 years and embraces building styles ranging from medieval to Victorian.

The original peel tower was built by Thomas de Hoton, or Hutton, who died in 1362. He was the hereditary keeper of the Royal Forest of Inglewood, which sprawled from Penrith to Carlisle and provided excellent cover for Scottish marauders.

East of the tower stands a wing added by Sir Richard Fletcher early in the 17th century. On the south front a three-storeyed façade of classical elegance is sandwiched between the peel and a Victorian 'Gothic' tower whose drawing room retains its original 1870s atmosphere. One of the mansion's portraits depicts Sir Henry Vane, a radical who supported Parliament during the Civil War. Although pardoned after the House of Stuart's restoration, he had many influential enemies and was executed on Tower Hill in 1662.

In the grounds, stately oaks and other native hardwoods overlook lakes and a 17th-century dovecote, whose birds were an important source of food.

KENDAL

Cumbria
19 miles north of Lancaster

Known as 'the auld grey town' because of its many fine old houses and other buildings in grey limestone, Kendal lies at the foot of softly rounded fells south of the Lake District. It was made a barony by Richard Coeur de Lion in 1189. In 1331 the Flemish established a woollen industry in the town, from which came its motto: *Pannus mihi panis* – wool is my bread.

The 14th-century ruined castle was the home of Catherine Parr, Henry VIII's sixth and last wife. It stands on a green hill where its overgrown moat and battlements create an impressive sight. Abbot Hall, an 18th-century mansion with period furniture, is an art gallery, with a collection of modern paintings and sculpture. A museum of Lakeland life and industry is in the stables.

George Romney, the painter, died in Kendal in 1802 and seven of his portraits hang in the town hall. Catherine Parr's silver-bound prayerbook is also displayed there.

Holy Trinity Church, one of the largest in England, was built in the 13th century and restored in the 19th century. According to legend, the helmet on the north wall of the church belonged to Robin the Devil – the Royalist Sir Robert Philipson. After being attacked at his home, Belle Isle on Lake Windermere, by Colonel Briggs, the Roundhead magistrate of Kendal, 'the Devil' led a band of armed men into the town the following Sunday, and rode into Kendal church in the middle of morning service in search of his enemy. Briggs was not there, but in the confusion Robin lost his sword and helmet. The incident was later used by Sir Walter Scott in his poem *Rokeby*.

There are many lovely river walks by the Kent, on the south side of which, 1 mile from the town centre, is the site of the Roman fort of Alauna. Above the town, Serpentine Woods provide magnificent views of the valley.

Other interesting walks in the area are along Scout Scar, 2½ miles southwest, which gives views of Lakeland and the Yorkshire Dales; and to Benson Knott, a 1041ft hill, 2 miles northeast. Potter Fell, above Burneside village, 2 miles northwest of Kendal, is a beautiful wilderness of bracken and heather.

KENTMERE

Cumbria
4 miles north of Staveley

Kentmere Hall, built in the 16th century and now a farm, was the birthplace in 1517 of Bernard Gilpin, a parson whose evangelistic travels earned him the nickname of 'The Apostle of the North'. The fells surrounding Kentmere are among the loveliest in the Lakes – easy to reach, easy to walk, and all graced with solitude. A mile west of the village, the 1475ft Garburn Pass, a bridleway linking Kentmere and Windermere, gives a superb view into Troutbeck Valley.

KESWICK

Cumbria
18 miles west of Penrith

Derwent Water, its surface dotted with little wooded islands, lies south of Keswick, a greenish-grey stone market town, often known as the Jewel of the Lakeland. In the 19th century the town and its surroundings were loved by poets, artists and writers.

One of the first poets to discover Keswick was Samuel Taylor Coleridge (1772–1834), who came to live in Greta Hall in 1800. The hall, now part of Keswick School and overlooking the River Greta, later became the home of Coleridge's brother-in-law, the Poet Laureate Robert Southey – who lived there for 40 years until his death in 1843. Among other writers who stayed in the town were Sir Walter Scott (1771–1832), Lord Tennyson (1809–92), John Ruskin (1819–1900) and Robert Louis Stevenson (1850–94).

The Keswick Museum and Art Gallery has a rare collection of manuscripts by Southey – as well as some by William Wordsworth and Sir Hugh Walpole (1884–1941), whose *Herries Chronicle* series of novels has introduced thousands to Derwent Water and Skiddaw – which looms to 3054ft north of the town.

Another museum, The Cumberland Pencil Museum, has a display of the lead pencils which are made in Keswick. They have been manufactured since the 16th century, when graphite – from which pencil leads are made – was first mined from the slopes of nearby Borrowdale. The local supply is now exhausted, but pencils are still made with imported graphite.

Overlooking the Market Place is the Moot – or Town – Hall, built in 1813 on the site of an old market building. The bell in the hall's tower is dated 1001.

For a fortnight each July a convention of thousands of Christians from all over the world is held in Keswick. One of their meeting places is the 16th-century Church of St Kentigern, in Crosthwaite, the northwest corner of the town. The church is on a site where the 6th-century Scottish saint set up a cross on a journey south. Indeed, the area owes its name, meaning 'clearing by a cross', to Kentigern's cross.

The walks around Keswick are superb. Castle Head, a 529ft hill half a mile south, gives a glorious view of Derwent Water and Bassenthwaite Lake; a mile northeast, 1203ft Latrigg provides a higher, wider panorama; and Friar's Crag, a headland on Derwent Water's eastern shore, was said by the writer John Ruskin to be one of Europe's best scenic viewpoints. A memorial to John Ruskin stands on the crag.

Closer at hand in the lake, and often fringed in the early morning with a wisp of mist, is St Herbert's Island. In the Middle Ages there was a shrine here dedicated to Herbert, a 7th-century hermit who lived on the island – and died on March 20, AD 687, the same day as his close friend St Cuthbert of Lindisfarne. Beatrix Potter modelled Owl Island in *The Tale of Squirrel Nutkin* on St Herbert's Island.

IDYLLIC SETTING *Wooded hills surround Derwent Water, which is the widest of all the lakes* (overleaf).

83

Lakes and fells at Cumbria's heart

Five of Cumbria's loveliest lakes are linked by a tour which climbs from Borrowdale over a spectacular mountain pass, then visits Wordsworth's birthplace before finally skirting lofty Skiddaw.

Ashness Bridge

A buzzard's mewing 'kiew' can often be heard in the hills

Whinlatter Pass

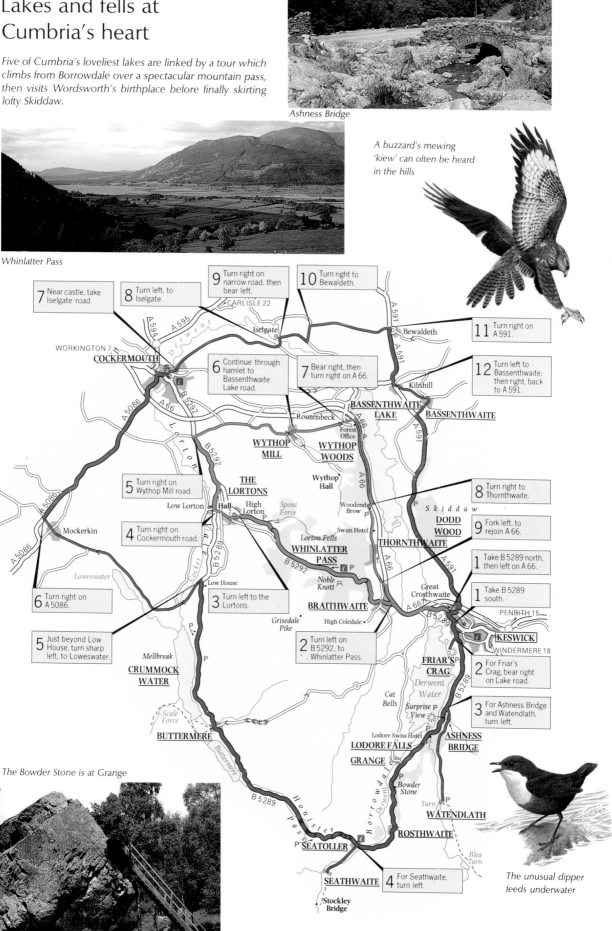

7 Near castle, take Iselgate road.

8 Turn left, to Iselgate.

9 Turn right on narrow road, then bear left.

10 Turn right to Bewaldeth.

CARLISLE 22

Iselgate

Bewaldeth

11 Turn right on A 591.

WORKINGTON 7
COCKERMOUTH

6 Continue through hamlet to Bassenthwaite Lake road.

7 Bear right, then turn right on A 66.

Kilnhill

12 Turn left to Bassenthwaite; then right, back to A 591.

Routenbeck

Forest Office

BASSENTHWAITE LAKE

BASSENTHWAITE

WYTHOP MILL

WYTHOP WOODS

5 Turn right on Wythop Mill road.

THE LORTONS

Low Lorton

Hall

High Lorton

Wythop Hall

Spout Force

Woodend Brow

Swan Hotel

Skiddaw

DODD WOOD

8 Turn right to Thornthwaite.

4 Turn right on Cockermouth road.

Mockerkin

Loweswater

Lorton Fells

WHINLATTER PASS

THORNTHWAITE

9 Fork left, to rejoin A 66.

1 Take B 5289 north, then left on A 66.

6 Turn right on A 5086.

Low House

3 Turn left to the Lortons.

Noble Knott

Great Crosthwaite

1 Take B 5289 south.

PENRITH 15

5 Just beyond Low House, turn sharp left, to Loweswater.

Grisedale Pike

High Coledale

BRAITHWAITE

2 Turn left on B 5292, to Whinlatter Pass.

KESWICK

WINDERMERE 18

Mellbreak

CRUMMOCK WATER

FRIAR'S CRAG

Derwent Water

2 For Friar's Crag, bear right on Lake road.

Cat Bells

Surprise View

3 For Ashness Bridge and Watendlath, turn left.

Scale Force

Lodore Swiss Hotel

LODORE FALLS

ASHNESS BRIDGE

BUTTERMERE

GRANGE

Bowder Stone

Tarn

The Bowder Stone is at Grange

B 5289

Honister pass

Derwent

Borrowdale

WATENDLATH

ROSTHWAITE

Blea Tarn

SEATOLLER

4 For Seathwaite, turn left.

SEATHWAITE

Stockley Bridge

The unusual dipper feeds underwater

KILLINGTON

Cumbria
3 miles southwest of Sedbergh

A narrow lane, just wide enough for a single car and sunk deep between hedgerows fragrant in spring, dips suddenly into the hidden hamlet of Killington – little more than a cluster of cottages and farms. The partly ruined Killington Hall, built in the 15th century as a fortified residence, is now a farmhouse. Its attractive front wall, half covered in thick ivy, displays heraldic symbols and handsome trefoiled windows. Opposite is a 14th-century church believed to have been once connected to the hall by a secret passage.

The road out of the village climbs steeply. Soon, hedgerows give way to open moorland scenery, varied by conifer plantations and by the bleak waters of Killington Reservoir, built during the last century to feed the Lancaster Canal.

KIRKBY LONSDALE

Cumbria
16 miles northeast of Lancaster

St Mary's churchyard in Kirkby Lonsdale has an unusual feature – an elegant eight-sided gazebo, or pavilion. It was probably built in the 18th century to provide a sheltered point from which to enjoy magnificent views of the Lune valley, which the 19th-century art critic John Ruskin called 'one of the loveliest scenes in England – therefore in the world'. Another admirer of the views was the artist J. M. W. Turner (1775–1851), who painted the valley as seen from near the churchyard. A wall plaque marks where Turner worked.

The Norman church is noted for the distinctive diamond patterns on some of its columns on the north side of the nave. St Mary's was extensively restored in the mid-1880s, when workmen uncovered burn marks in the tower. The marks were probably made in 1314, when the church was set on fire by roving Scots celebrating their victory at Bannockburn.

Kirkby Lonsdale is on high ground overlooking a bend in the River Lune. It is a town of dignified, stone buildings, which spread out from the Market Square in narrow alleys and cobbled courtyards, with names like The Horsemarket, Salt Pie Lane, and Jingling Lane. According to local tradition, the lane acquired its name because it 'jingles' if someone treads heavily along it. This may be an echoing effect from an old tunnel said to exist beneath the surface. Market day is on Thursday, when the square is crammed with stalls.

Dotted among the more modest buildings are some on a grander scale. They include the mid-Victorian Market House, built on the corner of Market Street, and the early 18th-century Old Manor House in Mill Brow. There are several inns – including the 17th-century Sun Hotel, with three pillars at the front, and the Royal Hotel, named after William IV's widow, Queen Adelaide, who convalesced here in 1840.

The town has two bridges over the Lune – an ancient one called Devil's Bridge, supposedly built by Satan; and a new one, definitely built by man in 1932. It is said that when Satan put up his bridge, he claimed the first living thing to cross it – which turned out to be an old dog. More prosaically, local historians say that the bridge dates from before 1368 – there are records to show that repairs were carried out then – and that the vicar of St Mary's raised the money to pay for it.

KIRKBY STEPHEN

Cumbria
9 miles southeast of Appleby-in-Westmorland

Perched 600ft above the fertile Eden valley, Kirkby Stephen has been an important wool town since the Middle Ages. Today its long main street is often crammed with sheep being driven from the fells to market. Nearby, brightly painted shops and old coaching inns huddle among attractive cobbled squares.

Just off the Market Place is the 13th-century parish church of St Stephen, which is approached along a drive. Inside the church is a collection of stones dating from before the Norman Conquest, and part of an Anglo-Danish cemetery cross depicting Loki, the Danish form of the Devil. The figure was carved in the 10th century, and is the only one of its kind in Britain.

Across the road from the church is a house with an open gallery on which the women did their spinning and weaving to make the most of the daylight.

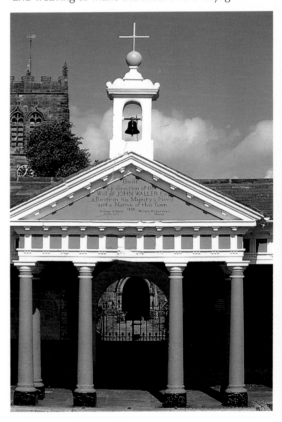

CHEERFUL COLONNADE *The portico above Kirkby Stephen's church gate was given in 1810 by a local purser.*

KIRKBY THORE

Cumbria
4 miles northwest of Appleby-in-Westmorland

A former meeting place for two Roman roads across the fells, Kirkby Thore was the site of the Roman fort of Bravoniacum. The medieval St Michael's Church was partly built of stones from the fort. Kirkby Thore Hall, to the east, was for 13 generations a seat of the Wharton family.

GREEN WALL *Fields and woods shield the secluded hamlet of Killington from the encircling moors.*

KIRKHAM

Lancashire
8 miles west of Preston

The town of Kirkham has an attractive view over the Fylde plain; the name 'Fylde' applied to this low-lying area of Lancashire comes from the Old English *gefilde*, meaning a plain. Kirkham is now an agricultural centre and commuter area for Preston and Blackpool, but its history dates back to the Domesday Book. The Church of St John the Evangelist, built in 1845, was the first Roman Catholic church to be allowed a peal of bells after the Reformation.

KIRK MICHAEL

Isle of Man
6 miles northeast of Peel

Probably the nearest of the Manx villages to being typically English is Kirk Michael, in the northwest of the island. Its long main street is flanked on either side by colour-washed cottages and small shops. Halfway down the street lies the English-looking stone church and bell tower. The entrance to the churchyard is through a wooden lych gate.

Kirk Michael has often been called the Bishop's village because on its outskirts lies Bishopscourt, until recently the residence of the Bishop of Sodor and Man, one of the smallest bishoprics in the Church of England. Bishopscourt was built sometime before the 13th century as a fortress. Courts were regularly held there to try offenders against Church laws, and so great was the power of the island's bishops that they not only had a particularly harsh dungeon on St Patrick's Isle, Peel, for their prisoners, but they also held, and still hold, a seat on the Legislative Council, the upper house of the Tynwald, the Manx Parliament.

Opposite Bishopscourt are the 13½ acres of Bishopscourt Glen, in which there is a mound topped by a commemorative stone. A shelf of rock in the glen is thought to have been used by earlier bishops as a seat for rest and meditation.

A small turning to the east from the village leads to a craft pottery. A turning to the west leads to the vast expanse of shore where the marine biologist Edward Forbes, born at Douglas in 1815, began his studies.

In June each year, Kirk Michael echoes to the thunder of high-powered motorcycles as competitors in the Tourist Trophy races roar through the village. The sharp, right-hand turn there provides an exacting test of judgment for the riders before they accelerate towards Ramsey.

KIRKOSWALD

Cumbria
7 miles north of Penrith

So that local people can hear them ringing, the bells of St Oswald's are hung in a detached stone tower on top of a grassy hill south of the village. The church itself is tucked into the foot of the hill 200yds away. There is thought to have been a bell tower on the summit since Norman times, but the present tower – complete with flagpole and weather vane – dates only from the 1890s.

The village and its church were named after King Oswald of Northumbria, who converted the area to Christianity in the 7th century. The wooden Saxon church was replaced in the 12th century by one built of stone, and despite later alterations it still has its splendid chancel arch with a Norman base. A little way to the east are the ruins of Kirkoswald Castle, most of whose 13th-century moat is intact.

Kirkoswald is a pretty village built mostly of red sandstone, and its finest building is the College, the home of the Fetherstonhaugh family since the late 16th century. The two-storeyed house, with its sloping-ended roof, was originally built about 1450 as a peel tower, and was converted into a college for priests in the 1520s. The house stands back from the road and is not clearly visible. It can be visited by special written appointment.

Two miles northwest of the village is the Nunnery Walks nature trail. It winds through the surrounding woods and past Croglin Water, which crashes over stony rapids. The 13th-century nunnery was rebuilt in 1715 in Georgian style and is now a guesthouse.

KIRKSTONE PASS

Cumbria
5 miles south of Patterdale

The highest pass in the region open to motorists, Kirkstone Pass links Windermere to Patterdale. It reaches 1489ft at its summit near the Kirkstone Pass Inn, with a gradient of 1-in-4 in places. The road from Ambleside starts with a minor road stretch, aptly named The Struggle. It joins the road from Windermere at the inn and is then only moderately steep and sufficiently wide for cars to pass.

On the descent to Patterdale, rugged fells sweep down towards the small lake of Brothers Water, an idyllic scene which can be admired from a car park which lies to the west of the road. Also to the west is Dove Crag, a rock face 2603ft up in the hills.

KNOTT END-ON-SEA

Lancashire
Opposite Fleetwood, on the eastern side of the Wyre estuary

A wide sandy beach, with stretches of softer mud, has made Knott End-on-Sea a popular resort. For the energetic, there are long walks along a footpath above the foreshore to Pilling, 2½ miles east, and upriver to Hambleton, 4 miles south. The foreshore walk is particularly attractive on a sunny evening at low tide, when the beach gleams like a sheet of gold.

KNOWSLEY SAFARI PARK

Lancashire
7 miles northeast of Liverpool

Trumpeting elephants, grazing wildebeests and acrobatic monkeys leaping onto the boots and bonnets of slow-moving cars make a visit to Knowsley Safari Park feel like a tour of the African bush. Five miles of roads wind through parkland in the grounds of Knowsley Park, owned by the Earl of Derby. Herds of eland, buffalo, bison and zebra graze alongside the road. Lions and tigers are enclosed except for one pride of lions in the drive-through area. The safari park is open from March until October.

L

LANCASTER
Lancashire
23 miles north of Preston

In the middle of the 18th century, Lancaster was a busy port, trading with the West Indies and shipping more cargoes than any port in the country except London, Bristol and Liverpool. But its history goes back much further: the Romans built a fort on the hill overlooking a bend in the River Lune, and the Norman military engineers followed their example centuries later, when they founded a castle of their own, which still stands. The view from its tallest tower embraces a huge sweep of the coast and, on a clear day, extends as far as the mountains of the Isle of Man.

John of Gaunt, Duke of Lancaster and father of Henry IV, enlarged the castle, and Elizabeth I strengthened its fortifications. The castle has been a courthouse and prison for centuries. It contains the Well Tower where prisoners languished while awaiting trial; they included the ten Lancashire witches convicted and hanged in 1612. On show are grim relics such as the clamp and iron used to fasten a criminal's arm while the initial 'M' (for 'malefactor') was burned into his hand; this was last used in 1811.

The Georgian Old Town Hall houses the Lancaster City Museum and the museum of the King's Own Royal (Lancaster) Regiment, and the Judges' Lodgings on Castle Hill contain a Museum of Childhood which gives a fascinating glimpse of what it was like to grow up in old Lancashire. In the Market Square, Charles II was proclaimed king in 1651. A period cottage, 15 Castle Hill, shows what sort of lifestyle a respectable but not affluent household could expect during the early 19th century.

The Friends' Meeting House dates from 1690, and the famous 18th-century divine, George Whitefield, often preached there. St Peter's Cathedral was built in 1859, and is chiefly noted for its Victorian frescoes.

Tree-lined St George's Quay is the centre of the old river port. Its tall, gabled, 18th-century warehouses have doors at top-floor level allowing goods to be raised and lowered with block-and-tackle. Nearby is the Old Custom House, but although small craft are still able to moor there, the old port died because of the silting up of the navigable channel. Later trade was carried by the Lancaster Canal, which ran northwards to Kendal on the edge of the Lake District, and southwards to a new outlet nearer the sea at Glasson.

In Williamson Park, on the eastern side of the town, is the Ashton Memorial, built in 1909 by Lord Ashton in memory of his wife.

LANERCOST PRIORY
Cumbria
3 miles northeast of Brampton

The minor road from Brampton sweeps down through a leafy tunnel to reach a few cottages clustered around the red sandstone Lanercost Priory in the River Irthing's deep, green valley. Most of the priory has

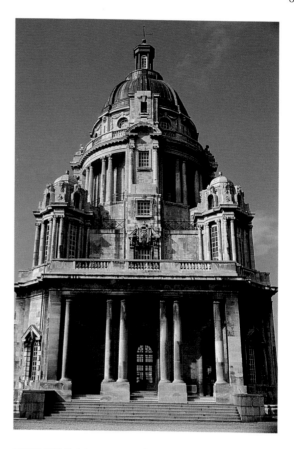

LOFTY DOME *Ashton Memorial has been called 'the Taj Mahal of the North'. Views from the top are superb.*

been a lofty ruin since Henry VIII ordered the Augustinian canons to be driven out in 1536. It soon became a convenient source of materials for local builders. The church's north aisle survived, however, and served as the parish church until the nave was restored in the 18th century. The north aisle's windows have stained glass by the Victorian artists William Morris and Sir Edward Burne-Jones.

Lanercost's peaceful setting contrasts with the priory's turbulent history. Founded in 1169, it was built largely of stones taken from nearby Hadrian's Wall. It was attacked by the Scots in 1296 and 1297, then ransacked by David II of Scotland's army in 1346.

GRACEFUL ARCHES *The medieval bridge at Lanercost, like the abbey, includes stones from Hadrian's Wall.*

LANGDALE

Cumbria
4 miles west of Ambleside to 2 miles west of Skelwith Bridge

Beyond Chapel Stile, a pretty slate-quarrying village on the Great Langdale Beck, the road twists, rises and plunges until it comes to an abrupt end at the greystone Dungeon Ghyll Hotel. The great arc of the Langdale mountains, Pike of Stickle, Harrison Stickle, Great Knott and the rest, fill the sky behind.

From the car park beside the hotel a steep path leads up to Dungeon Ghyll Force. Ribbons of water drop into an abyss, nearly 100ft deep, whose form really does suggest a dungeon. From there, the route follows a steep minor road up into fells dressed in russet, faded green and old gold, with a pale tumble of sunlit cloud over the pikes.

The road grows narrower and goes through gates and over cattle grids to Blea Tarn, mirroring a topknot of firs in its water, then goes on to Little Langdale, with its handsome valley farms and Three Shires Inn.

LANTY'S TARN

Cumbria
1½ miles south of Glenridding

Lanty's Tarn is tiny, tucked away and unknown to most visitors to the Lake District, and even in the height of summer it offers the determined walker a rare peace and solitude, wrapped in the deep quiet of the mountains. The walk across the fells leads south from the village of Glenridding, at the southern end of Ullswater. Take the road past the shops, keeping the car park on the right, and cross the stream beyond the cottages. Through the gate the path climbs very steeply upwards into typical fell countryside. Outcrops of rock stand bare and forbidding among patches of bracken; scattered trees, including oaks, ashes, birches and Scots pines, raise their branches to the sky. In early summer tormentil and sheep's sorrel add a twinkle of colour to the dark undergrowth.

The tarn, ringed with conifers, is wasp-waisted, heavily sedimented and full of fish – though most are very small. It is possible to walk on past its quiet waters, following the path through the bracken. Turn left where the path forks – the right-hand fork leads up to the heights of Striding Edge and then on to Helvellyn, a spectacular but long ascent.

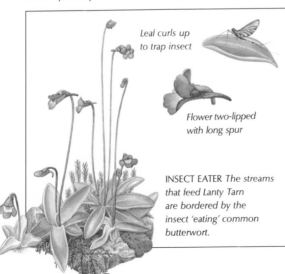

Leaf curls up to trap insect

Flower two-lipped with long spur

INSECT EATER The streams that feed Lanty Tarn are bordered by the insect 'eating' common butterwort.

REVOLUTIONARY *Laxey's water wheel, Britain's biggest, was built in 1854 – its axle alone weighs nine tons.*

LAXEY

Isle of Man
6 miles northeast of Douglas

Snaefell, the Isle of Man's highest mountain, rises to 2036ft in the northern part of the island, and from it springs the Laxey river which runs through the grassy glen to the valley below.

The little stone harbour where cabin cruisers and dinghies lie on the shingle at low tide was once busy with fishing boats, and Laxey cattle fairs were among the most important on the island. The only vestige left of them is the Laxey Fair held in July, though it is now an occasion for carnival rather than cattle. Some of the stallholders dress in Manx Victorian costume. Like most fairs on the island it is a relic of earlier pagan rituals practised by the ancient Celts. The water of Chibbyr Niglus – a well on the site of an early Keeill, or chapel, near Laxey harbour – was believed to have powers to heal eye troubles.

Laxey is the site of the 'Lady Isabella', a water wheel 72½ft in diameter – the largest in the United Kingdom. It was built in 1854 to pump water from a depth of 1000ft out of the now defunct lead mines, and named after the wife of the Lieutenant-Governor of the island at that time. The wheel still turns but now only for the railway tourists to watch.

From the tree-lined station which connects Laxey with Douglas to the south and Ramsey to the north, visitors can travel on the only electric mountain line in the British Isles. Trains run to within 30ft of the summit of Snaefell. Close by the station is the Mines Tavern, with a bar-counter resembling a tramcar.

LEASOWE
Merseyside
3 miles west of Wallasey centre

Leasowe's lighthouse tower stands on flat ground behind a rampart of dunes and a sea-wall, but when it was built in the late 18th century this was a soft and treacherous area of shifting sand which was unable to support a structure tall enough to give ships warning of the dangerous banks and shoals offshore. In the end, it took a disaster to put matters right. It is said that in 1760 a ship loaded with cotton was stranded on the sands, and its cargo left to rot on what was then the beach. The tough cotton bales served to bind the sand and the vegetation into a base solid enough to support a tower.

This whole area is now the North Wirral Coastal Park, in which shrubs and plants are being used to create picnic areas and homes for wildlife. From Leasowe it is possible to walk along the coastal path as far as Hoylake promenade to the west, or, to the east, to the start of the New Brighton coastal defences and thence along the promenade wall as far as Wallasey.

LEIGHTON HALL
Lancashire
3 miles north of Carnforth

From a distance, the turrets and roof castellations of Leighton Hall stand out sharply against a backcloth of rolling park and woodlands, and a horizon tinged by the purple of distant fells. The neo-Gothic façade was added to this classical mansion in about 1800.

In the public rooms are many fine examples of antique furniture including pieces by Richard Gillow, a member of the family whose home the hall has been for more than four centuries. The elegant curved stone staircase is Georgian, and delicate pillars supporting a gallery are a fine example of early Gothic revival.

The grounds include parkland, a shrubbery walk and a long, narrow lawn originally designed for archery. An aviary contains birds of prey, including kestrels, owls and eagles, and most afternoons in summer visitors can watch the birds in a display of hawking.

MEDIEVAL MOCK-UP *The 'Gothic' façade of Leighton Hall conceals its classical origins.*

LEIGHTON MOSS

Lancashire
About 1 mile east of Silverdale

One of the rarest of English bird calls may sometimes be heard rising from a wooded valley between the villages of Silverdale and Yealand Redmayne. This is the deep resonant 'boom' of the male bittern, which breeds on the Leighton Moss bird reserve.

The reserve, administered by the Royal Society for the Protection of Birds, is open daily, but not Tuesdays.

LEVENS HALL

Cumbria
5¼ miles southwest of Kendal

Yew and box trees sculptured to look like cones, corkscrews, circles, pyramids and other curious shapes make Levens Hall's topiary garden unique in Britain. 'Queen Catherine and her Maids of Honour' stand in one part of the garden, and another group of clipped trees is known as 'Coach and Horses'.

The topiary was created in the late 17th century by the Frenchman Guillaume Beaumont, who had been gardener to James II and was trained by de Nôtre at Versailles. Some of the mature trees are 20ft tall.

Overlooking the garden is the old stone-built Levens Hall, the largest Elizabethan mansion in south

SCULPTURED SYMMETRY *Neat flowerbeds and immaculate box hedges surround the topiary at Levens Hall.*

Cumbria, built around an earlier, 13th-century peel tower. Woodcarvings on the overmantel in the drawing room represent the four elements, the four seasons and the five senses.

In the grounds the hiss and clank of steam engines is heard each Sunday – weather permitting – when the hall's collection of working model steam engines is brought to life. The collection illustrates the progress of steam from 1820 to 1930, and includes traction engines, a steam wagon and a steam car. The house and gardens are open on most summer afternoons.

LINDALE

Cumbria
2 miles north of Grange-over-Sands

The iron obelisk near the centre of Lindale is a tribute to the engineer John Wilkinson, who built the famous iron bridge over the River Severn. Before he died in 1808 'Iron-Mad' Wilkinson had an iron coffin built for himself, and in it he lies buried in an unmarked grave in the parish church.

LITTLE SALKELD AND LONG MEG

Cumbria
5 miles northeast of Penrith

A narrow winding road just outside Little Salkeld leads to a meadow in which stands a 15ft tall column of sandstone. Long Meg, as the stone is called, together with her 66 'daughter' stones form a Neolithic circle some 300ft in diameter – one of the largest and oldest in Britain. It was possibly used for rituals associated with the changing seasons, and the setting midwinter sun is aligned with Long Meg herself. She bears some cup and ring carvings which are thought to be about 4500 years old.

In the village, red-sandstone cottages cluster near a restored 18th-century water mill, once used to grind oatmeal. It now grinds wholemeal flour throughout the year and is open to the public on certain afternoons in the summer. Visitors can watch the mill at work and sample freshly baked bread, scones and cakes in the tearooms.

There has been a hall in Little Salkeld since the Middle Ages, and the present hall stands near the small, triangular green. A large walled building, it dates mainly from the early 19th century and is now mostly divided into holiday apartments.

LIVERPOOL

Merseyside
178 miles northwest of London

When Chester was a thriving port, Liverpool was a small fishing village, but from the early 18th century, when the silting up of the Dee cut off Chester's trading lifeline, Liverpool began to grow into one of the biggest and most prosperous ports in the world. By 1880 lines of docks stretched for 7 miles along the banks of the Mersey, and 40 per cent of the world's trade was carried in Liverpool ships. Today much of this vast industrial system has fallen into disuse, with the shift to bulk-carriers and containerisation, and for the first time it is possible to take a closer look at this part of Britain's maritime history.

Liverpool Maritime Museum, opened in the old Liverpool Pilotage Headquarters beside the Pier Head, is the nucleus of a major preservation scheme for the old dock area. The museum houses a good collection of objects from the past, including the original builders' scale-model for the ill-fated *Titanic*, a Liverpool ship. The museum also incorporates part of the Albert Dock Warehouses. Exhibitions tell the story of

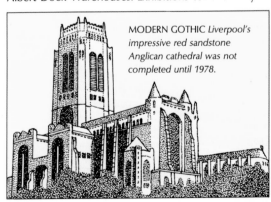

MODERN GOTHIC *Liverpool's impressive red sandstone Anglican cathedral was not completed until 1978.*

LIVERPOOL CREST *Two images of Father Neptune guard the Liver bird, the city's mythical protector.*

the docks, and restored ships are on display. These include the *Edmund Gardner*, a pilot boat, and the *De Wadden*, a schooner that was built in Holland in 1917.

A different viewpoint is obtained by approaching Liverpool from Birkenhead on the other side of the Mersey. The ferries unload at Pier Head, where disembarking passengers are faced by three massive buildings. To the left is the Royal Liver Insurance Company headquarters, crowned by the largest clock in Britain and by effigies of the mythical Liver birds. To the right are the Dock Board offices, and in the centre stands the Cunard Building.

Apart from regular ferry services across the river, there are frequent cruises up and down the Mersey. The wide, open area of the Pier Head is a good point from which to watch coasters, passenger boats, tankers and container ships making for the refineries of Stanlow and for the Manchester Ship Canal.

Inland from the waterfront, there are other reminders of Liverpool's maritime past. In an alley called Hackins Hey, off Dale Street, an inn called Ye Hole in Ye Wall was renowned in sailing-ship days, and the scene of at least one pitched battle between merchant seamen and the Royal Navy's press-gangs.

Liverpool became a city in 1880 and now has two cathedrals. The Anglican cathedral was originally intended to be larger than St Peter's in Rome, and even though the plans were later cut back, it still took 75 years to finish; it has the largest organ and the heaviest peal of bells in the world. At the other end of Hope Street stands the Roman Catholic cathedral, remarkable for its unusual circular design. Liverpool's original parish church of Our Lady and St Nicholas, close to the Pier Head and known as the 'Sailors' Church', was built in 1360. In 1810 the tower collapsed, and a replacement built the following year was the only part left standing after the air raids of 1941; the rest of the church was rebuilt after the war.

Liverpool has an outstanding museum, a concert hall, three art galleries and Botanic Gardens. Sir Andrew Barclay Walker, Lord Mayor of Liverpool in 1873, provided the money to build the Walker Art Gallery which contains one of the largest collection of paintings in Britain outside London. Among the famous works on display are: *And when did you last see your father?* by W. F. Yeames, Rubens' *Virgin and child with St Elizabeth and the child Baptist*, Martini's *Christ discovered in the Temple* and a Holbein portrait of Henry VIII. Other paintings include works by Hogarth, Reynolds, Turner and George Stubbs, who was born in Liverpool. Also on view are sculptures by Rodin, Renoir, Le Hongre and Epstein.

The Merseyside County Museum in William Brown Street contains an aquarium and transport gallery in the basement, while the ground floor is devoted to the development of the city and the port. The first floor covers the history of the ship and on the third floor is the Time Keeping Gallery with a fine collection of watches and clocks and a reconstruction of a Chinese water-clock. There is also a planetarium.

Speke Hall, near the southeast border of the city and close to the airport, was started in 1490 by Sir William Norris. The house was completed in 1610 in its present form of four wings surrounding a cobbled courtyard. It escaped 18th-century modernisation, and looks today as it did towards the end of the reign of Elizabeth I. With its black-and-white half-timbering it is one of the best houses of the period in existence. Much of the interior furnishing reflects the tastes of Richard Watt, a wealthy merchant who acquired the house in 1797, and his successors in the 19th century. The kitchen includes an array of copperware and a collection of smoothing irons.

LODORE FALLS
Cumbria
At the south end of Derwent Water

The waters from Watendlath Tarn drop into Borrowdale close to the Lodore Swiss Hotel. For those in a hurry the twinkling cascade of Lodore Falls – 'dashing and clashing and splashing', as Robert Southey described it in a tongue-twisting poem – can be reached through a turnstile, but for those with time to spare, a stroll through the delicate greenery of Lodore Wood is well worth while.

The upper falls can be reached along a path which follows the stream, the haunt of wagtails and dippers. Towering above is the massive bulk of Shepherds Crag, a popular practice area for climbers.

LONGSLEDDALE
Cumbria
6 miles north of Kendal

Among the most charming of the Lake District valleys, Longsleddale is lonely yet well inhabited, intensely private and yet easy to reach. The narrow road into the valley drops steeply away from the A6, winding through the trees to Garnett Bridge. As the road probes deeper into the valley, the impression grows that nothing has changed here for centuries.

The narrow valley, with its string of old stone farms and its pleasant patchwork of fields, forms a passage between the steep fells. Norman Nicholson, the modern poet and topographer of the Lake District, has said that in wet winters 'water pours down gill after gill till the dale looks like a street of terraced houses with the roof gutters all burst'. This mighty deluge of waterfalls feeds the aptly named River Sprint and enriches the fields on the narrow valley floor. The church, built in 1712, is in a lovely setting halfway along the valley, with broad-leaved woods closing in on both sides.

Beyond, the fells gradually close in and the landscape becomes starker. In front, visible through the roadside trees, the ferocious mountain masses of Goat Scar and Buckbarrow Crag tower over the valley head. The road ends at Sadgill, the highest farm, but on the east side of the valley a track leads on towards a distant col. This is Gatescarth Pass, between the heights of Harter Fell and Artle Crag. This path linked the valley with Mardale Green, the village drowned beneath Haweswater Reservoir.

THE LORTONS
Cumbria
4 miles southeast of Cockermouth

The two villages of Low and High Lorton lie in a green valley carved by the River Cocker and known as Lorton Vale. Lorton Hall is partly a 15th-century peel tower, built as a refuge for the villagers against raiding Scots during the Border wars. The rest of the house is part 17th century and part 19th century.

A beech tree in the garden is said to have been planted by Mary Winder, Lady of the Manor at the time of Charles II's Restoration. She had entertained the future king when he was seeking support against Cromwell after the execution of Charles I.

Outside the walled garden the surrounding village consists of trim white cottages, all within a pebble's throw of the babbling Cocker. At Lorton Bridge is Low Mill, now a private house, dating from the late 18th century when the river was diverted to provide a series of weirs and millraces.

TURRETED SHELL *The appearance of Lowther Castle is misleading – it is a 19th-century fake, abandoned in the 1930s.*

Lorton Bridge House was once the hall's working farm and, though largely Georgian, it is still attached to medieval farm buildings and cottages. Next door to the village store are Pack Horse Cottages, once an ale house used by drovers.

High Lorton, just to the east, is an attractive tangle of rambling cottages, some with steps leading up to their doors and with fuel stores beneath. The Horseshoe Inn sells an ale the brewing of which dates back to the 18th century, when the Jennings family at High Swinside Farm had a reputation for a good 'home brew'. This became so popular that the family bought a building in the village and used it as a malt house. The brewery is now based in Cockermouth, and the old malt house has become the village hall.

At the rear stands an ancient yew tree under which the founder of the Quaker movement, George Fox, preached pacifism to a large crowd that included Cromwellian soldiers. William Wordsworth in his poem *Yew Trees* wrote:

> *There is a yew tree, pride of Lorton Vale*
> *Which to this day stands single, in the midst*
> *Of its own darkness, as it stood of yore.*

In the centre of High Lorton is Lorton Park, a Regency mansion now a guesthouse. It was visited by Prince Arthur, Duke of Connaught and son of Queen Victoria, in 1863. In the garden he planted a horse chestnut tree, which is now so large that its massive trunk has split and distorted the surrounding railing.

LOWTHER

Cumbria
4 miles south of Penrith

When the 1st Earl of Lonsdale decided to build his castle at Lowther – on the site of Lowther Hall, which was destroyed by fire in 1725 – he chose a rising young architect who would do the job in the grand manner. Lowther, which had been in the earl's family since the 13th century, was the first major work of Robert Smirke, who later designed the British Museum. Starting in 1806, Smirke lavished upon it all the splendours and embellishments that a castle worthy of the name should have. The north front was 420ft long with a battlemented parapet, and a small forest of towers and turrets rose high above the roofline. It was later the home of the 5th Earl of Lonsdale, an amateur boxer who gave his name to the Lonsdale Belt – one of the sport's most coveted trophies. The Earl was also the first president of the Automobile Association.

DEER PARK *In springtime white-spotted calves can be seen at Lowther, where red deer have lived for over 700 years.*

Unfortunately, in the 1930s such grandeur became a bit too much for the Lonsdales – whose family name is Lowther – and they abandoned it for Askham Hall on the opposite bank of the River Lowther. In 1957 much of the castle was demolished and now only the shell remains.

North of the castle stands the Church of St Michael, dating from the 12th century but rebuilt by Sir John Lowther in 1686. Inside the porch is a Viking tombstone with a carving showing the souls of great warriors arriving in Valhalla. At the same time as rebuilding the church, Sir John Lowther pulled down the old village and built a new one, called Lowther New Town. Later, much of this village was, in its turn, pulled down because it blocked the view from the 1st Earl's new castle. Yet another village, called Lowther Village, was started in 1806–7. It was based on a design by Robert Adam, which was adapted by the 1st Earl.

The houses and cottages, around two squares with greens in the middle, are occupied by estate workers. The estate has had red deer roaming through it since 1283, when Edward I granted Sir Hugh de Louther permission to create a 200 acre deer park. In Lowther's amusement park archery ranges provide another link with medieval days, while a ride on a miniature steam train is a reminder of a more recent era. Peacocks and macaws are among the birds that can be seen in the park, which has two nature trails.

LUNE ESTUARY COASTAL PATH

Lancashire
Begins 4 miles south of Lancaster

The clearly marked Lune Estuary Coastal Path begins just beyond The Stork pub in the hamlet of Conder Green. It follows a disused railway line and is banked with hawthorns and stands of yellow gorse. There is a picnic site by the coast, and not far away brightly painted boats rock at anchor.

Across the bay is the tiny port of Glasson, built in the 18th century for trade with the West Indies. Today its prosperity comes mainly from trade in animal feed, grain and fuel in northern and southern Europe. A bustling marina links the Lancaster Canal to the estuary, and a colourful assortment of boats – some with sails flapping in the breeze, some with gently purring diesel engines – often waits to pass through the locks and out into the open sea.

LYTHAM ST ANNE'S

Lancashire
12 miles west of Preston

The twin resort of Lytham St Anne's stands well back from the sea, almost as if ignoring its presence, and the wide green between the town and its sandy beaches is broken only by the outlines of a large windmill and the old lifeboat house.

This is a place for walking, with views across the Ribble estuary, or for stretching out on the grass on a warm summer's day. For the sportsman there are the golf courses for which the town is famous; they include the Royal Lytham and St Anne's, where major international tournaments are played, the Fairhaven and the Green Drive.

At the western end of the seafront in Lytham is Fairhaven Lake, a large body of water used for yachting, motorboating, rowing and canoeing. There are bowling greens and tennis courts nearby. At the eastern end a windmill stands on the wide expanse of Lytham Green, facing the Ribble. In 1929 a freak gust of wind set the sails spinning the wrong way, wrecking the machinery and putting a stop to the mill's working life which had begun in 1805.

At the end of a long avenue is the late-Georgian mansion of Lytham Hall, built on the site of a farming cell belonging to the Abbey of Durham which passed to the Clifton family after the Dissolution of the Monasteries. The gateway of 1850 was built at the north side of the town's cheerful market square, the centre of a thriving community before it found a new prosperity as a seaside resort.

The beach becomes muddier towards the Ribble estuary, where strong currents and fast-flowing tides make swimming and walking across the sands less safe than it is further west.

The smaller scale and more peaceful seaside resort of St Anne's, the western part of Lytham St Anne's, offers a quiet alternative to the brasher delights of Blackpool. The pier dates from 1885, but the pier entrance was built this century – a quaint, mock-

WELL PLACED *Lytham's windmill is well-sited to catch the wind right on the front, by the lifeboat house.*

Tudor building with gables and imitation timber framing. Solid red-brick Victorian and Edwardian villas and genteel private hotels face a broad stretch of sandy beach, which has become renowned as a centre for the fast and spectacular sport of sand-yacht racing. Beginners can take lessons before trying their hand at this exhilarating sport.

There is safe bathing for those favouring more traditional seaside recreation. The Promenade Gardens overlook a boating pool, and there is a miniature railway. In the centre of the town Ashton Gardens has treelined walks, wide lawns and a watercourse with rock pools and waterfalls.

TRAGIC REMINDER *This memorial in St Anne's marks Britain's worst lifeboat disaster, when two lifeboats and 29 men were lost answering the same distress call in 1886.*

LYTH VALLEY

Cumbria
Between Crosthwaite and Brigsteer

At Crosthwaite, on the north side of the Lyth Valley, a footpath from a bridge over the sparkling River Gilpin leads in both directions along the river bank.

The sheltered valley is noted for its damson orchards. The trees are magnificent in full bloom in spring, and in September and October the fruit can be bought from farm shops by the roadside. Damsons can be stewed, bottled, jellied, made into jam, or eaten raw. An impressive view of the valley, flanked by the blunt shoulder of Whitbarrow Scar, can be seen just beyond Brigsteer as the road rises before entering a strip of woodland.

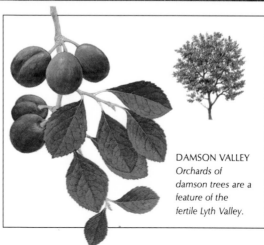

DAMSON VALLEY
Orchards of damson trees are a feature of the fertile Lyth Valley.

MALLERSTANG

Cumbria

About 4 miles south of Kirkby Stephen

The parish is named after the Welsh *moel*, or 'bare hill' and the old Norse *stong*, or 'boundary mark', and lies in a lonely but lovely valley close to the Yorkshire border. The Norman Pendragon Castle was razed by the Scots in 1541 and restored by Lady Anne Clifford in 1660. The remains include a fortified peel tower.

The skyline is dominated by the 2324ft mountain of Wild Boar Fell and all around is superb walking country, with views of the Settle to Carlisle railway crossing the 1169ft Aisgill summit.

MANCHESTER

Greater Manchester

164 miles northwest of London

Manchester, birthplace of the Industrial Revolution, has always held surprises for visitors. When Benjamin Disraeli (1804–81) saw the extent of new factories and mills that were being built, he was so impressed that he declared Manchester 'the most wonderful city of modern times'. Manchester is still wonderful. Today some of England's finest architecture is springing up in place of old bomb sites and slums, complementing important Victorian buildings such as Ryland's Library, the Art Gallery and the Free Trade Hall. Stretches of the canal and a handful of Manchester's 11 major parks have been transformed into beautiful recreation areas, while the city's Roman origins and Victorian heritage have been recaptured in museums and exhibitions at Castlefield in Liverpool Road.

The heart of modern Manchester is Piccadilly, a great square which was almost totally destroyed by bombing in the Second World War. Hotels, shops and the towering Piccadilly Plaza building loom over the square, but its centre is a green oasis of lawns and flower beds where the roar of the encircling traffic is reduced to a whisper.

In contrast to Piccadilly, the area bounded by Princess Street, Mount Street and Lower Mosley Street carries a strong reminder that Manchester is a Victorian city. The Town Hall, covering nearly 2 acres, stands facing Albert Square and is surmounted by a clock-tower 281ft 6in tall. The building was completed

in 1877 to the design of Alfred Waterhouse (1830–1905) and is in Gothic style. Above the Lord Mayor's entrance, in Princess Street, is a carving of Edward III, whose introduction of Flemish weavers laid the foundation of the city's traditional industry.

Inside the Town Hall are statues of men who played an important role in Manchester's history, including John Bright (1811–89), who was MP for Manchester in 1847 and 1852; Richard Cobden (1804–65), who was closely associated with Bright as an opponent of the

MUSIC MAN *Sir John Barbirolli conducted the Hallé Orchestra for 27 years.*

ALL FOR ART *Manchester's City Art Gallery is housed in a colonnaded 'temple'.*

Corn Laws, and several other prominent members of the Anti Corn Law League.

The league opposed the law which banned the import of cheap foreign wheat. Their headquarters was the Free Trade Hall, in Peter Street, built in 1843. A new hall was built in 1856, and it was here that the orchestra founded by Sir Charles Hallé (1819–95) gave its first concert in 1857. Second World War bombing almost totally destroyed the hall, but it was rebuilt in 1951 in its original Palladian style. The Free Trade Hall is still the home of the Hallé Orchestra, which gained international repute in the 1950s and 1960s under the leadership of Sir John Barbirolli (1899–1970).

Another of Manchester's benefactors was Humphrey Chetham (1580–1653), who bequeathed funds for founding a school for the poor and for a public library. The school, Chetham's Hospital, was opened in 1656. It now operates as the Chetham School of Music, developing the talents of musically gifted children. Chetham's Library was the first free library in Europe. It contains printed books and manuscripts, including a collection of works of the 16th–18th centuries.

Manchester's Central Library has been a favourite

CONTRASTING STYLES *The circular Central Library, dating from the 1930s, sets off Manchester's Victorian Town Hall and its lofty Gothic turrets. Together they frame the angular Town Hall, erected shortly after the library.*

meeting place for Mancunians since it was opened in 1934. The circular building is one of the largest municipal libraries in England, having a stock of more than nine million books. In contrast to the nearby Town Hall, the library has classical lines, with a portico of Corinthian columns and Tuscan columns around the upper storey. The tiny Library Theatre, seating 308, stages repertory productions in the basement.

Manchester's most revolutionary theatre is in the Royal Exchange building in St Ann's Square. The building was opened in 1921 as the city's cotton exchange, replacing an earlier one in Market Street. The floor space of the main hall covers about an acre, which earned it the claim when built of 'the biggest room in the world'. The roof has three glass domes and is supported on giant marble columns. Cotton trading ceased in 1968, and the theatre, which opened in 1976 and which seats 740 people, now occupies the hall. The complete theatre is a steel capsule weighing 100 tons. Because the floor was unable to bear the weight, the structure was suspended.

At the junction of Victoria Street and Cateaton Street stands Manchester Cathedral, a 15th-century building in Perpendicular Gothic style. It is dedicated to St Mary, St Denys and St George, and was given cathedral status in 1847. A tower was added in 1868, enhancing the striking majesty of the church, but its chief glory is its early-16th-century carved woodwork – particularly the canopied choir stalls.

St Ann's Church dates from 1709–12. It overlooks St Ann's Square, dating from the same period and now an elegant part of the city's shopping area. Barton Arcade connects the square with Deansgate.

Manchester has a wealth of art galleries, six municipally controlled and one administered by the university. The City Art Gallery, in Mosley Street, was originally the headquarters of the Royal Manchester Institution for the promotion of Literature, Science and the Arts, and was opened in 1829. The building was designed by Sir Charles Barry, the architect of the Houses of Parliament. Since becoming a public gallery in 1882 it has constantly added to its fine collection of paintings, specialising in the development of English art from the 16th century to the present day. There are also some early-Italian, Flemish and Dutch paintings and works by 19th-century French Impressionists. Sculptures include a bronze bust of C. P. Scott, the former *Manchester Guardian* editor, by Sir Jacob Epstein. The adjoining annexe to the gallery, the Athenaeum, contains ceramics, silver and glassware. The Fletcher Moss Art Gallery contains a selection of paintings by British artists, including Thomas Rowlandson, J. M. W. Turner, Augustus John and L. S. Lowry. There is also a display of 19th-century English domestic silver and porcelain. Victorian dresses are among those on show in the Gallery of English Costume in Platt Hall. The Georgian building makes a fitting setting for an exhibition that covers the changing styles of everyday clothing of the last 350 years.

Manchester University's own art collection is housed in the Whitworth Art Gallery. It includes English watercolours, Japanese woodcuts, textiles, and contemporary paintings and sculptures. The Manchester Museum is also part of the university. A geological gallery occupies most of the ground floor, and there are large galleries dedicated to zoology, entomology, botany, archaeology and ethnology.

A city that has its roots in the Industrial Revolution is a natural place to find a museum of science and

GLASS HOUSE *Barton Arcade's elaborate roof has sheltered shoppers from the elements since 1871.*

technology. The North Western Museum of Science and Industry in Grosvenor Street was opened in 1969, and is the largest of its kind in northwest England. A large part of the museum is devoted to textile machinery, with the emphasis on cotton spinning, and the allied trades such as calico printing and dyeing. The development of steam power is represented by exhibits ranging from a one-third scale model of Newcomen's first engine to a modern steam turbine.

Engineering exhibits include machine tools, railway locomotives and an atmospheric gas engine. The second motor-car engine built by Henry Royce is in the museum. The Industrial Revolution brought two historic transport systems to Manchester, the Liverpool to Manchester Railway and the Manchester Ship Canal. The railway opened in 1830 and was the world's first commercially successful line. It was built by George Stephenson (1781–1848) whose locomotive *Rocket* heralded the railway age. The Manchester Ship Canal once enabled sea-going vessels of up to 15,000 tons to sail almost to the city centre. The canal was opened in 1894 and runs the 36 miles from Manchester to Eastham on the Mersey Estuary. Ships no longer sail as far as Manchester, but the Eastham to Runcorn stretch is still kept busy.

MARPLE

Greater Manchester
5 miles east of Stockport

The rocky, wooded ravine of the River Goyt forms the background to this delightful town, where houses cling to the river banks or perch on the hilltop. There are pleasant walks through woods, and across wild moors, with splendid views of the Peak District.

The Peak Forest and Macclesfield canals, which meet in Marple, helped the town to develop as a centre of the cotton industry in the 19th century. Cotton has gone, but the canals remain as quiet byways for pleasure-boating and as monuments to the engineers who built them.

Until recent years, horses towed the boats on Britain's canals and occasionally special bridges were necessary to accommodate the sturdy beasts. Where a towpath changed from one side of a canal to the other, a 'snake' bridge was built so that the horse could be taken across without unhitching its towrope. When the canal went under the main road, the horse had to be unhitched and led through a tunnel beneath the road. At Marple, there are examples of both types of bridge. Where the Peak Forest Canal crosses the River Goyt at Marple, there is also an aqueduct.

MARTINDALE

Cumbria
4 miles southwest of Pooley Bridge

The two churches of Martindale village just south of Ullswater – St Martin's, built in 1633, and St Peter's, built in 1880 – are among the loneliest in Britain. This is wild and mountainous country, worth visiting for its rugged solitude. The best approach is along the winding road down the south bank of Ullswater, reached by turning off the A592 just north of Pooley Bridge.

MARTIN MERE WILDFOWL TRUST

Lancashire
4 miles northeast of Ormskirk

The tone of the Martin Mere conservation centre is set at the entrance buildings, built of Scandinavian pine with a turfed roof in the style of a traditional Norwegian log house. The mere itself is a 20 acre man-made lake, and also within the 360 acre site are a swan lake and pens for flamingos, black swans, geese and rare species such as the Laysan teal.

Among the lakes and gardens some 1500 tame wildfowl are on view, and for the dedicated bird-watcher there are hides out on the marsh along two half-mile-long nature trails. In winter the marsh comes to life with up to 15,000 pink-footed geese, thousands of teal and large flocks of wigeon, ruff and pintail. Whooper swans fly here from Iceland, and Bewick's swans cross the North Sea from Russia.

An exhibition in the Southport Hall illustrates the natural history of the mere, the work of the Wildfowl Trust, and many aspects of wildlife conservation.

MARYPORT

Cumbria
6 miles north of Workington

A few small fishing boats, stranded on glistening mudbanks at low tide, mingle with private craft in the extensive docks whose exports of coal and iron made Maryport a flourishing town for nearly 200 years. The ships have gone, but the old sandstone quays with their fishing nets, iron bollards and huge, abandoned anchors are reminders of the port's heyday. One anchor, flanked by a pair of carronades – stubby, large-calibre 'ship smasher' guns used by Nelson's navy – stands outside Christ Church as a simple but moving memorial to local men who died at sea.

Nearby, a former dockside pub now houses the town's excellent maritime museum whose exhibits include a brass telescope from the *Cutty Sark*, the best known of all clipper ships. The museum also contains old paintings, sailmakers' tools and several reminders of Fletcher Christian, leader of the *Bounty* mutineers, who was born in Cockermouth in 1764.

The museum also pays tribute to a Maryport man, Thomas Henry Ismay, who founded the White Star Line. He was born in a small Wood Street house in 1839. The White Star fleet, which eventually merged with Cunard, included the *Titanic* which sank on her maiden voyage in 1912.

Maryport's gridiron street pattern and neat terraces of sandstone houses and shops indicate a town that is new by British standards. It was founded in 1749 by Humphrey Senhouse and named after his wife, Mary, the Bishop of Carlisle's daughter. Trade thrived sufficiently for new docks to be opened in 1854 and 1880 but the town never really recovered from the First World War and was hit very hard during the depressed 1930s.

On a hill just north of the town stand the remains of the Roman fort of Alauna, part of Hadrian's defences against the Picts across the Solway and an outlying bastion of Hadrian's Wall.

RUFF TIME *In spring, the courting male ruff (left) raises his collar in a display that rivals the exotic glamour of flamingos (right) at Martin Mere.*

Flower tube has a pouch at base

Seed has a parachute

CALMING INFLUENCE
Common valerian has been used as a sedative for centuries.

MAUGHOLD

Isle of Man
3 miles southeast of Ramsey

Fuchsias, roses, foxgloves and valerian glow in the hedgerows and bury the dry-stone walls that divide the country up into a great counterpane that slides into the sea in Port Mooar Bay. Above the bay rear the massive cliffs of Maughold (pronounced 'Maccold') Head, with a splendid lighthouse on top. A path from Maughold village churchyard leads to the top of the headland and the lighthouse.

Headland and village are named after St Maughold who, so the story goes, landed there at some time in the 5th century, having drifted, possibly from Ireland, in a coracle, allowing the winds of God to blow him where they would. Safe ashore, he gave thanks for his deliverance, and where he did so, a spring gushed forth so pure that he used it later for baptisms. The spring is still there, and people used to say that if a Manx girl gazed into it she would see the man she would wed.

The saint established a monastery on the site now occupied by the churchyard. The remains of three ancient Celtic chapels can be seen here, and the partly 12th-century church itself stands on the foundations of a fourth. Also in the churchyard is the Cross House, sheltering an astonishing collection of Celtic and Norse monuments from the 6th to 13th centuries. All were found within the parish, indicating the importance of the Christian community here during the early Middle Ages. The stones are much worn, but look closely and you can still discern carvings of abbots, a Viking ship and episodes from Norse sagas.

In its way, the churchyard is a monument to

PATCHWORK FIELDS *Dry-stone walls frame the fields on Maughold Head, at the eastern tip of the Isle of Man.*

Manxdom; the gravestones are a long parade of such Manx names as Kerruish, Quayle, Kermeen and Christian. Among them lies an island novelist famous in his day, Sir Hall Caine (1853–1931), whose works include *The Woman thou Gavest Me.*

At the entrance to the village, a notice reads 'Failt erriu dys skyll Maghal – Welcome to Maughold'. The village is tiny indeed, but pretty, consisting of no more than a dozen pink or whitewashed stone houses grouped about a triangular green. Even so, it is large enough for a few minor mysteries. There is the little cottage by the churchyard that has a rose garden, glazed windows, but no roof; and the imposing pedestal on the green that is surmounted by a tiny sundial enclosed by impenetrable mesh.

MELMERBY

Cumbria
8 miles northeast of Penrith

A sandstone village at the foot of the Pennines, Melmerby surrounds a green planted with clusters of trees. The village is in the path of what can sometimes be an 80 mph gale from Cross Fell, known locally as the Helm Wind, which may strike even when the air 6 miles away is scarcely moving.

The Romans built a road here, the Maiden Way, which can be followed across the fells. In places it is 20ft wide and reveals traces of the original paving. Melmerby Hall, a private residence, dates from the 17th century.

MIDDLETON

Cumbria
5 miles north of Kirkby Lonsdale

The scattered and far-flung parish of Middleton occupies the eastern side of the Lune Valley, along which Roman legionaries marched on their way to the border. Green meadows by the riverside give way in the east to the high ground of Middleton Fell, rising to nearly 2000ft and forming a natural barrier between the Lune Valley and Yorkshire.

A Roman milestone marking the 53rd mile from Carlisle was found just off the main road to Sedbergh from Kirkby Lonsdale in 1836: it now stands in a field close to where it was discovered. Nearby is an ancient cross called the Standing Stone of Whilprigg.

MILBURN

Cumbria
6 miles north of Appleby-in-Westmorland

Sandstone buildings, mottled with green and yellow lichen, form a defensive rectangle around Milburn's spacious central green. All face inwards, a reminder of the days when bands of bloodthirsty outlaws roamed the wild borderland between England and Scotland, killing, burning and rustling sheep and cattle. Defending the village successfully was vital and the narrow entrances at each corner were easily sealed against border raiders, leaving a few even-narrower 'through gangs' as the only means of communication with the outside world.

The shop and post office is housed in what was originally a stone barn. It looks out across the green to a lofty maypole, which stands on the base of a long-vanished preaching cross and is topped by a weathercock. The village school, at the top of the 400yd long green, faces a small Wesleyan chapel at the opposite end. Both were built in the 1850s.

Milburn's setting does much to enhance its charm. The great wall of the Pennines rises steeply behind the village, reaching 2930ft above sea level at Cross Fell, only 4 miles away and the highest point in the chain.

MILLOM

Cumbria

5 miles southwest of Broughton in Furness

An unassuming little town on the western side of the Duddon estuary, Millom grew up around its 14th-century castle and the adjacent 12th-century Church of the Holy Trinity, which is notable for its fine windows, box pews, and monuments to the Huddleston family. One is thought to be of Sir Richard Huddleston, 'Terrible Dick', who fought at Agincourt. Both the castle and the church are situated near a bend in the road leading to Duddon Bridge, which is

about a mile or so north of the present town centre.

In later years, the local mining industry made Millom prosperous. During the late 19th century, when most of Millom was built, its iron mines had 11 working shafts, making them the largest and busiest in Britain. The last of the workings closed only in 1968. Among the exhibits at Millom's folk museum are a reconstruction of a miner's cottage and a replica of one of the working levels of the old Hodbarrow Iron Mine, at nearby Haverigg, 1 mile south.

While the town has a somewhat wistful air, there is much beauty surrounding it. Black Combe, 4 miles northwest, makes an impressive backcloth and there are superb sands from Haverigg to Silecroft, 3 miles northwest, and beyond.

MILNTHORPE

Cumbria

10 miles west of Kirkby Lonsdale

Milnthorpe was a notorious traffic bottleneck on the A6 road into Lakeland, until it was bypassed by the M6 motorway. Unknown to most of the motorists suffering delays, there was – and is – a delightful detour round the village through an avenue of massive old beech trees, alongside a well-stocked deer park by the bank of the River Kent.

Ironically, the road that tried the tempers of motorist and villager alike helped in the 18th century to bring the prosperity which created the village much as we now see it. Several turnpikes were installed, and it captured the coach traffic from an older Kendal to Burton route. Nine inns catered for the coaches, their crews and passengers, and also for the thriving local industries along the smaller River Bela. These industries and the village's seaport – the Bela was then navigable for small vessels – were the other source of its prosperity. Nowadays, although the estuary sands have silted up the port, and the canals, railways and other roads have bypassed the village, Milnthorpe still earns its keep as a working community. Local industries include quarrying and comb-making.

Although many of the stone cottages either side of the market square date from the 18th and early 19th centuries, the village is truly ancient. Earthworks in parkland surrounding Dallam Tower, a Queen Anne-style manor house on the southwest edge of the village, were probably built by Iron Age settlers.

Colonised successively by Celts, Romans, Angles and Norsemen, the village owes its name to the Norse-Irish, who arrived 1000 years ago and called it the 'village by the mill'. Despite this long history, Milnthorpe took on an independent identity only in the 1830s, when St Thomas's parish church was built in the market square. Previously it had been part of the nearby parish of Heversham. Milnthorpe's Friday market maintains a tradition going back to 1280. So does the annual funfair on May 12, which preserves an ancient right which was originally granted in the same year for holding cattle fairs.

A gentle stroll will reveal how the old builders, working in local limestone and without too many rules and regulations, managed to create a village that has both human scale – odd nooks and crannies and narrow twisting lanes – and a feel of spaciousness.

RIVERSIDE GRAZING *Sheep graze while the River Kent meanders between beech trees in Dallam Tower's park.*

LOW TIDE AT DUSK *Morecambe Bay's golden sands lie deserted when the holidaymakers have gone home.*

MOOR DIVOCK
Cumbria
5 miles southwest of Helton

From earliest times the wide, windswept plateau of Moor Divock, off the northeast shore of Ullswater, has had a strange fascination for man. This seems curious in a countryside noted for its mountains, lakes and valleys. And yet it is the emptiness of the place that appeals to the imagination, and the unchecked wind blowing across the blanket of bracken and heather that makes it so refreshing.

The surface of the moor is littered with cairns, standing stones, stone circles, mounds and pits, all of them dating back some 3000 to 4000 years. Many of the smaller relics are almost lost in the bracken; but the larger ones, such as the Cop Stone, stand up from the moor like the last, indestructible memorials to an otherwise forgotten people. The relics suggest a purpose, but the purpose remains unknown. Why prehistoric man dug the Wofa Holes, the Pulpit Holes and the Dewpot Holes is as much a matter of mystery as his reason for raising the Cop Stone or any other of the stones round about it.

The Romans also left their mark on the moor, but they were chiefly concerned with crossing it, not with stopping there. The Lake District was strategically important to the Romans because of its proximity to Hadrian's Wall. The old Roman road called High Street ran across the moor, on its way south to the Troutbeck valley and the central lakes. To this day the huge mountain over which the road ran is still called High Street. Careful searching of the moor can still reveal traces of the old road. This is perfect walking country, crisscrossed with green paths of springy turf. Lapwings and curlews call plaintively from above, and skylarks spiral into the sky delivering their clear, warbling song.

Wild ponies roam the moor. Nothing expresses the spirit of the place better than the sight of a herd of these shy creatures wheeling away from one of the tiny moorland becks, and galloping into the distance.

MORECAMBE
Lancashire
3 miles northwest of Lancaster

Like neighbouring Heysham, Morecambe is one of the 'lungs' of Lancashire. Its wide bay and spacious beaches have attracted holidaymakers from the industrial towns of the north since the beginning of the century, and still draw visitors today.

Most of the traditional seaside entertainments are in Morecambe. Funfairs, amusement arcades and theatres overlook the broad, 4 mile long promenade where illuminations light up the seafront from August to mid-October. Marineland, on the stone jetty, claims to be Europe's first oceanarium and has a well-stocked aquarium and performing dolphins. The Leisure Park has an outdoor heated swimming pool, paddling pools and terraces where you can sunbathe. The Superdome is a venue for indoor sports during the day and a variety of entertainments in the evening. The promenade gives a panoramic view across the width of the bay, from Piel Island to the heart of the Lakeland hills beyond.

Morecambe developed in Victorian times from three small fishing villages and fishing boats still bob in

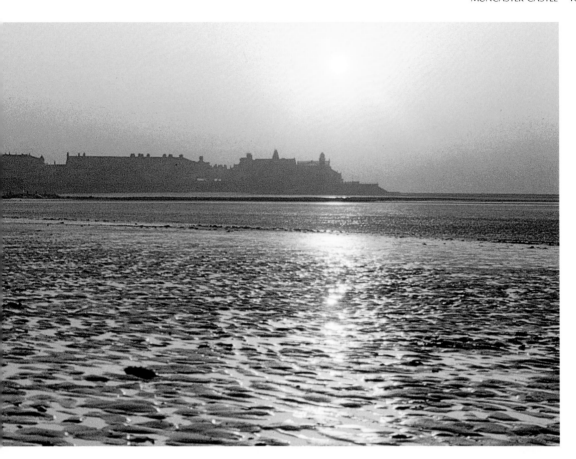

the bay, providing a colourful spectacle as well as supplying whitebait, codling and shrimps.

At low tide it is possible to walk across the bay from Hest Bank to Grange-over-Sands, on the estuary of the River Kent, a distance of about 8 miles. Walkers must be accompanied by an official guide as there are fast-flowing channels to ford, but the journey is worth-while, especially for naturalists. The rivulets and creeks teem with marine life, preyed upon by flocks of oystercatchers and other wading birds.

MUNCASTER CASTLE
Cumbria
15 miles southeast of Whitehaven

A fine collection of antique furniture, tapestries and portraits is housed in Muncaster Castle, perched on a hilltop 1 mile east of Ravenglass. The house dates from about 1200, but was rebuilt and extended in the 1860s. During the Wars of the Roses, shepherds found Henry VI wandering the nearby fells after the Battle of Hexham and took him to Muncaster Castle, home of Sir John Pennington. The room in which the king was hidden is still called King Henry's Room, and the gold-and-white enamelled glass bowl he presented to his hosts on leaving nine days later still remains in the castle. Known as the Luck of Muncaster, the bowl has been treasured by the family ever since. It is said that as long as the bowl remains unbroken, a Pennington will hold the castle. Understandably, the bowl is not on view, but there are fine paintings, tapestries and furniture. The oak panelling in the billiard room is said to have been taken from HMS *Téméraire*, one of Nelson's fleet at Trafalgar.

Muncaster Castle and its surrounding gardens are open on most afternoons in summer. Muncaster Mill, 1 mile to the north where the road crosses the River Mite, is an old water mill, restored to working order, which grinds wholemeal flour.

ROYAL HIDEAWAY *Henry VI hid in Muncaster Castle for nine days during the Wars of the Roses. In gratitude, he gave his hosts a glass bowl, preserved to this day.*

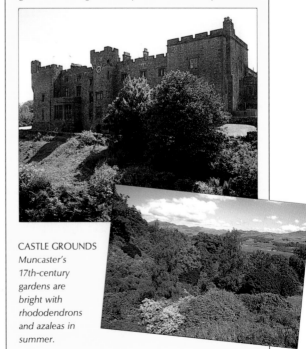

CASTLE GROUNDS *Muncaster's 17th-century gardens are bright with rhododendrons and azaleas in summer.*

N

NAWORTH CASTLE
Cumbria
2 miles east of Brampton

A brief climb from Greenhead leads to a long straight section of road with views to the west across the River Eden's valley to the Solway Firth and Scotland's distant hills. A short detour through wooded parkland leads to Naworth Castle, the home of the Earl of Carlisle whose ancestor, Lord William Howard, turned the stronghold into a mansion during the 17th century.

Battlemented sandstone towers flank the main part of the castle and overlook a gatehouse carved with the Dacre family's coat of arms. Naworth was built by Ranulph Dacre in 1335. It became one of the great border strongholds, and was a setting for Sir Walter Scott's *Lay of the Last Minstrel*. It was ravaged by fire in 1844, then restored by Anthony Salvin, and contains elaborate tapestries. Naworth Castle is open to the public on certain afternoons during summer.

NEAR SAWREY
Cumbria
2 miles south of Hawkshead

The pretty stone village of Near Sawrey lies in a green dell where the prevailing breeze streams horizontal ribbons of grey smoke from chimney pots. Just outside, guarded by an enormous cedar, is Hill Top Farm.

In 1900 Peter Rabbit, or his royalties, bought it for Beatrix Potter. During the 17 years that she lived here, this was the birthplace of Tom Kitten, Jemima Puddle-Duck and other childhood favourites.

Miss Potter was an early publicist of the ideals of the National Trust, and when she died in 1943, she bequeathed 17th-century Hill Top to the nation, together with her furniture, china and drawings. The house is as she left it, and a visit is like stepping back into the pages of a childhood story. Many of its contents appeared in picture form in Beatrix Potter's books, which she illustrated herself. Fans of *The Tale of Jemima Puddle-Duck* will recognise the Tower Bank Arms pub next door; this too is the property of the National Trust.

Far Sawrey, like its neighbour, is flanked by Windermere and Esthwaite Water and has its own, less publicised charm. It stands among trees on a lane which ends at the Windermere ferry. Another narrow lane runs southwards to the Victorian village church, set by a grassy hillock with pleasant views over Windermere to the hills above Kendal. Town End, opposite the churchyard entrance, is an attractive old pair of cottages whose whitewash gleams in the rich green landscape. The lane continues to Newby Bridge, rising and falling through woods where occasional breaks provide delightful views of Windermere.

TOM KITTEN'S BIRTHPLACE *Hill Top Farm gave Beatrix Potter the peace and solitude she needed to write.*

LUCY *An illustration from Mrs Tiggy-Winkle by Beatrix Potter.*

NENTHEAD

Cumbria
4½ miles southeast of Alston

The village of Nenthead was built during the 19th century by the London Lead Company as a model village for the miners working in the lead and zinc mines, which have long been derelict. One can still see the Miners' Reading Room and the Miners' Arms. There are also the blacksmith's shop and the old smelt mill just south of the main road.

Set 2000ft up among the Pennines, Nenthead claims to have the highest church, chapel and vicarage in England. Here the 18th-century civil engineer John Smeaton built an underground canal. But the chief attraction is the grandeur of the high moorlands.

NEWCHURCH IN PENDLE

Lancashire
3 miles northwest of Nelson

A quaint, steep, winding village of grey stone, Newchurch dovetails into the foothills of Pendle. It was once called Goldshaw Booth, but takes its present name from the 'New Church' of St Mary which was built around 1740 onto the existing 16th-century tower. A clock was added to the tower in 1946. A much older 'eye of God' is carved on the outer wall of the tower to warn off evil spirits.

In the churchyard is the reputed grave of Alice Nutter, a resident of nearby Roughlee Hall, who was among the ten Lancashire witches convicted and hanged in 1612. Roughlee Hall is privately owned and not open to the public. The village shop, called 'Witches Galore', is guarded by three life-size models of wrinkled crones; an inscription on a stone over the door urges customers to part with their money by the exhortation 'Gerrit spent'.

NEWLANDS PASS

Cumbria
About 2 miles southwest of Keswick

Father Thomas West, who wrote the first guide to the Lake District, published in 1778, described Newlands Pass as 'Alpine views and pastoral scenes in a sublime style'. Even today, the narrow road twisting through the fells, with some stretches steeper than 1-in-4, provides its excitements.

For almost 3 miles from Braithwaite, the road – which was built in the 1770s – runs along a ledge high above the Newlands valley, with fine views to the east and southeast of wooded Swinside and cosy-looking Cat Bells – the hill where Beatrix Potter's Mrs Tiggy-Winkle lived.

Stretching flat and green below, crisscrossed by stone walls, the Newlands valley is remote and peaceful. Yet 400 years ago in Elizabethan times it was a busy mining centre, with copper and some silver recovered from the local Goldscope Mine. The mine was worked by expert miners brought in from Germany by the Queen's Mines-Royal Company; the name Goldscope is said to be derived from the German *Gottsgabe* – 'God's gift'. The mining was at its height in the 16th century, and the ores were smelted near Keswick, the local woods being turned to charcoal to feed the furnaces.

After crossing Rigg Beck the road swings westwards from the Newlands valley along the much narrower Keskadale valley, below the steep fells of Ard Crags to the right. It is well worth parking by the hairpin bend over Ill Gill and scrambling up beside the beck for a glimpse of the Keskadale Oakwood. The 14 acre oakwood is now a protected area; in company with the Birkrigg Oakwood, on the slopes of Causey Pike to the northeast, it is thought to be the last surviving remnant of the great oak forests that once covered the Lakeland fells. The trees are small and windswept sessile oaks, recognised by their stalkless acorns.

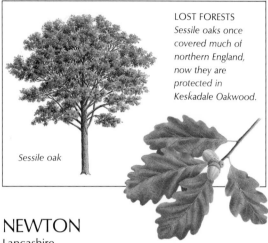

LOST FORESTS
Sessile oaks once covered much of northern England, now they are protected in Keskadale Oakwood.

Sessile oak

NEWTON

Lancashire
6 miles northwest of Clitheroe

This friendly village of limestone cottages crouches under the wooded slopes of Dunnow Rock. From the mid-17th century Newton was a centre for the Quakers and their meeting house, built in 1767, still stands. Among those educated at the old Quaker school was John Bright, the Lancashire-born politician. He was one of the leaders of a campaign in 1846 to repeal the Corn Laws which restricted grain imports. He carved his initials on the back of a bench in the House of Commons, where they can still be seen – together with the date 1826.

NEWTON ARLOSH

Cumbria
2 miles southwest of Kirkbride

Like every other old-established community on both sides of the Solway Firth, Newton Arlosh belies its tranquil atmosphere with memories of the Anglo-Scottish wars. The oldest parts of St Michael's Church date from 1303 and were built for defence as well as worship. The stubby sandstone tower, and the nave, where cattle were kept in times of trouble, have very thick walls and windows little bigger than slits for archers. The doorway has a pointed arch rising to barely the height of a man, and is less than 3ft wide.

St Michael's is one of the few Anglican churches in Britain whose altar is not on the eastern side. It was moved to the northern wall when a 19th-century extension, which now accounts for most of the building, made the church broader than it was long.

Newton Arlosh ('New Town on the Marsh') was founded at the same time as the church. People moved inland after the village's predecessor, a small port used by Edward I, was devastated by a storm.

NIARBYL BAY

Isle of Man
½ mile southwest of Dalby

A minor road leaves the main coast road at the village of Dalby and reaches the sea at Niarbyl Bay, where there is a small parking area by a group of cottages. The tiny, sheltered bay is guarded by a threatening promontory of rocks which projects out to sea.

A footpath climbs round the cliff-face to the south, eventually reaching a lane at the top of the slope; this lane rejoins the main road 3 miles further south, near the summit of Cronk ny Arrey Laa.

ROCKY NAMESAKE *The Niarbyl, a promontory jutting out to sea, means 'tail' in Manx and gives the bay its name.*

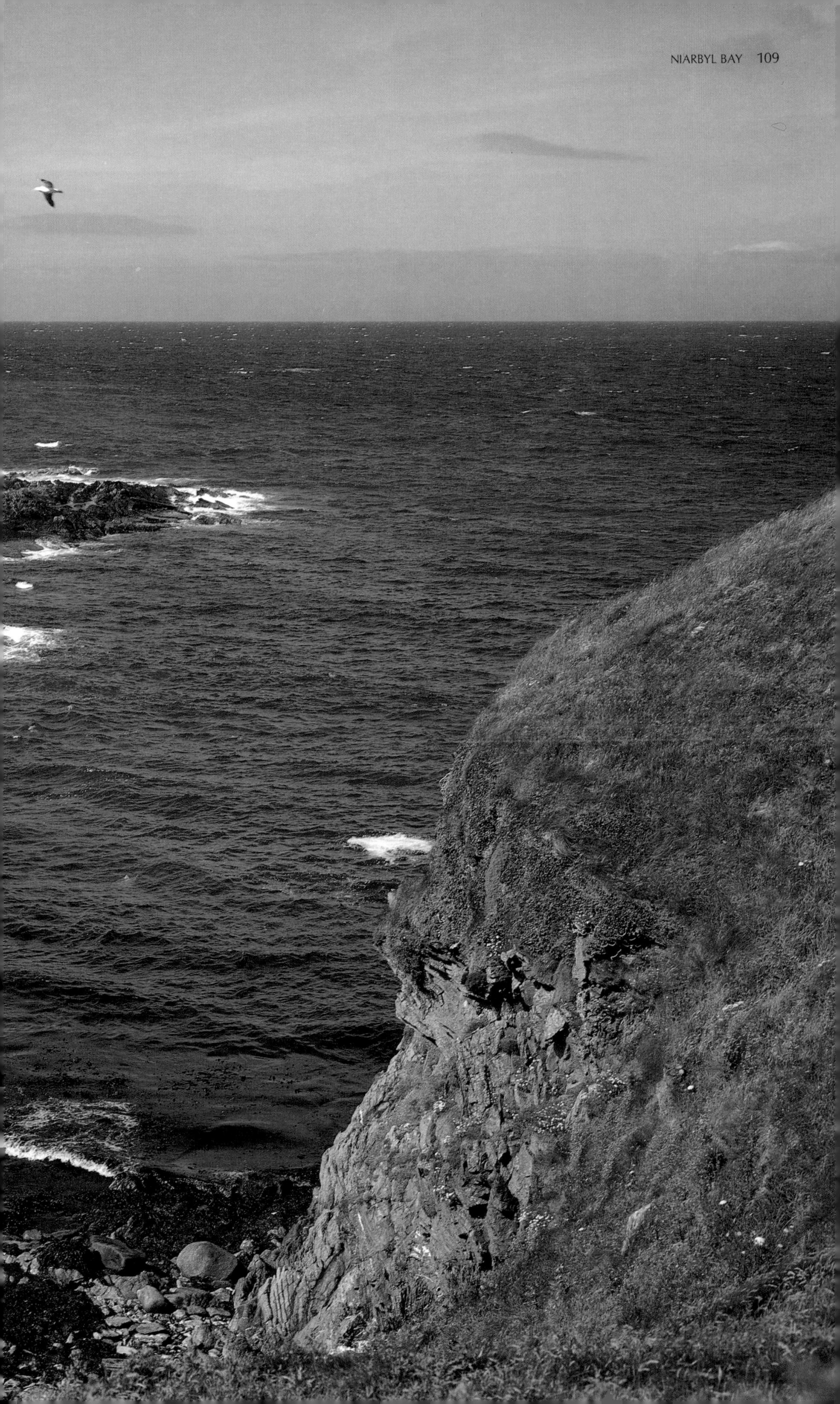

ONCHAN

Isle of Man
2 miles northeast of Douglas

The small town of Onchan spreads around the rocky mass of Onchan Head. Nowadays, it is virtually a suburb of Douglas, and offers the same kind of holiday facilities. Onchan Park's diversions include an amusement centre, golf, stock-car racing, and a boating lake and sports stadium.

The residence of the Lieutenant-Governor, the sovereign's representative on the island, is on the edge of the village, and the parish register records that in 1781, William Bligh, RN, was married to Miss Betham, daughter of the island's customs officer. At that time, Bligh commanded HMS *Ranger*, engaged in suppressing smuggling in the Irish Sea, and it was not until some six years later that he took command of HMS *Bounty* – an appointment that was to confront him with the Navy's best-known mutiny.

There are some pleasant walks about the village, to the wooded Groudle Glen and Molly Quirk's Glen, and from the Promenade through Calvary Glen to Lourdes Grotto and Onchan Park.

ORMSKIRK

Lancashire
7 miles southeast of Southport

Until 200 years ago, the land around Ormskirk was waterlogged moorland. After being drained, it became good agricultural land, and Ormskirk developed as a market town. In the market square, now a shopping precinct, stands a clock tower erected in 1876 by the Earl of Derby, and nearby stands the Church of St Peter and St Paul, the church of the Stanleys, Earls of Derby. It is unusual in having a low, square tower, erected, probably in 1540, to house the bells.

Inside the church the 16th-century Derby Chapel was built by the 3rd earl, and in it lies James Stanley, 7th Earl of Derby – in two coffins. A Royalist earl, he shared the fate of his king and was beheaded at Bolton for his part in the Civil War, and a short coffin holds his body while his head rests in a casket at its side.

Burscough Street has many fine Georgian houses, including 18th-century Knowles House.

Scarisbrick Hall, 3 miles northwest of the town, was rebuilt in neo-Gothic style in the 19th century. It was formerly the home of the Scarisbrick family, who were mainly responsible for draining the moorland. The hall, now a school, may be visited during the summer holidays. Rufford Old Hall, 5 miles north, is an outstanding half-timbered medieval mansion now a museum of Lancashire folk life, open in summer.

ORTON

Cumbria
13 miles northeast of Kendal

Climbing gently but steadily through a landscape dominated by limestone outcrops known as 'scars', the road from Crosby Ravensworth reaches 1100ft where it meets the main road north of Orton. The unfenced junction with its broad, turf-clad verges is a convenient stopping place from which to enjoy the fine views along Orton Scar and southeastwards across the Pennines to high peaks in the Yorkshire Dales National Park. A path leads to Beacon Hill, a craggy outcrop a few hundred yards east of the junction, where warning fires used to be lit when Scottish raiders were on the prowl.

Orton is a secluded village with stone houses and a spacious green. The Church of All Saints has an ancient parish chest of oak. It has three padlocks, each opened by a different key as a way of ensuring that three people were present when it was opened. There is also a fine stained-glass window by Beatrice Whistler, wife of the American artist James McNeill Whistler. The oldest of three bells, hung in a frame in the north aisle, was cast in 1530.

The Liberal Club, near the George Hotel, has a carving of William Gladstone above its doorway. The Old Hall, built in 1604, is largely intact. George Whitehead, co-founder of the Society of Friends, was born in Orton in about 1636.

Tebay, a long greystone village, 3 miles south, is also a good starting point for fell walks. Lune Gorge, stretching south from the village, is almost matched in its majesty by the magnificent gorge that has been artificially created through nearby cliffs to take the long, wide sweep of the M6 motorway.

UNUSUAL CHURCH *Hidden behind the stocky tower of St Peter and St Paul in Ormskirk is a slender spire.*

Sand and safaris on the Lancashire Plain

Golden sands bordered by pines provide a natural wind-break for fertile farms, while beasts from Africa roam in a country park. Inland from the promenades and beaches of Southport lies the Lancashire Plain which spreads to the marshy Ribble estuary.

Rhinos wander freely around Knowsley Safari Park

Rufford Old Hall still in its original splendour

Lancashire's red squirrels were disappearing fast until the Ainsdale Nature Reserve provided a haven where some at least can survive

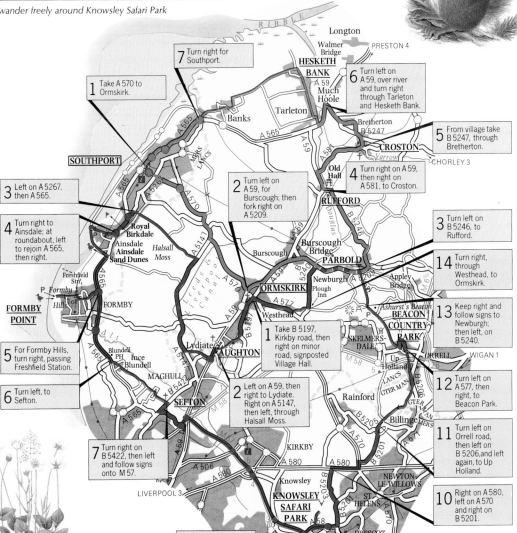

7 Turn right for Southport.

1 Take A 570 to Ormskirk.

6 Turn left on A 59, over river and turn right through Tarleton and Hesketh Bank.

5 From village take B 5247, through Bretherton.

3 Left on A 5267, then A 565.

2 Turn left on A 59, for Burscough; then fork right on A 5209.

4 Turn right on A 59, then right on A 581, to Croston.

4 Turn right to Ainsdale; at roundabout, left to rejoin A 565, then right.

3 Turn left on B 5246, to Rufford.

14 Turn right, through Westhead, to Ormskirk.

5 For Formby Hills, turn right, passing Freshfield Station.

1 Take B 5197, Kirkby road, then right on minor road, signposted Village Hall.

13 Keep right and follow signs to Newburgh; then left, on B 5240.

6 Turn left, to Sefton.

2 Left on A 59, then right to Lydiate. Right on A 5147, then left, through Halsall Moss.

12 Turn left on A 577, then right, to Beacon Park.

7 Turn right on B 5422, then left and follow signs onto M 57.

11 Turn left on Orrell road, then left on B 5206, and left again, to Up Holland.

10 Right on A 580, left on A 570 and right on B 5201.

8 At Junction 2 take A 58, then left for Knowsley Safari Park.

9 Left on B 5201, then B 5203.

Grass-of-Parnassus flourishes at Formby Point

SOUTHPORT · Royal Birkdale · Ainsdale · Ainsdale Sand Dunes · Halsall Moss · Freshfield Stn · FORMBY POINT · FORMBY · Blundell PH · Ince Blundell · MAGHULL · SEFTON · Lydiate · AUGHTON · KIRKBY · Knowsley · KNOWSLEY SAFARI PARK · LIVERPOOL 3 · ORMSKIRK · Westhead · Plough Inn · SKELMERSDALE · Newburgh · Appley Bridge · PARBOLD · BURSCOUGH · Burscough Bridge · RUFFORD · Old Hall · CROSTON · Bretherton · Tarleton · Banks · HESKETH BANK · Much Hoole · Walmer Bridge · Longton · RIBBLE · PRESTON 4 · CHORLEY 3 · Ashurst's Beacon · BEACON COUNTRY PARK · Up Holland · ORRELL · WIGAN 1 · Rainford · Billinge · NEWTON LE WILLOWS · ST HELENS · PRESCOT · WIDNES 5 · Leeds & Liverpool Canal

P

PAPCASTLE

Cumbria
1 mile northwest of Cockermouth

The pretty little village of Papcastle, in the River Derwent's valley, has many attractive stone-built houses, and is bright with flowers in the spring and summer. Once this was the site of a Roman fort and the start of a Roman road which leads to Carlisle.

Just before skirting Bothel, the road climbs Wharrels Hill – identified by a radio mast. From a layby near the mast there are panoramic views across the coastal plain to the Solway Firth and Scotland.

PARBOLD

Lancashire
7 miles northwest of Wigan

A humpbacked bridge spans the Leeds and Liverpool Canal in Parbold, and by it stand the stump of a tower windmill and the millhouse, both now used as business offices. Pleasure craft moor by the bridge, and at the canal edge there is a small car park from which a pleasant walk along the waterway leads to Burscough Bridge, 4 miles west.

Above Parbold looms the 394ft high brow of Parbold Beacon, and from the layby near its summit there are breathtaking views of the wide green valley with glimpses of the River Douglas appearing like fragments of glass among the soft folds of the hills.

PARLICK FELL

Lancashire
2 miles northwest of Chipping

It is a tough climb to the 1416ft summit of Parlick Fell, for the hill has convex slopes. The first 800ft of the climb is the steepest stretch and the most slippery, since it is over shale. But the views from the top make the climb well worth the effort. Parlick is among the southern Bowland fells and, jutting well out from the main mass, it commands tremendous views – over the valleys of the Loud and Ribble rivers, over the wide Lancashire Plain, across Morecambe Bay towards the southern hills of the Lake District, and even, when the weather is fine, as far as the Isle of Man and the distant mountains of Snowdonia some 80 miles away. Few other places in Lancashire survey such a wide domain.

Off the road that climbs up to Parlick from Chipping there is a rough farm track, just where the road makes a steep left bend at the foot of the fell. From the gate at the far end of the track, one path, with a gully on the right, climbs straight up the fell. A longer but easier path, to the left of the first, reaches the top of the fell in a series of zigzags.

Sheltering beneath the great rise of the fell is the village of Chipping. It lies in the valley of the River Loud, or rather perches over it, on a shelf about 50ft above the river. Everywhere the valley is lush. Cattle graze on the rich, green grass between the woods and

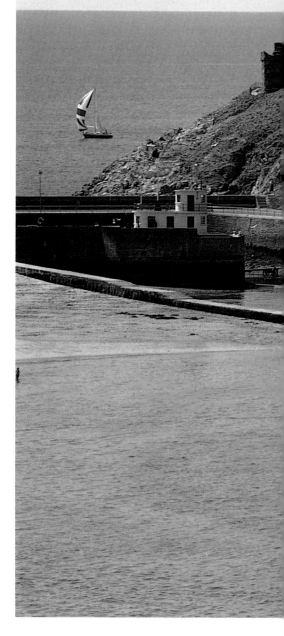

coppices, and lines of windbreak trees punctuate the landscape. In many parts of Bowland there are bluebells, and Leagram, the area of ancient forest that surrounds Chipping, has one of the finest bluebell woods in England. In winters long ago, it is said, the wolves that lived on nearby Wolf Fell used to come loping down to search for food in the village.

PATTERDALE

Cumbria
½ mile south of the southwest tip of Ullswater

An attractive tourist village surrounded by mountains, Patterdale is where St Patrick, the patron saint of Ireland, is said to have preached and baptised converts. His holy well is at the roadside 1 mile north of the town. There are steamer trips along the 7-mile Ullswater, which is in a delightful setting; and there are

many footpaths including shoreline walks through woods and hills on the eastern bank of the lake.

The village is an excellent base for climbing 3118ft Helvellyn – the third-highest peak in the Lake District and the most popular climb. It can be tackled by any fully equipped and hardened hiker, but a head for heights is needed along the 1 mile long ridge of Striding Edge. The approach is along the Grisedale Valley and starts from a side-turning off the A592, near the police station at Patterdale. The walk to the summit is a distance of about 3 miles.

An easier climb to the summit, avoiding Striding Edge, can be made from the west. The footpath starts from Thirlspot on the A591 on the east bank of Thirlmere. This route is also about 3 miles long, taking 2 hours. The view from the summit is breathtaking. On a clear day, almost every fell in Lakeland can be seen, as well as the Pennines to the east and the mountains of Scotland which lie 60 miles away to the northwest.

RUINS ON THE HORIZON *The forbidding walls of Peel Castle punctuate the harbour's skyline.*

PEEL
Isle of Man
11 miles northwest of Douglas

Castle, cathedral and kippers – these are the great landmarks of Peel, but some of its less well-known aspects linger with equal affection in the memory. For example, behind the harbour there are steep lanes of little shops and cottages, built from red sandstone boulders of all shapes and sizes, crammed and mortared together. Or there is the beach of red-gold sand running before the wide, old-fashioned promenade where cafés and restaurants sell such nostalgic dishes as cod and chips and pie and chips – as in the days before hamburgers and fried chicken were dreamt of.

FAMOUS FISH *Peel smokeries turn a humble herring into a Manx kipper.*

Finally there are the pleasant, chatty, friendly people.

Peel makes its living from the sea. The long harbour shelters all kinds of vessels; yachts and catamarans, big stern-loading trawlers and little drifters bearing the registration letters PL for Peel, RY for Ramsey, and maybe a stocky gunboat of the Fisheries Protection Squadron. Over all drifts a fragrant cloud of wood-smoke to alert the gourmet that he has arrived at the birthplace of the Manx kipper.

The herrings are taken straight from the boats to the smokeries, from which they may be purchased, posted or packed into parcels for the journey home. Behind the smokeries is *Odin's Raven* Boathouse, containing a replica of a Viking longship that was sailed and rowed from Trondheim to Peel by a crew of Norwegians and Manxmen in 1979, to celebrate the millennium of the Manx Parliament.

Drifts of fishing nets lie before the masonry bastions of St Patrick's Isle – truly an island, though it has long been connected to Peel by a causeway. This is the very heart of Manxdom. Stone Age people lived on the islet; St Patrick himself is supposed to have visited it in AD 444 (when he converted the heathen population and banished all snakes); and here too, so it is said, the Vikings made their first horrendous raid on Man in AD 798. Rather surprisingly, this episode is still commemorated with a re-enactment each July.

Behind the mighty medieval walls of Peel Castle at the harbour mouth is one of the most astonishing ranges of buildings in all of Britain. Recent investigations have revealed a Viking palace, among other discoveries, beneath the steep mound – but what stands on the surface is also remarkable. There is the roofless 10th-century Church of St Patrick, and beside it a 50ft round tower of the same period – rare outside Ireland. It is built of hefty sandstone blocks, and the entrance is 7ft off the ground. Monks would seek refuge in the tower, drawing a ladder up after them, when Viking raiders landed.

Nearby is the partly ruined St German's Cathedral, started by Bishop Simon of Argyll in 1226. The crypt was the prison of the ecclesiastical court. There are monuments to drowned sailors, and to a number of bishops too, for though there is a more complete cathedral church in the town, this is still the official seat of the Bishops of Sodor and Man. Among several other buildings within the curtain wall, the most imposing is the Gatehouse which, despite its name, is the principal fortification of the islet.

Along the Douglas Road, 2½ miles from Peel, stands tiny Tynwald Hill, shaped like a wedding cake. All new laws for the island must be proclaimed from this hill in the English and Manx languages.

PENDLETON AND PENDLE HILL
Lancashire
2 miles southeast and 3 miles east of Clitheroe

A story persists around Pendleton that a regular customer at the Swan with Two Necks village pub once auctioned his wife to the highest bidder. The pub was built in 1776 and, wife-auctioning stories apart, life in this busy farming community seems little changed over the years. The pub's unusual name probably has no local connection – there are others similarly named around the country. It may have originated as the Swan with Two Nicks, a reference to the method used by the Vintners' Company of London to mark the bills of its Thames swans.

The Swan stands at the west end of Pendleton, which has four dairy farms in its main street. At milking time the narrow village lanes are crowded with cattle coming in from the fields around. Once these lanes were used by monks travelling between the early 14th-century abbey of Whalley, to the south, and the 12th-century abbey of Sawley, to the north.

Set low on the western flank of Pendle Hill, the village is built astride a moorland stream, channelled down the middle of the main street and spanned by stone footbridges. Many of the sturdily built stone cottages and farmhouses, some distinguished by mullioned windows, date back 200 or 300 years, and the village itself is mentioned in the Domesday Survey of 1086 as 'Peniltune'. Relics of a far earlier culture have been discovered in a Bronze Age burial site found in one of the village gardens.

The tiny village school at the east end of the village, near the 19th-century parish church of All Saints, was one of the first National Schools in the country, built in 1837. But in 1981 it had only eight pupils and was closed. Beyond the school the slumbering lion shape of Pendle Hill – 7 miles long – sprawls to the east, its

LAND OF WITCHES *Pendle Hill dominates local history as much as the surrounding countryside.*

head pointing northeast, its rump southwest.

The rise of the rump – the 'Little End' of Pendle – is grooved by a col called the Nick of Pendle. The moment the village is left behind and the first cattle-grid crossed, the scene changes instantly to one of bleak, sweeping moorland. Clumps of rushes and sedge dot the poor, close-cropped grass, and rocks stick up through the thin soil.

From the top of the pass, where the small quarries just over the crest make convenient car parks, climb the sloping slabs of rock to the west. Enormous views spread in every direction. The cotton towns lie to the south, and to the west stretch the crops on the plain of Fylde with the Irish Sea beyond. The Pennines

HARDY SHEEP *The Swaledale thrives in the cold northern winter weather.*

dominate the eastern skyline, and to the north is the beautifully wooded valley of the Ribble, planted 200 years ago with more than a million oak trees. Beyond this belt of green rise the purple crags and moors of the Forest of Bowland, filling the whole horizon.

On the east side of the Nick, a path runs away to the bulk of Pendle Hill. It climbs and climbs, and then suddenly steepens to scramble up the lion's flank. It is a rough track of gritstone fragments, and fairly hard going, but it is a wonderful, exhilarating walk all the way and well worth the effort. The only animals you will see are rabbits, hares and Swaledale sheep, and

the common birds are the skylark, meadow pipit and the plaintive lapwing. The summit reaches 1827ft, and is capped by a flat, east–west sloping plateau of gritstone. There are no trees, only the small, erect shrubs that bear the delicious orange-coloured fruits called cloudberries, so named, it is said, because they so often grow on cloud-capped hilltops.

Pendle Hill has always been a natural barometer for local people, 'a vast black mountain which is the morning weather glass of the country people', according to the 18th-century traveller William Stukeley. It is easy to imagine that something sinister lingers here – perhaps a spell cast by the poor women, known as the Witches of Pendle, who were tried for sorcery and hanged at Lancaster in 1612.

At haymaking time the people of Barley, on the eastern side, used to post a sentinel with a flag on the hill. If he saw a storm brewing in the west, he would wave the flag as a warning to the farmers, telling them to bring in the hay as quickly as possible.

PENRITH

Cumbria
18 miles southeast of Carlisle

The squat, pyramid-topped tower on Beacon Hill, whose wooded slopes rise steeply above Penrith, is a reminder of the old town's turbulent history. Although not built until 1719, the tower marks the spot where many a warning fire was lit before peace finally came to the Anglo-Scottish border at the end of the 16th century. In 1804, when invasion was feared during the Napoleonic Wars, Sir Walter Scott hurried home to join his regiment after, it is said, seeing the flames flickering above Penrith. There is a footpath to the top of Beacon Hill, from which there are fine views over the Lake District.

Penrith is the northern gateway to the Lake District. The old streets on its perimeter are narrow, because that made them easy to defend against raiders from over the border. The open spaces of Sandgate and Dockray were there to protect cattle during raids.

Penrith's sandstone castle, in ruins for more than 400 years, was built at the end of the 14th century after the town had been sacked by the Scots. Its keepers included Richard Neville, Earl of Warwick – 'Warwick the Kingmaker' – and the future Richard III when he was Lord Warden of the Western Marches. The weathered walls, set in a public park, overlook the former Castlegate Foundry, established in the 19th century. The old foundry now houses the Penrith Steam Museum's traction engines, vintage farm machinery, and a working blacksmith's shop.

The partly Norman Church of St Andrew is a notable survivor of the border wars, though much of it was rebuilt in the 18th century. Its Norman tower, with walls 6ft thick, casts its shadow over stones marking the so-called 'Giant's Grave'. These two ancient crosses – both 11ft high – and four hogback tombstones are said to be the burial place of Owen Caesarius, King of Cumbria in the 10th century, but may be a collection of medieval memorials.

Near the church, a restaurant now occupies the Tudor building where Dame Birkett's School was attended by William Wordsworth, his sister Dorothy, and his future wife, Mary Hutchinson. Wordsworth twice revisited Penrith in the late 1790s and stayed at the Robin Hood Inn, where there is a plaque to him.

PICKUP BANK

Lancashire
2 miles east of Darwen

The tiny hamlet of Pickup Bank perches on a breezy hillside dotted with sheep farms and old shepherds' cottages, many now restored. At the centre of the hamlet is the imposing Old Rosin's inn, the name of which derives from the resin used around the turn of the century to polish the inn's dance floor and musical instruments. Local people called the inn 'Old Rosin's' and this name was adopted in place of the former 'Duke of Wellington'.

Pickup Bank overlooks a fertile valley lined with trees which screen disused mills and their ponds.

PIEL ISLAND

Cumbria
On the south side of Piel Channel

Standing in the gap between the mainland and the southern end of the Isle of Walney, Piel Island was ideally placed for the defence of Barrow Harbour. A castle was first built there in the 12th century, but 100 years later the monks of Furness Abbey set up a fortress and a warehouse for the goods traded from the abbey, such as food, wine and wool.

MONKS' CASTLE *Piel Island's castle was built by monks to protect their profitable wool trade.*

In 1486 Lambert Simnel, impersonating the imprisoned Earl of Warwick, landed at Piel Island in an attempt to seize the crown from the new king, Henry VII. He was later defeated and captured at Stoke, and was given a job as a servant in the royal household.

The island can be reached by boat from Roa Island, or at very low tide by walking across the sands from the Isle of Walney.

POINT OF AYRE

Isle of Man
7 miles north of Ramsey

The 4 mile stretch of coast between Rue Point and Point of Ayre is called The Ayres, from an old Norse word meaning a bank of sand or gravel. A road from the village of Bride leads after 3 miles to the lighthouse on the point, from which there is a wide view of sea and low-lying land round three-quarters of the horizon and, behind, to the frowning bulk of the mountains in the island's interior. The picnic site is a fine vantage point from which to watch the ferryboats passing between Douglas and Ardrossan in Scotland and Belfast in Northern Ireland.

Two miles west of the point, a turning off the coast road runs north to a car park near the sea, where a visitor centre and picnic site mark the start of the Ayres Nature Trail. The trail, arranged by the Manx Nature Conservation Trust, illustrates the geology and natural history of this wild part of the island.

POOLEY BRIDGE
Cumbria
5 miles southwest of Penrith

A large pool in the River Eamont, just before it flows out of Ullswater, gave the name Pooley – a corruption of 'pool by the hill' – to the little farming and fishing community which stood on its banks. Then, in the 18th century, a bridge was built across the river, and the village became Pooley Bridge. Today, the pool has disappeared, but the bridge, commanding superb views of Ullswater, still stands. Beside it, the village is spread out along two principal streets, both of which are lined with many delightful old stone houses.

South of Pooley Bridge, Ullswater is a shimmering 7 mile stretch of water that mirrors the wooded fells rising from its shores, and is hemmed in by craggy peaks thrusting higher than 2000ft. The waters of the lake are home to the schelly, a freshwater herring cut off from the sea many thousands of years ago; and living along its banks are two species of fish-eating duck. They are the goosander and the red-breasted merganser, which has a handsome, double-crested green head. Both have bills with serrated edges, which enable them to hold their wriggling, slippery prey.

Leading out along the lakeside from Pooley Bridge are some attractive walks. They pass through woods and copses – where the unusual, tree-hole nests made by the goosander can sometimes be seen – and bring magnificent views at every turn. But perhaps the best way to see Ullswater is from a boat.

The lake is classed as a public highway, and anyone is free to launch a small boat on it, and to explore its creeks and islands. Or you can take a lake boat which calls at Pooley Bridge's little pier, and goes also to Howton and Glenridding.

Back in the centre of the village, St Paul's Church dates only from 1868. Before that time, the nearest church was St Michael's at Barton, 2 miles northeast off the Penrith road. St Michael's was built in about 1150 and was added to over the centuries, especially between 1318 and 1536 when it belonged to the Augustinian canons of Wartre Priory, near York. In the churchyard are buried the poet William Wordsworth's grandfather, Richard, and two of his aunts, as well as his grandson. Near the church stands Church Farm, which probably dates partly from the 17th century.

PORT CARLISLE
Cumbria
11 miles west of Carlisle

A lonely little village, Port Carlisle comprises little more than two terraces of cottages flanking a late Georgian house. The village is a memorial to a commercial venture ruined by the unpredictability of nature. As its name implies, Port Carlisle was established in 1819 to provide a harbour for coastal shipping, with a fast and efficient link by canal to markets in Carlisle and beyond. But in the 1860s the tidal currents changed, the harbour silted up, and the canal was abandoned when the estuary's deep water channel moved away from the shore. The railway which replaced it closed in 1924, after the viaduct which crossed the firth near Bowness-on-Solway became unsafe.

Today the visitor has to search carefully for signs of the old harbour and the remains of the canal, while the traces of the railway are also fast disappearing.

FISH EATERS
Goosanders live on Ullswater.

COLOURED DUCK
Red-breasted mergansers have a green double crest.

PORT CORNAA
Isle of Man
3 miles northeast of Laxey

The tiny but beautiful cove of Port Cornaa is not easy to find. Driving south along the Ramsey–Douglas road, look out for a pub on the right-hand side, about 4 miles south of Ramsey. On the other side of the road, a narrow lane descends steeply across a level crossing, then loops back on itself before turning seawards through a deep tree-lined glen down to a pebbly beach flanked by cliffs. There is limited parking on the shingle bank which overlooks the beach.

PORT ERIN
Isle of Man
5 miles west of Castletown

A pleasant and decorative resort, Port Erin's chosen role is to instruct as well as entertain; or so it would seem from the large number of museums here. There is the Railway Museum, for example, crammed with painted steel and wood, gleaming brass and the hushed, reverential train buffs found in all such museums. In fact, this is a very good one, devoted entirely to the island's own railways, and it is open daily in the summer.

There are gallant little tank engines like *Sutherland*, that first went into service in 1873, brightly painted coaches – the first to be fitted with electric light – and a fascinating collection of posters, photographs and other memorabilia. Outside is the station, all red Victorian wrought iron, and bearing large notices saying 'Purt Chiarn' (Port of the Lord) as well as the English name of Port Erin. The station doubles up as a street market, but in summer you can also board a steam train stopping at all stations to Douglas.

There is the Motor Museum, open occasionally in summer, which maintains a large collection of ageing vehicles in full roadworthy condition; the Erin Arts Centre, open on weekdays throughout the year; and the Marine Biological Station of the University of Liverpool. This not only instructs students but also

QUIET SEA *The sun's last rays catch the waves gently lapping on Port Erin's deserted beach (overleaf).*

monitors fish stocks in the Irish Sea, and has a fine aquarium that is open from April to October.

Following similar though commercial lines is the Clearwater Sea Farm carved out of the side of the cliff. It has large seawater tanks in which lobsters, scallops and other marine creatures may be observed.

Yn Shooylaghan, whose splendid name means simply 'The Promenade', leaves the little shopping centre behind and climbs up the steep green cliffs, whose summits are battlemented with tall Victorian and Edwardian hotels. They are magnificently situated, high above the elegant sweep of the bay that culminates in mighty Bradda Head.

The curious, key-shaped monument on the summit is in memory of William Milner, of the safe-making firm, who was a generous local benefactor. A footpath round Bradda Head gives a panoramic view of Port Erin, while further round the headland there are magnificent views out to sea from Milner's Tower, and the area near the coastguard lookout. The path skirts the edge of Bradda Hill to the north, and eventually rejoins the road to Fleshwick Bay.

There is a little fishing and yachting harbour and, down by the shore, some good, straightforward stone houses with pretty front gardens divided from them by a walkway. Beside them, a little rill of water called St Catherine's Well runs out to the sand. It is fresh water and it was this, centuries ago, that made it possible for fishermen to settle and live in this part of the island. The crystal-clear water is ideal for scuba diving, and there are boat trips to the bird sanctuary on the Calf of Man, where many species of seabirds can be seen. The sanctuary is closed to visitors during the breeding season.

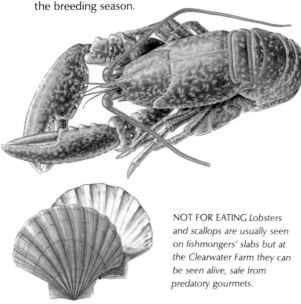

NOT FOR EATING *Lobsters and scallops are usually seen on fishmongers' slabs but at the Clearwater Farm they can be seen alive, safe from predatory gourmets.*

PORT MOOAR

Isle of Man
½ mile southwest of Maughold

A steep plunge down a narrow lane which leaves the main road leads to Port Mooar, a deep, funnel-shaped cove in the cliffs, where the waves roll up a beach of smooth, sparkling pebbles.

Cars can be parked on a broad grassy bank just above the beach, while the high ground behind it shelters the cove from all but southeasterly winds.

PORT ST MARY

Isle of Man
4 miles west of Castletown

Purt Le Moirrey (Port of St Mary) stands back to back with Port Erin, and faces southeast from the shelter of the gap between the twin headlands of Kallow Point and Gansey Point. To some extent it mirrors Port Erin in its fortunate possession of a grand bay and beach. Here, too, there are some tall and dignified Victorian hotels, but not so many as in Port Erin, and the harbour is bigger and somehow more workmanlike.

There are two harbours really, Chapel Bay, named after the little Celtic chapel that once stood on the cliff, and the Bay of Rocks. Both are crowded with fishing boats and yachts, and between them is a lifeboat station that operates both a deep-sea and an inshore craft; it is worth being there when the station holds its Lifeboat Day, usually in July.

Somewhere close by is a foghorn that rattles the teeth whenever the mist comes in – a not infrequent occurrence. This mist is still known as Mannanan's Cloak; Mannanan is the god, or king, or ancient hero after whom the island is named, and his cloak was traditionally flung over his isle to protect it from enemies. During the last century or so, however, it has been especially all-enveloping when royalty are about to arrive, giving rise to a newer saying that the mist is an indication that someone of royal blood is present. Fairly flattering, since almost every visitor will see the mist at some time during his stay.

Port St Mary is the headquarters of the Isle of Man Yacht Club – an offshore yacht race around the island takes place in May. One of the club's favourite cruises is the 36 mile voyage to the Mull of Galloway. In this, its members are echoing a much earlier connection between the two places, when Port St Mary was the island's chief smuggling outlet.

During the 17th and 18th centuries, customs dues on the island were far lower than those of mainland Britain; therefore, cargoes from all over Europe were landed here, and quietly shipped out again by local entrepreneurs to Galloway.

There are a number of fine old limestone houses and tenements in Port St Mary, some of the best being by The Underway, leading down to Chapel Bay, where bright, flowering shrubs tumble over rough stone walls. Someone, too, has made cunning use of old lifebuoys as flower-basket holders.

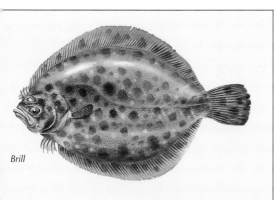

Brill

RECORD CATCH *Trawlers moor side by side in Port St Mary. A new British record was set in 1950 when a brill weighing 16lb was caught just off the bay. Brill always fetches a good price for the fishermen in the local restaurants.*

Paths lead westwards to the spectacular cliff scenery of Spanish Head and The Chasms, and eastwards to Black Rocks. There is good sea-fishing – especially for cod, skate, dogfish and pollock – from boats that can be hired off The Carrick and Langness.

PORT SODERICK
Isle of Man
3 miles southwest of Douglas

A walk down from the A25 Douglas-Ballasalla road leads through an attractive glen to the east-facing shingle beach of Port Soderick. A small stream flows down the glen over grassy slopes, and at the lower end are a café, shops and an amusement centre.

PORT SUNLIGHT
Merseyside
3 miles southeast of Birkenhead

Naming it after the trademark of the soap which made him rich, Lord Leverhulme built the garden village of Port Sunlight for his workers in 1888, and created one of the most spectacular examples of enlightened town planning of his time.

In the centre of the village is the Lady Lever Art Gallery, opened in 1922. It contains paintings, principally of the English School, watercolours and engravings, miniatures, antique Renaissance and British sculpture, Chinese pottery and porcelain and Wedgwood wares. There is also one of the best collections of English furniture outside London. Near the railway station there is an information centre and bookshop.

PRESTON
Lancashire
27 miles northwest of Manchester

Over the centuries, Preston has had an importance far beyond its size. It was once a prosperous inland port, and though in recent years its trade has declined, part of the old port area is now being redeveloped. It was also an important railway junction, and its position midway between London and the cities of Scotland led to the building of hotels where weary passengers could rest before completing their journey.

Richard Arkwright, born in Preston in 1732, was the inventor of the spinning frame, an innovation which helped to make the town a centre for cotton-spinning for 150 years. It is still a busy industrial town, with a shopping centre whose shop fronts are built on to Georgian, Victorian and Edwardian premises.

Street names such as Fishergate, Friargate and Stoneygate are about the only relics of Preston's medieval beginnings, and the great houses of the gentry have long since been replaced by warehouses and shops. But the fine buildings to be found in the centre of the town date from a later period of prosperity when Preston led the way in textiles.

Preston's heart is Market Square, perhaps the most noble site bearing such a humble name in England. It is dominated by the Harris Museum and Art Gallery, completed in 1893 from funds donated by Edmund Robert Harris, a local benefactor. Standing high above the paved square, it is of classical design with tall fluted columns supporting a massive pediment along which are sculptured reliefs much in the style of the British Museum in London. The treasures of the museum and art gallery include 19th-century watercolours by British artists, Georgian drinking glasses and costumes, pottery, toys and games from the 18th century to more recent times, Bronze Age burial urns and coins from a Viking treasure hoard found buried near a ford across the Ribble.

Preston was the second oldest borough in England and has been represented in Parliament since the 13th century. It was given the right to hold a Merchant Guild, a form of regular market for merchants, under the charter of Henry II in 1179, and the Guild has been celebrated every 20 years since 1542, with only one break during the Second World War. The Fulwood Barracks, at the northern end of the city, is the home depot of the Queen's Lancashire Regiment and also houses the Regimental Museum with uniforms, medals and weapons dating back to the regiment's beginnings.

At Goosnargh, 5½ miles north of Preston, is Chingle Hall, a 13th-century moated manor house built in the shape of a cross, and reputed to be haunted. During the Civil War, it was a place of Roman Catholic worship and there are four priests' hiding holes.

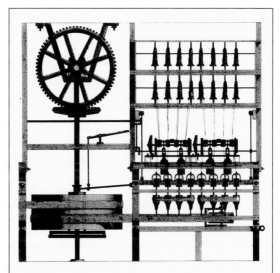

SPINNING FRAME *Richard Arkwright's water-powered frame tripled spinning output and won Preston a prominent place in the cotton industry.*

R

RAMPSIDE
Cumbria
3 miles southeast of Barrow-in-Furness

The single main street of Rampside runs along the edge of a muddy shingle beach, which at low water extends 2 miles out to sea. Deep pools and gullies have been scoured out by the fast currents which funnel out of this corner of Morecambe Bay, and bathing is safe only at high water. The late-17th-century Rampside Hall has a row of prominent diagonally set chimneys, known as the Twelve Apostles.

RAMSEY
Isle of Man
12 miles northeast of Douglas

Ramsey sits by one of the island's loveliest bays, a wide, gentle curve of pale green breakers sweeping in to meet a vast beach of shingle and sand that stretches from the hooked cliff of Gob ny Rona in the south almost to the Point of Ayre in the north.

The town is second only to Douglas in size and, like Douglas, is a resort – though rather more dignified. No casinos or amusement arcades: well, not many, and those that do exist are discreetly disposed. Instead, the backdrop of the promenade consists of towered, deep-bayed Victorian buildings in immaculate cream, white and pale grey. The turn-of-the-century look is enhanced by the half-mile-long Queen's Pier, and the decorous, 40 acre Mooragh Park with its large boating lake and nodding palm trees.

The Sulby, the island's biggest river, sweeps through the town, under a huge iron swing bridge, and out to sea between two massive breakwaters with tall lights at their points. There are quays near the swing bridge with little shops and restaurants, and the harbour is a constant bustle of fishing boats and yachts about the shipwright's yard, where trawlers are pulled ashore and overhauled on slipways.

Almost everyone who invaded the Isle of Man – and there were a fair number – came by way of Ramsey Bay, attracted, no doubt, by its sheltered anchorage. Vikings landed here to plunder, and then settle; Robert Bruce came, to annex the island to the Kingdom of Scotland, and Cromwell's Ironsides arrived, emphasising the benefits of the Commonwealth with cavalry, infantry and artillery.

In 1847, Queen Victoria and Prince Albert also landed, inadvertently, at Ramsey when the sea was too rough to permit docking at Douglas. This invasion was a welcome one, however, and the inhabitants erected an Albert Tower to commemorate the event.

The town is sheltered from the prevailing south-westerlies and has a mild climate – palm trees grow on the seafront – while two sandy beaches, one on either side of the river mouth, offer safe bathing. There is also good fishing from the pier, from the beach or from boats which ply from the harbour. Catches include cod, pollack, flatfish, conger, dogfish and mackerel.

Every June, thousands of visitors flock to Ramsey to see the Isle of Man T.T. (Tourist Trophy) motorcycle races. The course, which snakes over the hills west of the town, is used again each September for the Manx Grand Prix races.

RAVENGLASS
Cumbria
4 miles southeast of Seascale

Three rivers, the Esk, the Mite and the Irt, converge at Ravenglass, and this dominating position must have been one reason why the Romans built a fort there, at the spot they called Glannaventa. The fort's bath-house still stands, its 12ft high walls making it the best-preserved Roman building in the north of England and the reason why it is sometimes named Walls Castle.

The curving estuary, its inner stretches sheltered from onshore winds by sandspits, made an ideal anchorage for fishing boats, and for generations the village of Ravenglass made its living from the sea. In the 18th century the harbour was also much used as a base for smuggling tobacco, French brandy and other contraband from the Isle of Man.

Today Ravenglass makes a peaceful, unspoiled refuge, but bathing is dangerous. The meeting of the waters from the three rivers, the curving estuary channels and the sweep of the incoming and outgoing tides create currents and tide-rips fast enough to sweep unwary bathers out of their depth in seconds.

The coastline here is particularly rich in animal and plant life. The Ravenglass dunes and beach are both nature reserves, where you can sometimes see shel-ducks, skylarks, oystercatchers, ringed plovers and a few gulls. There is a third reserve, the Eskmeals dunes, on the other side of the estuary. All three are home to a wide selection of coast-loving flowers, including harebells, the small, creamy, many-spined burnet rose, and the pink-flowered restharrow. Here, too, are ponds where natterjack toads breed – easily identified by the prominent yellow line along their backs. Natterjacks are also slightly smaller than common toads and they tend to have a smoother skin.

SMUGGLERS' RIVER *This quiet stretch of the Esk was almost certainly used to move contraband inland from Ravenglass.*

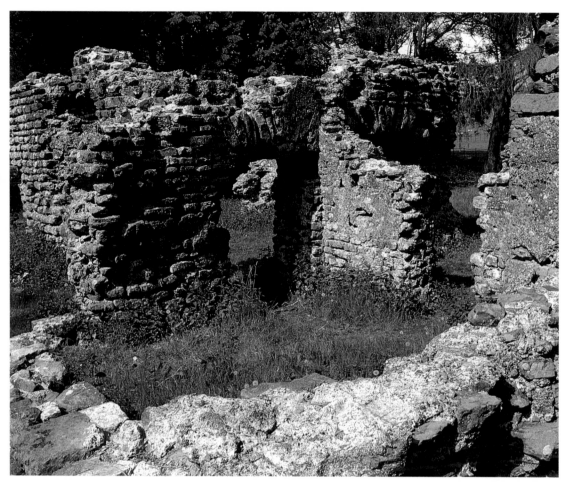

CLEAN BREAK *The bath-house of the Roman fort at Ravenglass is known as Walls Castle and stands over 12ft high.*

The layout of Ravenglass Main Street has changed little since the 16th century, but the harbour has long been silted up. Iron ore from the mines at Boot was occasionally shipped from Ravenglass until the opening of the Ravenglass and Eskdale Railway in 1875. Though the mines and quarries up the valley are no more, the line is now one of the most popular privately owned narrow-gauge lines in Britain. Each year it carries thousands of holidaymakers through some of the loveliest country in Lakeland. The road runs east to Muncaster, though the hamlet can be reached just as easily by footpath. The main reason for doing so is to visit Muncaster Castle, an imposing 19th-century building incorporating parts of a medieval castle.

RAVENSTONEDALE

Cumbria

4 miles southwest of Kirkby Stephen

The beautifully wooded village of Ravenstonedale lies near the source of the River Lune. The 18th-century Church of St Oswald has a three-tiered pulpit with a seat in it for the parson's wife. The village was the birthplace of Elizabeth Gaunt, the last woman to be executed in England for a political offence. She was burnt at Tyburn in 1685 for sheltering a follower of the rebel Duke of Monmouth.

Nearby, to the northeast, is the Iron Age settlement group of Crosby Garrett. Here three villages are set roughly in line, the overall distance between them being about 1000yds. The longest of the three is the southwest village; this consists of rectangular huts and a paddock. The middle village is similar but smaller, and the third compares closely with the second. All three villages are set in a complex of small square fields of characteristic 'Celtic' type, with boundary banks and pathways. The settlements probably continued into the Roman Age.

MAGICAL *In folklore, harebells are called 'witches' thimbles' and restharrow is said to have many medicinal properties.*

Restharrow

Harebell

RIBCHESTER

Lancashire
5 miles north of Blackburn

Beneath the streets of Ribchester is the site of Breme-
tennacum, one of the largest Roman forts in Britain. It
covered 5½ acres and was built around AD 80 to
garrison some 500 cavalrymen. It was near there that,
in the 18th century, a schoolboy found a magnificent
Roman ceremonial helmet. The helmet is now in the
British Museum, but there is a replica of it in the small
museum just outside St Wilfrid's churchyard, which
also contains Romano-British and Samian pottery,
coins, altar stones and lamps. Part of the fort's granaries can be seen in the museum gardens, and the
churchyard is situated directly over a corner of the
fort's treasury building. The churchyard sundial has
the inscription: 'I am a Shadow. So art Thou. I mark
Time. Dost Thou?'

The village lies in a curve of the River Ribble and is
encircled by the green hills of Longridge and Bowland
to the north and Darwen and Bolton to the south. It is
a pleasant jumble of multicoloured stone cottages in
long, twisting terraces, and has two pubs, the White
Bull, dated 1707, and the Black Bull. The White Bull has
a porch canopy supported by four columns said to be
from the Roman ruins.

Many stones from the fort went into the building of
the 13th-century church. Inside is a Jacobean pulpit
and a faded mural to St Christopher, the patron saint
of travellers. The saint was often invoked by those
about to cross the swift-flowing Ribble – a dangerous
undertaking in the past and which, in the 13th century, resulted in the drowning of Ribchester's first
recorded rector, who was named Drogo.

LIFE SAVER *Travellers risked drowning, trying to ford the Ribble at*
Ribchester, before the bridge was built in 1774.

RIVINGTON

Lancashire
3 miles southeast of Chorley

A long causeway spanning a vast, man-made lake
approaches Rivington from the west, and an early
glimpse of this captivating village is the stubby spire
and weathercock of its part-Elizabethan church
poking above the trees of a wooded knoll. The church
has Saxon origins, although it was rebuilt in 1591 and
altered in 1884. Half of old Rivington lies beneath the
2 mile long reservoir – formed in the 1850s to provide
water for Liverpool.

Opposite, and slightly downhill from the church, is
the village primary school, built in 1656 as a grammar
school, then rebuilt in 1714. At the centre of the village
is a triangular green, from which it is possible to peer
over the vicarage wall and see the remains of a set of
stocks. Overlooking the green is a graceful little
Unitarian chapel, built in 1703.

Rivington Hall, at the end of a long avenue of beech
trees, is a handsome Georgian mansion built in 1780
by Robert Andrews. A hall has stood on the site since
Saxon days. In 1900, the house was sold to the
Lancashire soap-maker and multi-millionaire industrialist William Lever, later Lord Leverhulme, who
restored and rebuilt the two vast barns that are among
the glories of Rivington. These barns – one next to the
hall, one at the other end of the beech avenue – also
date back to Saxon days. They needed to be large
because every winter they became Noah's arks, sheltering the farm animals and holding fodder to last until
the thaws of spring. Both barns are of cruck construc-
tion, with massive paired oaks supporting the roof and
walls. Lever, who turned most of the hall grounds over
to the public as Lever Park, built a replica of long-
vanished Liverpool Castle on a bluff towering over the
lower end of the lake. He also built a tower on the

1191ft summit of Rivington Pike. Another tower there, square-shaped and partly obscured by trees, was built by the Andrews family in 1733. The hall is now owned by the North West Water Authority, and permits for trout or coarse fishing can be bought there. The barns are used as tearooms for visitors.

The Rivington valley has been settled since the Bronze Age, and a winding but well trodden and gently sloping footpath leads to the summit of Rivington Pike, a beacon point since at least the time of the Armada.

HAMMER-BEAM ROOF *Rufford's 15th-century great hall has a ceiling richly carved with angels and a rare carved screen.*

ROA ISLAND
Cumbria
3 miles southeast of Barrow-in-Furness

Despite its name, Roa Island is very firmly part of the mainland, linked to it by a half-mile causeway which carries the road from Rampside. Another spit leads more than 1 mile to the southeast to Foulney Island, which is the home of the large nesting colonies of terns during the spring and summer. The shelter provided by the causeway has led to Roa Island's development as a yachting centre.

ROSTHWAITE
Cumbria
3 miles south of Derwent Water

The attractive grey-slate village of Rosthwaite is an ideal centre for the naturalist. Herons soar over the streams, and the path to Longthwaite leads across the Derwent to the National Trust's Johnny Wood, set on a knoll and rich in native oaks. The wood has a rich and varied plant life, including liverworts, mosses and ferns, and it is a Site of Special Scientific Interest.

There are splendid walks along the banks of the River Derwent, whose lovely green pools mirror birch trees. On the west side of the river is the 900ft Castle Crag, the summit of which – reached by a fairly easy 20-minute walk – provides a view of Derwent Water.

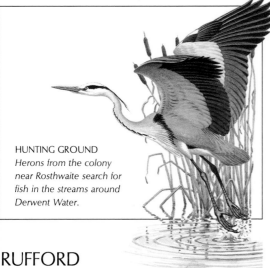

HUNTING GROUND *Herons from the colony near Rosthwaite search for fish in the streams around Derwent Water.*

RUFFORD
Lancashire
6 miles northeast of Ormskirk

In gardens ablaze in early summer with rhododendrons and the pinks, golds and yellows of other early flowering shrubs stands Rufford Old Hall, a medieval timber-framed manor house built in Rufford village by

the Hesketh family in the 15th century. From the large car park near the house, the first view of the black timbers and white infill of the oldest part of the hall almost overshadows the 17th-century wing built at right angles to it – but not quite, for this is a fine example of Jacobean brickwork with a hooded doorway, arched windows and gabled dormer windows. The two styles blend perfectly.

The folk museum in the house was begun in 1936 and contains ancient agricultural implements and items of local craftsmanship. Also on display are 17th-century furniture, the Hesketh Collection of 16th-century arms and armour, and Brussels and Mortlake tapestries. There is a doll and games museum as well.

The Church of St Mary is Victorian, built in Gothic style in 1869. It replaced an earlier church and contains several interesting monuments, including one of 1458 to the Heskeths, which includes 11 children and another by John Flaxman (1755–1826), the eminent neoclassical sculptor.

There are pleasant walks along the banks of the River Douglas. Wrightington Bar, 5 miles east, is an attractive village reached by narrow roads that were once the haunt of highwaymen.

RYDAL
Cumbria
2 miles southeast of Grasmere

In all weathers, a steady stream of anoraked and booted visitors marches up the hill above Rydal village to Rydal Mount, the stone farmhouse of pleasantly jumbled periods that was the poet Wordsworth's home from 1813 until his death in 1850. His wife Mary and sister Dorothy also spent the remainder of their lives there, and the presence of the three is everywhere in the house – in the furniture, the garden they created, in the portraits and mementos.

It is easy to see why Wordsworth chose Rydal, a stone and slate village with a humpbacked bridge, overlooked by the crag of Loughrigg Fell. An eye-catcher is Church Cottage, with its lattice windows, barrel-shaped chimney and garden of multicoloured heathers and fuchsias beside a little stream. St Mary's Church, dating from 1824, where Wordsworth worshipped, has windows glowing with pre-Raphaelite angels and cherubs. Just beyond the village calm, reedy Rydal Water reflects the surrounding hills. A path from the church gives views of the lake, sheltered by the slopes of Rydal Fell.

S

SABDEN

Lancashire
4 miles southeast of Clitheroe

The steep descent into the once flourishing textile village of Sabden is lined in season with sparkling gorse and aromatic heather buzzing with honey-bees.

The Church of St Nicholas, built in 1841, is surrounded by colourful masses of azaleas and rhododendrons framing splendid views over the valley to Padiham Heights.

From the Nick of Pendle that cuts through the upland moors there are breathtaking views over the silver ribbon of the sea lapping the Fylde coast to the west and the ever-changing colours of the Lakeland hills to the north. Hang-gliders soar over the valley, and there are artificial ski slopes – open all year round – at the Wellsprings Inn in the middle of Sabden.

ST BEES

Cumbria
4 miles south of Whitehaven

St Bees owes its name to the 7th-century St Bega. According to legend Bega was the daughter of an Irish king who, on the day she was supposed to be married to a Norse prince, fled from her father's court and was miraculously transported by an angel to the Cumbrian coast. On midsummer eve she asked the Lord of Egremont for some land on which to found a nunnery and was told that she might have as much as would be covered by snow on the following morning. Since he was a pagan and she an Irish saint, he should have known better; for sure enough on midsummer morning some 3 square miles lay under a blanket of white.

In a sheltered hollow between towering 300ft cliffs, St Bega founded a small nunnery that grew over succeeding centuries into the mighty priory of St Bees. However, after founding the nunnery, she was forced to flee again from her rejected suitor and seek refuge in the court of the king of Northumbria. There she helped to found the Abbey of Whitby, and ministered to the poor and oppressed.

Of St Bees Priory, only the church remains. It dates from the 12th century, when it was rebuilt by the Benedictines after the Danes had destroyed St Bega's nunnery in the 10th century. Although the church has been greatly altered since, there is still a magnificent Norman arch, and on a lintel between the church and vicarage is the carved Beowulf stone. This shows St Michael killing a dragon, and is thought to date from the Conquest.

Beside the church are the charming Abbey Cottage and St Bees School – built, like most of the village's old buildings, in red sandstone. The school stands around a courtyard above which rises an elegant clocktower of the 1840s. The north side of the courtyard dates from 1587, four years after the school was founded by Edmund Grindall, the son of a local farmer who became Archbishop of Canterbury.

East of the Barrow to Whitehaven railway, which divides the village, Main Street winds up a steep slope between old farms and cottages. There are magnificent views over a golden sweep of sands, thickly scattered with multicoloured pebbles worn to flat, oval discs like coins or sweets. Far out to sea is the silhouette of the Isle of Man, rising up to the peak of Snaefell. Seamill Lane leads down to a shingle beach, and Marsh House, at the end of the lane, looks straight out to sea. It once possibly belonged to smugglers.

North of the village, red-sandstone cliffs stretch out to St Bees Head, and beyond that is North Head, with a lighthouse on its crest. There is a noted nature reserve on the headland, whose cliffs are crowded with guillemots, razorbills, kittiwakes, gulls, gannets and skuas. Visitors should beware and keep to the footpath – the sheer cliffs drop straight to the sea.

ST JOHN'S

Isle of Man
3 miles southeast of Peel

The historical heart of the Isle of Man is the village of St John's. An open-air meeting of the Tynwald – the island's parliament, introduced by the Vikings 1000 years ago – is held in the village every year, on the first Monday in July. The term Tynwald derives from the Norse words *Thing*, meaning 'assembly', and *Vollr*, meaning 'meeting place'.

On Tynwald Day, the Lieutenant-Governor, members of the Tynwald and other civic officials walk in procession from St John's Chapel over a rush-strewn path to take up their appointed positions on the four-tiered Tynwald Hill. Then all the laws enacted in the previous year are read out in both Manx and English, newly elected coroners are presented with their wands of office, and an opportunity is given for anyone who wishes to present a petition of protest to do so. Several petitions have been presented in recent years. For the tourist, Tynwald Day is the most colourful day in the island's calendar, since on that day there is also a fair and folk festival with displays of Manx dancing and music.

St John's Chapel, at which a service of thanksgiving is held before the Tynwald ceremony, is worth a visit. Its primary function was originally that of a court house, and this can be seen clearly in the arrangement of the pews.

Although the village is small, its distinction in having the Tynwald field at its centre is because it sits at the junction of the main north–south road and the main east–west road. Its houses are colour-washed or rendered, with slate roofs, and its has three pubs. Perhaps the best known of these is the Ballacraine Hotel. It was through this hotel's door and into its bar that the comedian George Formby accidentally rode in a scene in his 1930s film, *No Limit*, about the Manx Tourist Trophy motorcycle race.

For most of the year, however, visitors are attracted to St John's chiefly by its crafts centre in the old woollen mills. There it is possible to watch potters and other craftsmen at work.

SAMLESBURY

Lancashire
4 miles east of Preston

Samlesbury sprawls over rolling farmland above the Ribble valley and may go almost unnoticed by travellers between Preston and Blackburn. But it is a district with an interesting history and is noted particularly for Samlesbury Hall.

The hall is a remarkable place, largely because it was built in two totally different styles. Its west side is red brick, with stone mullioned windows and tall chimneys; the other side is wood-framed, the blackened timbers set with panels cut with a quatrefoil (four-leaf) design to show the white plaster beneath. Inside the hall the timber roof is supported by huge oak pillars roughly carved from oaks chosen for their natural bent shape, and on a beam supporting the gallery is carved the name Thomas Southworth and the date 1532.

For 300 years Samlesbury Hall was owned by the Southworth family, but they sold it to pay a debt and it became in turn a tenement house for weavers and labourers, an inn called the Bradyll Arms, a school and then a house in which the author Charles Dickens (1812–70) is said to have stayed. The house was taken over by the Samlesbury Hall Trust in 1925 and was restored to its present glory. To the left of the hall is a chapel, and several rooms display antiques for sale.

WHITE AND BLACK 15th-century Salmesbury Hall is one of England's most intricate timber-framed buildings.

Standing in fields by the River Ribble is the Church of St Leonard, which dates from the 12th century with a stone-built, turreted tower of 1899. A helmet, crest and sword suspended high on a wall inside are believed to be those of Sir Thomas Southworth, who died in 1546 and whose grave is said to be below. A silver penny minted in the reign of Henry III (1216–72) is displayed in the two-decker pulpit.

A Roman Catholic church built in 1818 is dedicated to St Mary and St John Southworth, a relative of Sir Thomas. John was executed at Tyburn in 1654, the last English priest to be martyred. His body lies in Westminster Cathedral and he was canonised in 1970.

SATTERTHWAITE

Cumbria
4 miles south of Hawkshead

The hamlet of Satterthwaite is of Viking origin, and its name means 'the clearing of the saeter (summer farm)'. It is not much more than that today, for all about it lies the vast Grizedale Forest. But it is a pretty little place, built of the same local stone as the mossy dry-stone walls, so that it almost looks as though it has grown as naturally in its place as the trees.

RESILIENT *Herdwick sheep never stray far from their bleak fells where they live all year round.*

SEASCALE
Cumbria
11 miles south of Whitehaven

A partly Victorian seaside resort, Seascale appears to have been dropped, without any visible attempt at planning, onto the windy shores of the Irish Sea. The background, at a picturesque distance, is the lovely hillscape of the Lake District National Park. The beach is dark gold, boulder-strewn sand, and bathers may or may not be encouraged by the Sellafield nuclear processing plant peering over the rooftops to the north. Boating is popular, the breakers are ideal for surfing, and there is golf and riding on the dunes.

A rare breed of sheep known as Herdwicks is found only in the Lake District. Their origins are unknown, but legend claims that they first appeared in Britain in 1588 when several swam ashore from a Spanish Armada ship wrecked near Seascale. Another legend says that they were brought from Scandinavia by Vikings who landed on the Cumberland coast many centuries earlier. Herdwicks, if moved elsewhere, always wander back to the same 'heaf', or plot of land, on which they have been reared. Once there the sheep will not wander, so they do not have to be fenced in.

SEATHWAITE
Cumbria
5 miles south of Derwent Water

The tiny village of Seathwaite in Borrowdale – not to be confused with its near neighbour, close to Broughton in Furness – is reached at the end of a narrow winding road. Fringed by dramatic hills and a few straggling pines and birches, Seathwaite is renowned for having one of the highest average annual rainfalls in England, 157in, but this does not diminish its popularity with fell walkers. A footpath from the village leads in less than a mile to a packhorse bridge at Stockley, from which signposted but difficult paths lead to Sty Head Tarn, Great Gable and Scafell Pike. These walks should not be attempted by anyone on their own, and even experienced walkers should wear waterproof clothing and have a map and compass.

On the fellsides to the northwest are the spoil heaps left by mining in earlier days for plumbago, or graphite. In the 17th century it was used to make moulds for the manufacture of cannonballs and as 'lead' in the pencil industry based at Keswick.

SEATHWAITE
Cumbria
6 miles north of Broughton in Furness

While its namesake village in Borrowdale is known for its record annual rainfall, this Seathwaite is famed for a past vicar. The modern church occupies the site of an old chapel where Robert Walker was vicar for more than 60 years. William Wordsworth immortalised Walker by describing him as a hard-working preacher who raised a family of eight children on a stipend of less than £50 a year.

The minor road through Seathwaite follows the river, and there are many grassy places beside small waterfalls where you can stop to enjoy a picnic. Wallowbarrow Gorge, half a mile to the west, is spectacular in flood, while the Walna Scar track that strikes out eastwards half a mile north of the village gives a mountainous 5 mile walk to Coniston. Forestry Commission woodlands lie about a mile north of Seathwaite, blending with the 2140ft Harter Fell Peak to provide a glorious alpine setting.

SEATOLLER
Cumbria
3 miles south of Derwent Water

The Lake District National Park Information Centre makes Seatoller a good stopping place before the 1176ft Honister Pass – a narrow, twisting route.

The climb is spectacular, with streams and waterfalls down to the left and towering fells on the right. At the summit is a youth hostel in an old slate quarry, and behind it a car park. The descent towards Buttermere is even more dramatic, with tumbling slate scree on the left and hills rusted with bracken to the right.

PACKHORSE BRIDGE *Horses laden with ore from Coniston mines once crossed the Duddon at Seathwaite, near Broughton.*

DOLL'S HOUSE *In Sedbergh's busy main street a tiny cottage has been squeezed in between two more typical houses.*

SEDBERGH
Cumbria
9 miles east of Kendal

A small country town, Sedbergh stands beneath the protective, dome-shaped peaks of Howgill Fells, on raised ground above the meeting point of the Lune and Rawthey rivers. Elegant houses and gardens on the outskirts give way to a narrow main street of tall houses and busy shops and pubs. In the centre, the magnificent parish church of St Andrew, dating back to Norman times, is flanked by the playing fields and meadows which surround Sedbergh public school, founded in 1525.

Steep paths lead to the top of Winder, some 1100ft directly above the town, from which the views are spectacular. The sides of the fells are scarred with blue-black scree, and, in autumn, the tops are tawny with bracken. To the south are the Pennines, deeply cut by the valleys of Garsdale and Dent, and farther west the broad valley of the Lune sweeps away towards the distant hills of the Forest of Bowland.

SEFTON
Merseyside
3 miles northeast of Crosby

A tiny hamlet clustered round a 16th-century church with a lofty spire, Sefton retains a medieval tranquillity. The Church of St Helen has a ceiling which has been restored by 20th-century craftsmen; the new bosses and moulded beams match the quality of the 16th-century screens and the ornately carved pulpit of 1635. Medieval stained glass unearthed in the vestry is incorporated into the windows, and there is a beautifully preserved display of 16th-century brasses.

The box pews are among the finest in the county. They include those occupied by the dog whippers whose job was to exclude unwanted animals from the church and to control those brought by members of the congregation to protect them on their walk to and from church.

The church contains a so-called 'Treacle Bible', with some mis-translations which were corrected in the Authorised Version of 1611. For example, Jeremiah 8 v 22 reads: 'There is no more triacle (AV *balm*) in Gilead.' Another curious rendering occurs at Psalm 91 v 5: 'Thou shalt not need to be afraid for any bugges (AV *terror*) by night.' The translation was the work of Miles Coverdale, later Bishop of Exeter, in 1535.

SELLAFIELD
Cumbria
2 miles southwest of Calder Bridge

The site of the controversial nuclear fuel reprocessing plant, formerly known as Windscale, Sellafield also includes Calder Hall, which in 1956 became the first nuclear power station in Britain to generate electricity on a commercial scale. The four cooling towers of the Calder Hall reactors, which are still generating electricity, can be seen from the coast road. There is an exhibition centre and there are organised tours.

SHAP ABBEY
Cumbria
9 miles south of Penrith

The ruined tower of the abbey church appears suddenly through the trees as the narrow road dips down into the secluded valley of the River Lowther.

Shap Abbey's tranquil setting is a world apart from the lonely fells over which many a medieval traveller struggled in search of a night's shelter with the white canons. Founded in 1199, the abbey administered large estates until it was closed in 1534 during the Dissolution of the Monasteries. Its isolation did not prevent a 15th-century abbot, Richard Redman, from becoming successively Bishop of St Asaph, Exeter and Ely. A short walk across the fields south of the abbey leads to Keld, a hamlet whose modest little 16th-century chapel belongs to the National Trust.

In Shap village is the Church of St Michael, parts of which date from the 12th century. A stone in the churchyard is dedicated to the memory of the workmen 'who lost their lives by accidents' during work on the Shap section of the Lancaster and Carlisle Railway.

In the grounds of Shap Wells, a hotel built in 1850, $3\frac{1}{2}$ miles south of Shap, is a charming statue (1842) of Queen Victoria as a young girl. It was the work of a mason from Lowther, a village 6 miles north of Shap, where there is now an amusement park.

Superb walking country stretches on each side of the A6 around Shap, and motorists can park in valleys that strike off the road. South Cumbria's Borrowdale, for example, 7 miles south of Shap, is a fascinating

LONELY REMINDER *The west tower rises defiantly above the rest of the ruins of 13th-century Shap Abbey.*

peaty valley, and the surrounding Bretherdale, Round-thwaite and Whinfell commons are full of wildlife and rugged beauty. At High Borrow Bridge, just west, the Duke of Cumberland's forces routed those of Bonnie Prince Charlie in 1745.

SILLOTH
Cumbria
6 miles northwest of Abbeytown

There is an air of spaciousness in the little seaside resort of Silloth, with its wide, tree-lined streets, pleas-ant promenade, small harbour, pinewoods and a green covering 40 acres with well kept flowerbeds and rose gardens. Most of the town as it is today was built in the late 19th century after the coming of the railway from Carlisle in 1859; but there are still a few old cobbled streets from a much earlier period.

A railway guide published in 1854 dismissed Silloth as nothing more than 'a rabbit warren inhabited by rabbits'. But the village grew rapidly over the next few years and the dock, opened in 1859, was the depart-ure point for regular steamer services to Liverpool, Dublin and other ports in the 19th century. Today it is used mainly by coasters visiting the nearby flour mill.

Grain stored by the Cistercian monks from Holme Cultram Abbey gave the village its name – the grain was placed in stores called laths, and being by the sea 'Sea Lath', later corrupted to Silloth, was derived.

On clear days there are fine views from Silloth across the mouth of the Solway Firth to Scotland where Criffel, 1868ft high, is a major landmark to the northwest. The coast south between Silloth and Allon-by is one long bank of shingle, with muddy sand and a scattering of rocks below the high-water mark. The tide goes out more than a mile at low water, leaving vast areas of sand and rock pools, but care must be taken when the tide turns.

At Backfoot, about halfway down the coast, are the fragments of a Roman fort, part of the coastal de-fences intended to prevent the Picts to the north from making a landing behind the line of Hadrian's Wall.

SILVERDALE
Lancashire
16 miles west of Kirkby Lonsdale

'I think that one is never disappointed in coming back to Silverdale', novelist Elizabeth Gaskell wrote in 1858. She gave as her reasons 'the expanse of view . . . such wide plains of golden sands with purple hill shadows, or fainter wandering filmy cloud shadows, and the great dome of the sky'. Mrs Gaskell lived in Silverdale at the house called Lindeth Tower, and Charlotte Brontë stayed with friends in the village when she was a young girl.

Twisting, leafy lanes flanked by old limestone walls meander around Silverdale, and a labyrinth of foot-paths crisscrosses the surrounding woods and craggy broken ground which, from springtime, are carpeted in a profusion of wild flowers. This is a naturalist's paradise, especially for birdwatchers. Along the shore-line the salt marshes are internationally renowned for several species of ducks and waders, including the handsome black-and-white oystercatcher and the colourful shelduck.

Signposted walks lead from the railway station to

OYSTERCATCHER
This long-billed wader probes Silverdale marshes for food.

SHELDUCK
Britain's largest duck, it also feeds on the Silverdale marshes.

beauty spots such as Jack Scout, a headland over-looking Morecambe Bay and owned by the National Trust, and the Pepper Pot, a monument on Castle-barrow built for Queen Victoria's Diamond Jubilee. Visitors can also enjoy golf on a nine-hole course, or fish along the shore or in the many dykes.

The village's scattered buildings include none of great age, but St John's parish church, built in 1885–6, has some exuberant carvings and the Trinity Methodist Church, a little older, has among its features an imposing rose window.

Silverdale was a fishing port until the 1850s, and craft would tie up alongside the harbour just below the Silverdale Hotel. Here, too, cattle drovers would come ashore at low tide after crossing the northeast corner of Morecambe Bay from Kent's Bank, 3 miles west on the other side. They preferred to risk navi-gating the treacherous paths across the shifting sands rather than face the often more arduous and longer route that led through Kendal.

Silverdale's earlier inhabitants also included wild-fowlers, quarrymen and miners. A splendidly pre-served old copper-smelting furnace stands on an isolated spot named Jenny Brown's Point, after an old lady who lived on the shore. Known locally as 'the chimney on the shore', it is a survivor of a business established in the late 18th century to smelt ore mined at nearby Crag Foot. The surrounding springy, close-textured grass is much in demand for garden lawns and bowling greens. There were plans during the last century to enclose large areas of the salt marsh between Park Point, near Arnside, and Bolton-le-Sands to reclaim the land, in the manner of the polders which the Dutch have reclaimed from the Zuider Zee. A length of the old wall out on the mud flats is the only remaining evidence of the £84,000 spent before the scheme was abandoned.

ACROSS THE WATER *A stand of Scots pines frames Silloth's view of Scotland over the Solway Firth (overleaf).*

SINGLETON
Lancashire
2 miles east of Poulton-le-Fylde

The clue to the origins of Singleton lies in the splendid cream-painted Miller Arms at the entrance to the village, for it was the Miller family, wealthy Preston cotton-mill owners, who built the village in the 19th century. The Millers lived in Singleton Hall, out of sight from the village and not open to the public; the imposing wrought-iron gates of its south lodge stand beside the road just past the pretty little post office.

The single street running through the village is lined on one side by white-painted houses and cottages standing behind neat front gardens. On the corner of Church Road there is a little black-and-white building with red double doors, and on the beam above the doors are carved the words 'Fire Engine'. This was the village fire station, looking quaintly medieval but built in Victorian times, and now an electricity substation.

At the top of Church Road, almost hidden by trees, is St Anne's Church, built in 1860 by Thomas Miller. It occupies the site of an earlier church, whose lych gate stands by the road opposite the church.

SIZERGH CASTLE
Cumbria
3¼ miles south of Kendal

Round the massive creeper-clad walls of a 14th-century peel tower at Sizergh, built to keep out Scottish raiders, clusters a group of buildings added over the following four centuries. Together they form three sides of a rectangular courtyard. The peel tower is easily recognisable by its turret rising above the castellated parapet.

Sizergh has been the home of the Strickland family since 1239, and its name stems from even earlier settlement in the area; it comes from the Scandinavian *Sigarith*, a personal name, and *erg*, 'a dairy farm', and dates from Viking occupation in the 9th and 10th centuries.

Several rooms have Elizabethan oak panelling from floor to ceiling, and the dining room has a richly carved overmantel bearing the date 1564. The top floor of the peel tower is now a museum, where 14th-century fireplaces and windows survive unaltered. A number of portraits of the Stuart royal family are on display, and there are also Stuart and Jacobean relics.

WAR AND PEACE *Once a bulwark against the Scottish warriors, Sizergh Castle is now flanked only by beautiful gardens.*

The Sizergh estate covers about 1500 acres and includes a rock garden of hardy ferns and dwarf conifers. A footpath leads through the grounds to Brigsteer Woods, where daffodils carpet the glades in spring. The estate is administered by the National Trust, and both the castle and the grounds are open to the public daily in summer.

SKINBURNESS

Cumbria
2 miles northeast of Silloth

It is very difficult to imagine that the tiny village of Skinburness, dominated today by a large hotel, was the spot chosen by Edward I as a base from which to attack his turbulent enemies in Scotland. In 1303, however, a flood swept away most of the settlement and the villagers moved to Newton (or 'Newtown') Arlosh, founded on a safer site farther inland.

Today the sea to the east and south has retreated, leaving a wild tract of salt marsh on which sheep and cattle graze. Nearby Grune Point gives a wide view of the estuary and of the waders and wildfowl which live along its borders.

SLAIDBURN

Lancashire
7 miles north of Clitheroe

Cobbled pavements flank Slaidburn's narrow main street, which climbs from a stone bridge over the River Hodder. Slaidburn lies in a fold in the moors, where the Croasdale Brook joins the River Hodder below the Forest of Bowland. Rolling green pastures and, beyond, bracken and heather, almost encircle the village.

Many of its houses and cottages are built of grey stone, and two of the main buildings bear inscriptions which proclaim their age. An elegant two-storey building in Church Street, which was once the grammar school, has a carved plaque over the door saying that it was 'erected and endowed by John Brennand, late of Panehill in this Parish, Gentleman, who died on the 15th day of May in the year of Our LORD 1717'. It is now the local primary school. At the lower end of the village is a large stone barn bearing the words: 'Erected AD 1852 for the use of the industrious poor of the Township of Slaidburn, for ever.'

At the centre of the village, where Church Street and Chapel Street meet, stands an inn called the Hark to Bounty. The sign shows a clergyman listening to a dog baying at the full moon. Local legend says that Bounty was the name of a foxhound belonging to a 19th-century squarson named Wigglesworth, who was both squire and rector of the parish. Whenever he took a drink at the inn, Wigglesworth would leave the hound outside and, when it barked, would say to his companions, 'Hark to Bounty'.

Gisburn Forest, northeast of the village, is an extensive mixed coniferous plantation sloping down to the eastern shore of Stocks Reservoir, which takes its name from the village drowned during the early 1930s to create it. Sometimes, in dry summers, the level of the water falls enough to reveal cobbles in the ruins.

When the valley was flooded, some of the stones of the village church were removed, at the villagers' insistence, and incorporated in a new church built alongside the road through the forest. The reservoir is the winter haunt of large flocks of wildfowl, including whooper swans, goosanders and Canada geese.

WINTER VISITORS *Canada geese flock to Stocks Reservoir near Slaidburn where they spend the winter months.*

SMITHILLS HALL

Greater Manchester
2 miles northwest of central Bolton

Surrounded by a wooded nature trail, Smithills Hall stands on an easily defended hill above Ravenden Clough. The earliest building was the work of the Knights of St John, a military religious order founded during the Crusades in the 11th century, but the present structure dates from the 14th century. There have been alterations since, but the original medieval great hall is magnificent, its four-leaf, moulded decoration still in fine condition.

The hall is now a museum, containing fine Stuart furniture. The old stables and coach house have been converted into a restaurant reached through an archway and overlooking a courtyard colourful with restored and brightly painted stagecoaches. There are also a nature trail and a museum in the grounds.

SOUTHPORT

Merseyside
16 miles north of Liverpool

From the point where the mud flats and saltings of the Ribble estuary give way to the open Lancashire coast, a long stretch of flat, firm sand stretches as far as industrial Merseyside. On this wide beach is the resort of Southport, which despite a wide variety of modern holiday attractions still preserves much of the style and atmosphere of a Victorian or Edwardian watering-place. Its popularity goes back to the late 18th century, when William Sutton, an innkeeper in the village of Churchtown, used driftwood from the beach to build the first bathing house, in which people could change into the right clothes for a sedate paddle.

The main street of the town, the elegant tree-lined boulevard of Lord Street, was built during the 1820s, and tablets honouring William Sutton can still be seen in the wall bordering the gardens at the junction of Lord Street and Duke Street. For almost their entire length the shop fronts on the west side of Lord Street are shaded by glass-and-iron canopies, and at intervals glass-roofed arcades entice the shopper into cool passageways where polished antique furniture and glittering jewellery gleams. If an unusual number of shops seem to cater for the golfer, this is because Southport is the home of Royal Birkdale, a championship course to the south of the town, as well as four other 18-hole courses.

The promenade was added in 1835, and expansion has continued ever since. Now more than 300,000 visitors every year are attracted to Southport's sandy beach and its acres of sand dunes. Other attractions of Southport include a zoo, a model village, a Marine Lake covering 86 acres and a pier three-quarters of a mile long, served by its own miniature railway. There is also a vintage transport museum.

SPEKE HALL

Merseyside
¾ mile southeast of Liverpool airport

The Norris family built the magnificent half-timbered mansion of Speke Hall 8 miles away from what was then the tiny fishing village of Liverpool. In 1490, when the house was begun, this involved a long and tiring journey over rough roads for those working on the site.

The house was finished in 1612: its wings surround a central courtyard, and the entrance drive crosses the old moat by a small stone bridge. It has a Tudor Great Hall decorated with panels said to have been removed from the Palace of Holyroodhouse, beautiful plasterwork and tapestries, a fine carved chimneypiece, and two ancient yew trees in the courtyard.

STAINTON

Cumbria
7 miles south of Kendal

A narrow lane running between high hedgerows follows the grassy banks of Stainton Beck away from the busy main road to the tiny rural community of Stainton. There are only a few farmsteads and cottages – many of them adorned by colourful shrubs – and the atmosphere is tranquil. An old stone footbridge crosses the beck and a bench stands in the shade of a nearby sycamore.

Just beyond the village lies a disused leg of the Lancaster Canal. It resembles an overgrown lily pond, but once it was a busy waterway along which horses would draw a 'swift packet boat' to Preston, about 35 miles away, in less than seven hours.

STANDISH

Greater Manchester
3 miles northwest of Wigan

Shops large and small line the streets of Standish, a workaday village which gives the impression of a small market town. Beyond the crossroads, where two main roads meet, the shops on one side give way to a wide square and the impressive stonework of St Wilfrid's Church.

The church dates mostly from the 16th century, except for its octagonal steeple which is not the best example of Victorian creative restoration. Nevertheless, the church as a whole is extremely attractive, with a two-storey porch, buttressed tower and two domed turrets where the nave and chancel meet.

In the square stands the village cross, and below its steps the village stocks, whose well-worn holes suggest that many a miscreant must have spent unhappy hours of punishment there.

STANLEY GHYLL AND DEVOKE WATER

Cumbria
6 miles northeast and 5 miles east of Ravenglass

It is not its height but its spectacular setting in a narrow, thickly wooded gorge that has made Stanley Force, the 60ft waterfall in Stanley Ghyll, such an attraction. When Ice Age glaciers carved out the Lakeland valleys, they cut off many tributaries and left them hanging in the air – places today where lovely waterfalls tumble to the valley bottoms. Stanley Ghyll was created in this way when the glacier deepening the River Esk valley cut across its course.

A nature trail leads up to the falls by way of Stanley Beck, passing the old farmhouse of Dalegarth Hall, the home of the Stanleys from whom the ghyll takes its name. Attractive woodland that includes oaks, sycamores, rowans and hazels borders the beck, with bilberries, wood sage and mats of white-flowered heath bedstraw along the banks.

Pick your way through the boulders brought down by previous floods until the path meets the beck again. Mosses and liverworts, including the light green bog moss, thrive in the damp atmosphere. Rhododendrons bloom among the rocks in June, naturalised from earlier plantings when part of the ghyll was kept as a woodland garden.

All the way to the third wooden bridge across the beck the path remains steep and rocky, and beyond the bridge it becomes very wet and dangerous. But there is no need to go further. You are now standing at the bottom of the waterfall, with fine views from the bridge of the thin wall of water tumbling down its gorge of 400 million-year-old Eskdale granite.

High on Birker Fell above Stanley Ghyll lies the wild and lonely Devoke Water (it is pronounced 'Dev-ock'), surrounded by heather moors. Part of the Muncaster Castle estate, it is noted for its trout and its birds – red-throated and black-throated divers have been seen here. The many cairns around its shores (which are boggy in places) are remains of the Bronze Age settlements of more than 3000 years ago. The view northeastwards as you walk back to the road is staggeringly beautiful, with the peaks between nearby Harter Fell and Great Gable forming a backcloth.

DESOLATE OASIS *Rough Crag looks down on Devoke Water set high on Birker Fell and surrounded by wild moorland.*

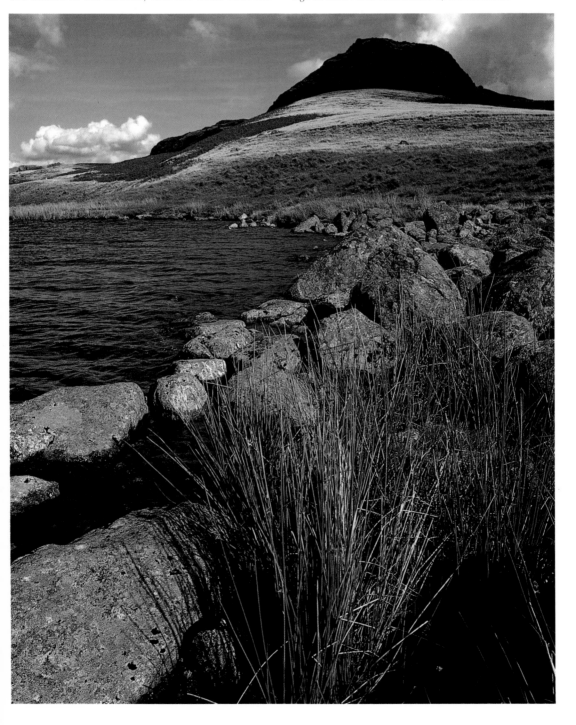

STONETHWAITE
Cumbria
7½ miles southeast of Keswick

Any walk around Stonethwaite is almost bound to be wet, for this was once the eastern limb of a great lake that covered the flat-lands of Borrowdale. The lake was connected by a river to Derwent Water in the north. Over thousands of years the streams rushing down from the ring of high fells around the lake swept more and more debris into it, and eventually filled it. Even today, after a spell of heavy rain, the flat-lands become a lake again and large boulders are carried there by the tumultuous, flooding becks.

Stonethwaite Beck is formed by two streams, Langstrath Beck and Greenup Gill, which meet below the fierce bluff of Eagle Crag. The crag can be reached by turning east out of Stonethwaite village, crossing the bridge, turning right and following the track through the woods. At the meeting of the two becks lies Smithymire Island, where the monks of Furness Abbey, 25 miles to the south, used to smelt iron ore. Beyond, rough, wet beck-side paths lead through wild, lonely country overhung by beetling crags.

By way of old packhorse trails, the Greenup Gill route leads eventually to Grasmere (6 miles away), and from Langstrath, a climb through Ore Gap and down Mosedale and the Duddon valley leads eventually to the distant Furness Peninsula.

STOTT PARK BOBBIN MILL
Cumbria
3 miles north of Newby Bridge

One of the country's more unusual museums, the Stott Park Bobbin Mill is the sole survivor of many similar factories in the area whose chief customers were the Lancashire cotton mills. From its opening in 1835, Stott Park turned out some 28,000 reels and bobbins a day until it closed in 1971.

Few alterations have been made, and the mill is still in working order. Former workers show visitors the venerable lathes, driven by flapping leather belts.

SUNDERLAND POINT
Lancashire
About 3 miles south of Heysham

This piece of land, almost entirely surrounded by water, where the River Lune enters the Irish Sea, is reached across the saltings from the quaint village of Overton. The Point was a port in the 18th century, when ships crossed to the West Indies, and the first cargo of cotton to reach England was landed here.

SWARTHMOOR
Cumbria
1 mile southwest of Ulverston

At first sight Swarthmoor seems simply a collection of semidetached houses straddling a main road. Those who pause here will, however, be amply rewarded. The cottages of old Swarthmoor sparkle white in the sun, and half a mile along a hedge-bordered lane stands historic Swarthmoor Hall, seen at its best from the well-kept garden.

Built around 1586 by George Fell, a wealthy lawyer and landowner, the hall housed some Roundhead soldiers during the Civil War. The main event in its long history came, however, in 1652 when Margaret, the wife of George's son, the influential Judge Thomas Fell, heard the Quaker George Fox preach. He was getting some rough treatment and so Margaret persuaded her husband to give him protection.

The hall became the first settled centre of the Quaker sect, where missionary journeys were properly organised and appropriate action taken. But in the mid-18th century it passed out of the Fell family and ceased to have anything to do with the Quakers for about 150 years. Then, in 1912, a descendant of the Fells together with the Society of Friends bought back the old house and restored it. Judge Fell died in 1658, and 11 years later Margaret married George Fox, who established a local meeting house, still used today.

MEETING PLACE *In 1642 George Fox took refuge in Swarthmoor Hall and held the first Quaker gatherings here.*

T

TALKIN TARN COUNTRY PARK

Cumbria
2 miles southeast of Brampton

A wooded hillock rises gently behind a Victorian boathouse and provides delightful views across Talkin Tarn to the Pennine fells. The 65 acre lake, more than 40ft deep in places, has been the headquarters of Cumbria's only rowing club for more than a century. It is also used by two sailing clubs, and visitors may hire rowing boats.

A delightful and undemanding nature trail starts from the boathouse. The trail leads through woodland, where deer can sometimes be seen.

Beside the lake is a sandy bay which is a popular spot for picnicking and swimming. Talkin Tarn is also an excellent fishing lake, containing pike, perch and eel. From the Tarn End Hotel there is a magnificent view down the whole length of the tarn.

The name Talkin is derived from the Celtic *tal can*, meaning 'white brow'. The word 'tarn' for a small lake is corrupted from the Norse word for 'a teardrop'.

TARNBROOK WYRE

Lancashire
7½ miles southeast of Lancaster

A narrow road winds for 1½ miles up the lightly wooded, shallow valley of the Tarnbrook Wyre, one of the two main tributaries which meet at Abbeystead to form the River Wyre. It is an attractive road beneath a canopy of mixed broad-leaved trees, and never strays more than a few yards from water. The road ends at the hamlet of Tarnbrook which consists of scattered sheep farms, sweet-scented wood smoke curling from their chimneys, and a mountain rescue centre which is kept busy when heavy snows fall on Bowland.

From Tarnbrook, a footpath leads up into the hills, to the highest points in the Forest of Bowland. This is moorland walking at its wildest and most lonely, with sweeping views to distant horizons. The path leads first across the open moor and then into the narrowing valley and towards the small waterfall at its head. The walk is not difficult, but steepens sharply as it climbs the side of the valley, known as the Black Side of Tarnbook Fell — while the other side of the valley is known as the White Side. The names derive from their winter aspects — one is dark, heather moorland; the other is lighter grass moorland. To the south is the broad, dark breast of Hawthornthwaite Fell at 1568ft, with Hareden Fell to its east; between them, farther south, rises the 1656ft summit of Fair Snape Fell. In autumn the hills glow with unexpected colour — the purple of flowering heather, and the gold of dying grass and bracken.

The path, one of the official access routes across private moorland, leads on to the heights of Mallowdale Fell and then, just at the watershed, it makes a T-junction with another concessionary path which runs along at 1500ft from Grit Fell in the west to Wolfhole Crag in the east. Only practised long-distance walkers

VORACIOUS
Pike eat anything — even water birds.

will carry on from here, making the long trudge westwards over the 1840ft summit of the moor, and reaching the road again 6 miles west of Tarnbrook. For most people it will suffice to reach the watershed, almost 3 miles from Tarnbrook, and then enjoy the downhill return, having tasted the true wilderness of Bowland and breathed its refreshing air.

TEMPLE SOWERBY

Cumbria
6 miles northwest of Appleby-in-Westmorland

A quiet village near an excellent stretch of fishing along the Eden, Temple Sowerby's mixture of 17th and 18th-century buildings huddles around a large sloping green. The village is named after the Knights Templar who ruled the community until their suppression in 1312. It was then taken over by the religious military order the Knights Hospitaller, who governed the lands until the Dissolution of the Monasteries in the 1530s.

Since the Middle Ages the village has had a reputation for herbal healing, and the tradition is continued today as the National Trust Gardens at Acorn Bank — an early 18th-century manor house — have a fine collection of medicinal and culinary herbs. The red-sandstone house is now a home for the elderly and is not open to the public. However, its walled gardens, reached by a path through a thick oak wood, are open daily in the summer.

THIRLMERE

Cumbria
4 miles southeast of Keswick

The road along the western shore of 3½ mile long Thirlmere lake is a conifer tunnel with feathery branches of softest green reaching over to touch the high bracken. Through the black columns of the trees there are only occasional glimpses of the deep, clear lake; yet this is still the best side to see it from, looking over to the vast, smooth hummock of Helvellyn.

The best views are obtained from Hause Point, where railed steps lead to the top of a rock overlooking the lake, and at Armboth, where a car park has been cut through the trees almost to the water's edge. There are other parking places along the western shore, while at the northern end a forest trail leads up to Castle Rock of Triermain, a crag near Thirlspot.

THORNTHWAITE

Cumbria
3 miles northwest of Keswick

A car park at Woodend Brow, north of the village of Thornthwaite, affords wide views of Bassenthwaite Lake, dominated by the brooding hulk of Skiddaw. From Thornthwaite village a pleasant stroll from the Swan Hotel follows a marked footpath to the lake shore. The tiny parish church can be glimpsed across green fields through an attractive belt of trees.

THRELKELD

Cumbria
4 miles east of Keswick

The narrow track which winds its tortuous way between Threlkeld's old stone cottages was once part of the main road from Penrith to Keswick. The pretty little village has now been bypassed, but in days gone by it must often have rung to the sounds of pack-horses, cattle and sheep drives, and regular stage-coaches. The white-walled Horse and Farrier Inn, dating back to 1688, would have done great business servicing the needs of travellers.

Links with the past are maintained in the form of sheepdog trials held during the summer, when the hills resound to the whistles of their handlers, the bleating of driven sheep and the applause of spectators.

The village was once famous for its tough Cumberland and Westmorland wrestlers. It is famous to this day for its team of fox hunters, the Blencathra Fell Pack. These men hunt not upon the backs of well-bred horses, but on foot – and in the old days they used to wear dull grey instead of scarlet. To them, far from being a mere pastime or sport, the fox hunt was, and still is, an essential job to protect their sheep, and demands great stamina from man and dog.

In St Mary's churchyard there are some fascinating tombstones and a monument to 45 fox hunters – among them the remarkable John Crozier, master of the hunt for 64 years until his death at the age of 80. Each man is listed and remembered by the verse:

> *The Forest music is to hear the hounds*
> *Rend the thin air, and with lusty cry*
> *Awake the drowsy echoes and confound*
> *Their perfect language is a mingled cry*

St Mary's dates from 1777, and replaced a 13th-century church; but a leather-bound Bible and a set of medieval bells survive from the older building, as do many of the parish records going back to the time of Elizabeth I. An unusual wedding vow is still sometimes quoted in the village. Apparently, there was a time when local couples married in Threlkeld used to agree that, if either of them ever broke their promises to each other, they would pay the considerable sum of five shillings (25p) for the benefit of the poor.

A belt of trees screens the church from an extensive granite quarry that until 1982 ate into the hillside. There were also lead mines in the district until about 1910, but Threlkeld bore industry with gentle dignity and remains unspoilt. Walks lead up to 2847ft high Blencathra – now usually called Saddleback – and Scales Tarn, set in isolated grandeur. Sir Walter Scott in his narrative poem *The Bridal of Triermain* and Sir Hugh Walpole in his tale *A Prayer for my Son* both used this magical setting.

A thousand feet up on these breezy slopes stands the Blencathra Centre, from which holidays in the Lake District are run. Originally the building was a hospital, which opened in 1904 as a tuberculosis sanatorium – the second to be founded in England – and closed in 1975.

INSPIRED AUTHOR *High above Threlkeld, Scales Tarn shimmers on Saddleback, like a diamond among the dark cliffs. The beauty of the setting so moved Sir Walter Scott he used it in his poem* The Bridal of Triermain.

THURNHAM

Lancashire
5 miles south of Lancaster

A sweeping drive through green pastures leads to Thurnham Hall, built around a 13th-century peel tower – the original building built to withstand raids from the sea and across the border. It is backed by wooded gardens and an avenue of yews. The Dalton family formerly occupied the mansion for more than 400 years and added a magnificent Elizabethan Great Hall, a fine Jacobean staircase and some beautiful panelling and plaster work. There is also a Gothic-style chapel, built in the mid-1850s. Thurnham Hall has been carefully restored and is now a private residence, not open to the public.

Just beyond the hall a narrow road on the left winds for about 3 miles through flat fields to the remains of Cockersand Abbey. The abbey was founded near the coast in the 12th century and is closed to visitors. Only a few wall fragments have survived, including part of the chapter house. This was built 40 years after the abbey and for a while the Dalton family used it as their burial chapel.

The road ends at the Wyre-Lune Bird Sanctuary, which is open throughout the year. It is noted for its sea birds, waders and wildfowl which roost on the sea covering the surrounding mud flats.

THURSTASTON

Merseyside
3 miles southeast of West Kirby

Thurstaston itself is little more than a tiny group of buildings just off the road from West Kirby to Heswall, centred on a church, a hall and several farms. But Thurstaston Hill, on the opposite side of the road, is a wilderness of sandstone rocks and sandy trails, ideal for children to wander in and for picnics. It is often used for orienteering events, and from its highest point offers fine views of the mountains of North Wales just across the estuary. On top of the hill is Thor's Stone, a 25ft high rounded pinnacle of red sandstone.

The road which leads through the village continues almost to the edge of the estuary, and its last stretch passes the site of the old railway station, now the centre for the Wirral Country Park. This is based on the route of the old branch railway line from Hooton, on the Chester to Rock Ferry line, to West Kirby. One station – Hadlow Road, on the edge of Willaston – has been restored to how it was in the 1960s.

TOCKHOLES

Lancashire
4 miles southwest of Blackburn

Turn off the main road to Tockholes at the Victoria Inn and go down School Lane. This descends steeply to the aptly named Ivy Cottages, draped also by sweet-smelling rambling roses. Next to the cottages is the United Reformed Chapel, founded in 1662 and a centre of nonconformity in the intolerant days of the 17th and 18th centuries.

A narrow lane beyond the chapel leads to the parish church, which has unusual lance-shaped windows. The church was rebuilt in 1832, and its outdoor pulpit is a relic of the days when large congregations could not be accommodated inside.

WOODLAND STREAM *A bower of trees shades the stream which runs beside the Roddlesworth Nature Trail near Tockholes.*

ON THE WING *Swallows swoop to drink while flying.*

TROUGH OF BOWLAND

Lancashire
3 miles northwest of Dunsop Bridge

If you want one place that sums up the whole of what the Forest of Bowland has to offer, take the winding road through the Trough of Bowland. Mountain, stream and fell combine in one delightful whole. The Trough of Bowland is the wild pass you travel on the switchback road through fells and valleys from Quernmore, near Lancaster, to Dunsop Bridge some 12 miles to the southeast. The name could apply to the whole length of the road, but it is generally given to the stretch between Winfold Fell and Blaze Moss.

From end to end the road is spectacular and full of interest, as much for the motorist as for the walker. In the northwest it climbs steeply out of the Conder Valley, then rushes headlong down the Grizedale Valley. It passes the Jubilee Tower, which commemorates the Golden Jubilee of Queen Victoria; the views from the top of the tower are among the most magnificent in the area. The prospect sweeps from the cloud-capped blue heights of the Lake District in the far northwest, then down the slate-grey line of Morecambe Bay to the ramparts of Blackpool in the south, overtopped by the 500ft spire of Blackpool Tower.

Behind you is the height of Ward's Stone, more than 1800ft above sea level and set off by the crags of Grit Fell. Climb to the top of Ward's Stone, and there you can sink on a cushion of heather and gaze up into the bowl of the sky, trying to pick out the soaring skylarks whose songs fill the air.

After Jubilee Tower the road crosses the upper arms of the River Wyre – a bubbling, infant stream here – and runs in splendour along the Marshaw Wyre, where it flows through stretches of close-cropped grass, shaded by an occasional oak, ash or pine.

Some of the best walks are in the last few miles down to Dunsop Bridge. A path runs up the wide valley of Rams Clough, to the north of the road about 3 miles from Dunsop, leading to Whin Fell and down the Brennand river to the River Dunsop, and so down to Dunsop Bridge – a solid 5 miles in all. The Dunsop is a delightful stream, dropped down rills and miniature waterfalls. Swallows and swifts dart and swoop low over it for evening flies, trout rise for newly hatched midges, and mallards bustle protectively around their chicks on the willow-hung pools.

Another lovely 5 mile walk starts on the south side of the road at the bottom of Hareden Brook, by Hareden Farm, and soon leaves the valley to strike up the side of Mellor Knoll, passing just below its 1100ft summit. From there it is an easy descent to the Hodder valley at Burholme Bridge, and the last 2 miles of gentle riverside walking leads to Dunsop Bridge.

TROUTBECK

Cumbria

3 miles north of Windermere

Like many Lake District villages, Troutbeck is spread along a hillside. For well over 1 mile, from Town End to Town Head, farms and cottages are scattered along a narrow lane bordered by dry-stone walls.

Townend — a farm with whitewashed walls and stone-mullioned windows — was built in 1623 and still has much of the original oak furniture. It remained in the Browne family for nearly 300 years, but is now owned by the National Trust. The lovely old house has the slate roofs and massive, tapering chimneys that are a feature of Lake District architecture.

Across the lane is one of several ranges of farm buildings that contribute much to Troutbeck's timeless character. Towards the far end of the village, farms and cottages cluster tightly round the Mortal Man, a 17th-century inn, and the delightful Clock Cottage.

Troutbeck's church and former school are down in the valley. The largely 18th-century church has an east window created in 1873 by William Morris, Edward Burne-Jones and Ford Madox Brown.

Troutbeck Bridge lies 2 miles south. In the 17th century, Calgarth Hall in the hamlet was the home of Myles Phillipson, a local JP. In order to gain possession of a rich farm near by, he invited the owner and his wife to a Christmas banquet at the Hall, and then accused them of stealing a silver cup which he had hidden in their baggage. Phillipson presided at their trial, sentenced the couple to death, and appropriated their farm. As she was led away, the wife cursed him, saying that his victims would never leave him and that his entire family would perish in poverty and distress.

After the execution, two skulls appeared at Calgarth.

In his attempts to get rid of them, Phillipson had them buried, burnt, smashed to pieces and thrown into Lake Windermere, but the skulls always returned to the Hall. True to the prophecy, the Phillipsons grew poorer and poorer and, in 1705, the family line died out. The Bishop of Llandaff, who later lived at Calgarth, finally performed a service of exorcism over the skulls and they were never seen again.

TURTON BOTTOMS

Lancashire
4 miles north of Bolton

The small village of Turton Bottoms lies in spectacular walking country. Humphrey Chetham, founder of a library and a school for poor boys in Manchester, lived in Turton in the 17th century. The old inn in the High Street is decorated with Chetham's family arms.

A drive bordered by beech and horse chestnut leads to a fine Tudor house, Turton Tower, built around an early 15th-century peel tower fortified against the Scots. It was used as a farmhouse during the 18th century and bought and restored by industrialist James Kay in the 1830s. When the Bolton to Blackburn railway was built in the 1840s Kay insisted that the bridges close by the tower should be castellated in keeping with its style.

The tower is now a museum, with fine collections of armour, Tudor and Victorian furniture and a remarkable German chandelier made from the antlers of fallow deer. It is open from Saturday to Wednesday, on summer afternoons.

WHITEWASHED VILLAGE *Troutbeck grew up alongside a line of wells which until recently were its only water supply.*

U

ULLOCK PIKE

Cumbria
4 miles northwest of Keswick

The shapely summit of Ullock Pike, 2230ft high, offers panoramic views across northern Lakeland. Yet, in spite of the mountain's proximity to Keswick, it remains one of the least visited of the Skiddaw and Saddleback mountain group. The final part of the ascent is the most exciting, along the heather-clad ridge, looking steeply down over the wilderness of Southerndale to the northeast, and over the 4 mile long Bassenthwaite Lake to the west – the most northern of all the lakes and the only one to be called a lake, and not a water or mere.

There are two routes up Ullock Pike from the road, both starting from a creosoted gate and stile 30yds south of the Ravenstone Hotel. The first path climbs to the right through the Forestry Commission plantation – first larch, oak, sycamore and Scots pine, then Sitka spruce and other softwoods – to the tree line at 600–700ft. Then follows a steep scramble through bracken and heather and bare outcrops of rock to the ridge about 1000ft above. The second path meets the ridge about a mile farther north, after climbing behind the hotel and following a wall northeastwards above the tree line, then following an old drove road.

The safest way back is to return along the ridge, for the sides are very steep and rocky. But it is possible to drop into Southerndale farther down, picking up the path on the east of the valley and following it to the footbridge below the natural standing stones known as The Watches. A path leads from the gate below the footbridge to the minor road leading from Orthwaite to High Side, a hamlet about half a mile north.

ULLSWATER

Cumbria
Southwest to northeast, from Patterdale to Pooley Bridge

A good view of Ullswater – Lakeland's longest stretch of water after Windermere – and of the mountains that surround it, is obtained from the narrow road which runs along the lake's eastern shore from Pooley Bridge. The road zigzags up to the remote hamlet of Martindale before reaching Sandwick on the lakeside.

A short detour south from Martindale enters a deep valley where slopes rise steeply above the 16th-century Chapel of St Martin. Walls of uncut stone shelter the 17th-century pulpit and pews. Outside is the grave of Richard Birkett, parish priest from 1633 until his death in 1699. St Martin's was the parish church until St Peter's, on the road between Martindale and Howtown, was consecrated in 1882.

Serious walkers can explore the lake shore between Sandwick and Patterdale, or make Martindale the base for long hikes over the mountains. Visitors seeking gentler exercise should follow the path round Hallin Fell from Sandwick to Howtown, a fine high vantage point for views across Ullswater's shimmering expanse.

SAFE GRAZING *Sheep graze on the pastures gently leading down to Ullswater beneath the rugged slopes of Swarth Fell.*

ULPHA

Cumbria
4 miles north of Broughton in Furness

The name 'Ulpha' derives from a Scandinavian word meaning 'wolf hill'. There is not much of the village – mainly a few cottages and some almshouses – but its setting among the wild fells is glorious, if lonely.

The Church of St John is handsomely set on high ground. It has wall paintings and an altar made from apple or pear wood.

ULVERSTON

Cumbria
9 miles northeast of Barrow-in-Furness

A Saxon landowner named Ulph gave the town of Ulverston its name. After the Norman Conquest it became the property of the monks of Furness Abbey, and a favourite target for raiders from Scotland under Robert Bruce, who burned the town twice, in

1316 and 1322. Ulverston suffered again in the Civil War, being fought over by both sides. By the 18th century, however, it had become a prosperous port and an important stopping place for the mail coach from Lancaster and the south, which in those days saved hours of pounding over rough roads by taking a short cut across the sands of Morecambe Bay.

The oldest building in Ulverston is the parish church of St Mary, dating partly from 1111. It was restored and rebuilt in the 1860s, and the chancel was added in 1903–4. The church is notable for its splendid Norman door and magnificent 19th and early 20th-century stained glass, including one window based on a design by the painter Sir Joshua Reynolds (1723–92).

The present tower was built during the reign of Elizabeth I (1558–1603). It has an inscription running: 'Pray for the sowle of William Dobson, Gen. Ussher to Queen Elizabeth who gave unto this work.' The original steeple was destroyed in a storm in 1540.

On Hoad Hill, northeast of the town, a replica of the Eddystone Lighthouse commemorates Sir John Barrow, geographer, explorer and Secretary to the Admiralty, who was born in Ulverston in 1764.

The cobbled streets of the old town, centred on its busy market square, became such a centre for trade that it was known as 'the London of Furness'; but the same sands which assisted one kind of communication were to inhibit another, when shifting sandbanks silted up the harbour. To avoid this bottleneck the 2 mile long Ulverston Canal was built in 1795, to link the town with the sea at Canal Foot. The canal gave Ulverston another century as a busy port and shipbuilding centre, but after the coming of the railway it fell into disuse and is now a haven for birds.

In 1890 Stan Laurel, the short, skinny half of Laurel and Hardy, was born here. His real name was Arthur Stanley Jefferson, and he spent his first 15 years in a small terraced house at No. 3 Argyle Street. It now has a plaque beside the front door commemorating him, and the local pub has been renamed The Stan Laurel.

In nearby Upper Brook Street is the Laurel and Hardy Museum, open most days in summer and by appointment in the winter. The museum displays photographs and relics of Laurel and of his Hollywood partner Oliver Hardy. It also has a writing case, with the original pens, that belonged to Stan's father, who was a travelling theatre manager. Part of the museum is a small film theatre, with wooden seats rescued from a 1920s cinema. Laurel and Hardy films are shown all day in the theatre while the museum is open.

WADDINGTON AND WADDINGTON FELL

Lancashire
2 miles and 4 miles northwest of Clitheroe

When the guns open up at the start of the grouse-shooting season on the 'Glorious Twelfth' of August, the footpaths on the moors round Waddington Fell are closed to the public. Red grouse are practically an industry hereabouts, but in spring and early summer it is the views that are the fell's main attractions.

A road climbs to the summit of the fell from the village of Waddington, which lies to the south. It was at Waddington that the unfortunate Henry VI was captured after he had spent a year in hiding, mostly in the fastnesses of the Forest of Bowland. His host at Waddington was Sir John Tempest, and, according to a strong local tradition, it was Sir John's son-in-law Thomas Talbot of Bashall who betrayed him. Sir John's house was surrounded by soldiers as the king was at dinner. He managed to escape into the woods, but was captured as he crossed the River Ribble by the steppingstones at Brungerley.

Just after the moorland road from Waddington has surmounted the fell and dropped over the other side, it passes a spring bubbling into a stone trough on the left – Walloper Well. Climb the hill above the well, and at once there is a lovely view of the Bowland fells across the River Hodder. Or park a little downhill and take the path that runs northwards down to the hamlet of Easington. From anywhere along the path, near the plateau edge, there are fine views across the water meadows of the Hodder to Beatrix and Burn fells, and to Dunsop Fell beyond the valley.

'QURRACK-RACK-RACK'
The red grouse's alarm call often rings out over Waddington Fell.

WALLOWBARROW GORGE

Cumbria
4–6 miles northeast of Broughton in Furness

In the most spectacular stretch of Wallowbarrow Gorge, between the villages of Ulpha and Seathwaite, the River Duddon flows straight through a fell instead of round it, walled in to the west by the 950ft high Wallowbarrow Crag, and to the east by the more than

700ft high Holling House Tongue. In the last Ice Age, glaciers following the line of a fault scoured out the deep cleft of the gorge. Both sides are very steep – in some places vertical – and thickly wooded with oak, ash, beech, birch and rowan. Alder trees and willows overhang the racing water, until the river breaks out of the gorge and begins to meander across the wide flood plain where it is joined by the Tarn Beck.

Shortly before the Newfield Inn, in Seathwaite, a signpost marked 'To the Stepping Stones' points the way to the gorge, which leads through a mixed wood with a variety of woodland flowers and fungi. In time of flood the steppingstones are usually under water and become impassable, but just a little farther upstream there is a single-arch bridge. The path carries on through another wood to the fields of the flood plain, with the southern end of the Wallowbarrow Crags towering above them. From here it is possible to walk up the gorge, although the going is rough.

Another path striking off to the west of Wallowbarrow Crags leads, after about a mile, to Grassguards Farm and through the conifer forest beside it. Then it drops down to more steppingstones below Fickle Crag, before climbing back southeastwards through bracken and a scattering of small oaks to the road – about three-quarters of a mile north of Seathwaite. An alternative path leads from Grassguards Farm through the woods to a beauty spot, Birks Bridge, which lies on the same road about 2 miles north of Seathwaite.

WALNA SCAR ROAD

Cumbria
Begins at Coniston, 6 miles southwest of Ambleside

Walking across Coniston Fells by the Walna Scar Road is like travelling back through time, for this is one of the oldest roads in the Lake District. It has been walked or ridden throughout history by shepherds and weavers, pedlars and traders, wool-buyers, merchants and, of course, lovers of landscape.

But for a thousand years or more the chief traffic was provided by packhorses, heavily laden with copper ore from the Coniston mines. They are the oldest mines in the Lake District, dating from Roman times. The route from them crossed the Duddon at Seathwaite and led on over Birker Fell to Eskdale and then down to the Roman port of Ravenglass. In the early 19th century, when the mines were at their peak, several hundred men and boys were employed. The boys were trained to wash and sort the ore, using water diverted from mountain streams and tarns. Some of the old waterways can be found above the mine workings on the Coniston Fells. The adult miners were known as 'old men' – perhaps because they were prematurely aged by the appalling working conditions deep inside the mountain. Mine entrances, often no more than about 5ft high and 18in wide, can be found in the area. It is unsafe to enter them so visitors should

RUSHING RIVER *The waters of the Duddon hurtle through Wallowbarrow Gorge on their way into the Irish Sea.*

take care not to venture too close, in case they slip.

Walna Scar Road starts at the foot of the Coniston Fells. It can be reached by driving at least part of the way up the steep, rough road signposted from just south of the centre of Coniston. Beyond the second gate there is no choice but to walk. Walna Scar Road leads straight ahead; the track to the right along Church Beck climbs to the 2502ft summit of Wetherlam, a mountain 2 miles north of Coniston. The old road winds steadily upwards beneath the crags of Little Arrow Moor, passing various tiny stretches of water, including Boo Tarn. A path northwards leads to Goat's Water, in a magnificent example of an Ice Age corrie, with Dow Crag soaring 2555ft on its western shore. Once the col between Walna Scar and Brown Pike has been reached, the view ahead is breathtaking. Away in the far southwest is the huge bulk of Black Combe; across the foreground lies the lovely expanse of the Duddon valley. To the northwest is Harter Fell, behind which and farther to the north is the mighty jumble of mountains leading to Scafell Pike, at 3206ft the highest peak in England.

The return to Coniston can be made by walking back along the road, or by following the ridge walk north to the summit of Dow Crag, and then swinging round to the top of The Old Man of Coniston. From there the path down is steep but passable, though the area around is riddled with old mine workings and shafts, and is dangerous.

WARCOP

Cumbria
3 miles west of Brough

A village green is overlooked by a colourful maypole and surrounded by a tangle of cottages and sandstone houses. Warcop lies between the main road and the River Eden, which is spanned by a fine 16th-century bridge with three graceful arches.

The partly Elizabethan and partly Georgian Warcop Hall stands to the northwest of the village, opposite the 12th-century Church of St Columba. The hall is not open to the public. The path to the church is lined with yew trees, whose upper branches are linked, thus creating a leafy umbrella, which provides shade from the sun and shelter from the rain and snow.

WARTON

Lancashire
1 mile north of Carnforth

The long main street of Warton contours the lower slopes of a hillside crowned by the exposed limestone terraces of Warton Crag. Cottages and more substantial houses, all built from local stone, lead towards a parish church with important transatlantic links. George Washington (1732–99), first President of the United States, was a descendant of the local landowner who built the church tower in the 15th century. An old family crest, which includes stars and stripes, and a Stars and Stripes banner inside the church commemorate this bond.

In the vicarage gardens across the street are some carefully preserved remains of a 14th-century lay rectory. But there was a settlement here as long ago as the Bronze Age, when people made their homes among the rocky knolls high above the village.

WAST WATER AND WASDALE HEAD

Cumbria
3 miles northeast of Stanton Bridge

The most remote-feeling of all the English lakes, Wast Water is also the deepest, plunging to 258ft. Its slaty black waters reflect the mountains rising almost sheer from the surface, which is often broken by great slides of scree sweeping down from bare, rocky slopes. Sometimes the lake is smooth as glass; at other times cold spray can be felt hundreds of feet up the surrounding slopes.

The two ends of the lake are totally different. In the southwest, Nether Wasdale is sheltered and thickly wooded, with an abundance of flowers on the forest floor, and moss and lichen everywhere. Wasdale Head, in the northeast, is the very core of the highest part of England, rough and wild above the dry-stone walls of rounded boulders which surround some sheep pastures. Wasdale Head is said to possess the smallest parish church in England. It certainly is tiny, and is roofed with massive slate tiles over beams that may have come from Viking wrecks.

British rock climbing began at Wasdale Head in the 1880s, and the hamlet has an inn famed among climbers. A footpath runs from the car park up to Sty Head Pass and Great Gable. Wasdale is also a centre for climbing Scafell Pike (3206ft), England's highest peak. It is a safe mountain to climb, provided the recognised routes are followed. Perhaps the easiest of these, marked by piles of stones, starts a mile south, above Wast Water, and crosses Lingmell Gill. The summit can be reached in about three hours.

There are many places from which to view the lake, and one of the best is from the southwest end, in the area of Wasdale Hall. On the left the crags of Buckbarrow give way to the immense jumble of rocks – Long Crag – which forms the lower slopes of Middle Fell. The valley of Nether Beck slices through the heights, and beyond it are the crag-stepped ridge of Yewbarrow, the Mosedale Valley and Kirk Fell.

At the other end of Wast Water, the road to Ravenglass is idyllic, if a little narrow. It offers the lake and the savage mountains, sweet pastures governed by mossy stone walls, sudden vistas across country.

TROUT LAKE *Hills encircle the dark waters of Watendlath's tarn where many fish live including large numbers of trout.*

WATENDLATH
Cumbria
5 miles south of Keswick

When the novelist Sir Hugh Walpole visited and wrote about his beloved Watendlath it was a remote hamlet high above Borrowdale. It remains remote and unspoilt, its whitewashed cottages with their black painted woodwork clustered around a trout-filled tarn from which a chuckling stream spills out and under a stone bridge. Day permits are available to anglers, who can enjoy their sport with the reflection of Watendlath Fells shimmering on the tarn's waters.

Watendlath is reached by turning left off the Keswick to Borrowdale road, along a twisting track lined with high stone walls. By far the best way to approach the hamlet is along one of several footpaths from the spacious tree-fringed car park just over the tiny humpbacked Ashness Bridge.

Well-signposted, these flower-scented paths lead through leafy dells shaded by birch and Scots pine, home to red squirrels and song birds. Just before the village, a gate leads to the Churn, also called the Devil's Punchbowl. Here the continual splashing and whirling of the stream has eroded a bowl-shaped

hollow, and a drink from its crystal waters brings one much nearer to heaven than the Devil's abode.

For the motorist there is a National Trust car park at Watendlath itself, and a cluster of cottages and a couple of farms nestle around it. Foldhead Farm is generally agreed to be the setting for Rogue Herries' farm in Sir Hugh Walpole's tale of *Judith Paris*.

Clearly marked paths follow steep stony tracks to Blea Tarn and Wythburn, the climb often being en-livened by the chattering notes of meadow pipits and the bubbling sound of curlews. Not long ago, hares could be seen scampering over the grassy slopes, but they have now vanished – to the puzzlement of local people. So have starlings and sparrows.

On the opposite side of Watendlath Bridge, tracks lead down to Rosthwaite village and the Lodore falls. From the highest point on the Rosthwaite route there are towering views over Borrowdale towards Lakeland's highest peaks, the magnificent Scafell Pike, Great End and Great Gable.

WETHERAL
Cumbria
4 miles east of Carlisle

A steep road leads from Wetheral's triangular green and ends at the edge of the River Eden. Near the site of an old ferry crossing now stands the high, five-arched viaduct carrying the Carlisle to Newcastle railway across the river.

A well-signed riverside walk to National Trust wood-lands provides colourful flashes of kingfishers, and herons fish in the deeper pools. Along the riverbank are three man-made caves in which a saint called Constantine is said to have lived in the 6th century. He was probably the Cornish saint of royal birth who visited the area when it was a part of Scotland.

Nearby is the dignified Gothic Church of Holy Trinity, restored in the 1880s. A chapel to the Howard family of Corby Castle, on the opposite side of the river, stands at the north side of the chancel and behind a wrought-iron screen. The chapel was built in 1791 to house a monument showing the figure of Faith, by the sculptor Joseph Nollekens. It stands above the Howards' mausoleum, which was in use until the mid-19th century and sealed in the 1960s.

BLUE FLASH *Kingfishers can be seen diving for fish in Wetheral's pools.*

RUINED ABBEY *The abbot's residence survives intact, but Whalley Abbey itself is just a pattern among the lawns.*

WHALLEY
Lancashire
4 miles south of Clitheroe

At the foot of a wooded hillside on the northern banks of the River Calder, a jumble of architectural styles – from traditional stone cottages to mock-Tudor fronted shops – blends happily together in Whalley.

For many centuries Whalley has been a focus of Christian worship, but it is the 13th-century Cistercian abbey that draws most visitors to the village. Nowadays the ruined but majestic walls and gateways stand carefully preserved amid lovingly tended lawns and gardens. Happily not all is in ruins, and what was once the abbot's lodging is now a conference centre and retreat run by the diocese of Blackburn.

Another building known locally as the Catholic Hall was originally a dormitory for lay brothers. Now it is used for social occasions, including bingo, and the local Catholic priest delights in the thought that he may have the oldest bingo hall in Britain.

The monks who built the abbey started their work in 1296, but it was not until 1380 that a great consecration mass was held, and the whole complex was not completed until the 15th century. By this time, the influence of the abbot was considerable and the abbey lands were extensive.

Disaster came after the Pilgrimage of Grace, the northern uprising in 1537 against the seizure of Church lands by Henry VIII. The monks of Whalley did not take part, but an excuse was found to implicate the abbot nonetheless and he was hanged at Lancaster Castle. Later the abbey was confiscated and eventually almost demolished. Fortunately some of the abbey's treasures were saved, among them the richly carved choir stalls now in the nearby parish church of St Mary and All Saints.

WHINLATTER PASS

Cumbria
2 miles west of Braithwaite

From Braithwaite, the road rises sharply to 1043ft at Whinlatter Pass, but the road is wide and there are several lay-bys. Noble Knott picnic site, on the left, is the starting point for many marked footpaths that often ring with bird song. At the summit of the pass a sharp right turn leads to a large car park and a well-appointed Forestry Commission visitor centre, the starting point of miles of lovely woodland walks.

The descent into Lorton Vale is dramatic. On the right, close to an old quarry, is a lay-by from which a marked footpath leads after half a mile to Spout Force, which is spectacular after rain. In the summer dippers bob on the shores of the Aiken Beck, larks sing above the fells and buzzards circle overhead, scanning the ground below for small mammals.

WHITEHAVEN

Cumbria
8 miles south of Workington

The satirist Jonathan Swift (1667–1745) is said to have conceived the kingdom of Lilliput in *Gulliver's Travels* after looking down on seemingly tiny figures moving about on the beach below Whitehaven cliffs. He often watched the poor locals, who scoured the sand for sea coal to put on their fires, and he imagined them as a race of very small people, such as the Lilliputians in his book, published in 1726.

Swift – born in Dublin – spent some of the first four years of his life in Bowling Green House, perched high on the clifftop, and he returned there several times as a man. His old home later became an inn – the Red Flag – and today it is a private house.

Farther along the cliffs is a ruined fan house, built in 1747 to drive fresh air into a now disused coalmine, Duke Pit. The medieval-looking building is kept as a memorial to 136 miners, boys among them, who were killed in an underground disaster in the nearby Wellington Pit in 1910. The entrance lodge to Wellington Pit, which closed in 1933, is now a café.

Towering behind it is the tall, stone Candlestick Chimney, an air vent to the mine. The man who suggested its unusual shape was Lord Lonsdale, whose family owned the pit and built Whitehaven Castle (now an age concern centre) in 1769. Apparently, his lordship was dining when the architect of Duke Pit asked him what type of 'chimney' he should put up,

Green coast and green hills of Cumbria

Along the Cumbrian coast the journey ends for the rivers which flow down from the Lakeland fells. On their banks men have been building for centuries, from the Romans who established a naval base at Ravenglass to the 20th-century builders of the nuclear power station at Sellafield.

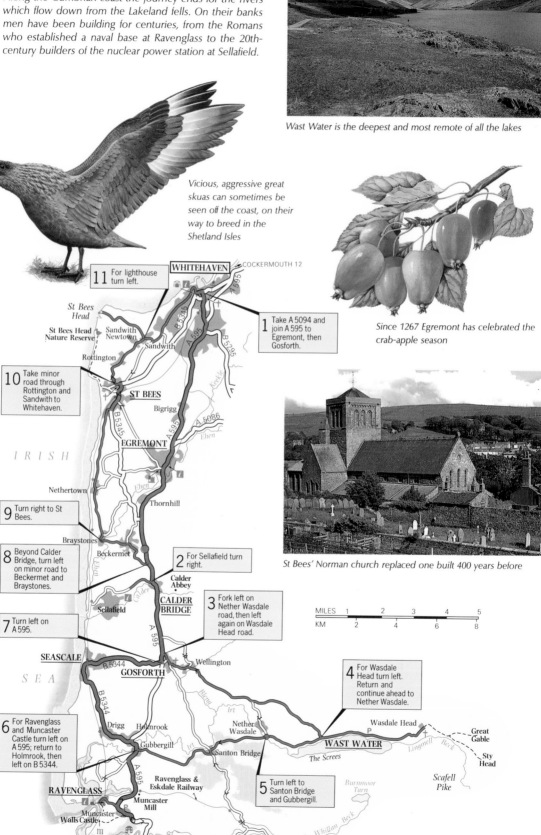

Wast Water is the deepest and most remote of all the lakes

Vicious, aggressive great skuas can sometimes be seen off the coast, on their way to breed in the Shetland Isles

Since 1267 Egremont has celebrated the crab-apple season

St Bees' Norman church replaced one built 400 years before

COCKERMOUTH 12

WHITEHAVEN

11 For lighthouse turn left.

1 Take A 5094 and join A 595 to Egremont, then Gosforth.

St Bees Head

St Bees Head Nature Reserve

Sandwith Newtown

Sandwith

Rottington

10 Take minor road through Rottington and Sandwith to Whitehaven.

ST BEES

Bigrigg

I R I S H

EGREMONT

A 5086

Ehen

Nethertown

Thornhill

9 Turn right to St Bees.

Braystones

8 Beyond Calder Bridge, turn left on minor road to Beckermet and Braystones.

Beckermet

2 For Sellafield turn right.

Calder Abbey

CALDER BRIDGE

3 Fork left on Nether Wasdale road, then left again on Wasdale Head road.

7 Turn left on A 595.

Sellafield

Calder

MILES 1   2   3   4   5
KM   2   4   6   8

SEASCALE

B 5344

Wellington

GOSFORTH

A 595

4 For Wasdale Head turn left. Return and continue ahead to Nether Wasdale.

Wasdale Head

6 For Ravenglass and Muncaster Castle turn left on A 595; return to Holmrook, then left on B 5344.

B 5344

Drigg   Holmrook

Gubbergill

Nether Wasdale

WAST WATER

Great Gable

Sty Head

Santon Bridge

The Screes

Lingmell Beck

S E A

Irt

Blind

RAVENGLASS

Ravenglass & Eskdale Railway

5 Turn left to Santon Bridge and Gubbergill.

Burnmoor Tarn

Scafell Pike

Muncaster Mill

Walls Castle

Muncaster

A 595

Whillan Beck

Esk

whereupon Lord Lonsdale pointed to the candlestick in front of him and said, 'Like this'. Though the coal and iron trades which founded the town's prosperity have vanished, the harbour still handles cargo – mostly phosphate rock from North Africa for the chemical works on the hill above the sea.

A steep flight of stone steps leads down from the cliffs to Whitehaven harbour, which originally exported coal from the town and imported tobacco from the Americas. Warehouses and miners' cottages stood on either side of the steps and some of the buildings remain. The harbour has twice been attacked by enemy vessels. The Scottish-born hero of the American Navy, John Paul Jones, had served his apprenticeship as a seaman in Whitehaven. In 1778, during the American War of Independence, he sailed the privateer *Ranger* into the harbour, landed and set fire to several ships.

The second attack was in 1915, when a German U-boat surfaced close to shore and shelled the area causing some damage, but no deaths. Today the harbour contains Britain's last coal-fired dredger, which works alongside the fishing smacks, cargo ships and pleasure boats which also shelter there.

Whitehaven developed in the 12th century as the port of nearby St Bees Priory. But most of the town was built by the Lowther family in the 17th and 18th centuries, along lines devised by Sir Christopher Wren. At that time it was second only to London as a port, and there are many elegant Georgian houses which survive – including some in Lowther Street, the main and most impressive thoroughfare. The town was laid out to a regular gridiron pattern – the first deliberately planned town in England since the Middle Ages.

Known as 'The Gateway to the Western Lakes', the town used to have two parish churches, St James's and St Nicholas's. The Church of St James was built in 1752–3 and has a fine Georgian interior. St Nicholas's Church was built in 1883 on the site of an earlier church. It was mostly destroyed by fire in 1971 and there is now a garden surrounding the ruins.

WHITEWELL

Lancashire
6 miles northwest of Clitheroe

A village of grey cottages, Whitewell nestles in the lovely, wooded Hodder Valley. There are riverside walks, but the road also closely follows the river. It leads south into a thickly wooded ravine, and north through a more open valley to Dunsop Bridge, 2 miles away. Eastwards from Whitewell, the road climbs swiftly into limestone country to give views over the whole sweep of the valley. Then, in $2\frac{1}{2}$ miles, it leads to the fine 17th-century mansion of Browsholme (pronounced Brewsome) Hall, for centuries the home of the Parker family.

WINDERMERE

Cumbria
7 miles northwest of Kendal

The Lake District's busiest tourist centre was a tiny farming hamlet until the railway arrived in 1847. Now holidaymakers, walkers and climbers fill many of Windermere's guesthouses in summer, and hotels have spread over the surrounding countryside.

The focal point in the mountainous scenery is the lake itself, more than 10 miles long and England's largest. Pleasure steamers, yachts and rowing boats ply its surface, and fishermen probe in its depths for pike, perch and the salmon-like char. The lake has been the scene of several water-speed record attempts. In 1930 Sir Henry Seagrave was killed there while attacking the world record.

Orrest Head, 784ft, easily reached by a footpath which starts opposite the railway station, gives fine views of the lake and Belle Isle, a landscaped island estate with a round 18th-century mansion. Based on the Villa Vicenza in Rome, the house has a domed roof and an elegant columned portico.

Another easy climb is to the top of Biskey How, a 300ft hill just east of the Windermere suburb of Bowness, which has quaint, narrow streets, a 15th-century church with some good stained glass, and beautiful views across the lake. Bowness is the headquarters of the Royal Windermere Yacht Club. About half a mile north along the lakeside road is the Steamboat Museum, open from Easter to October. Its roofed harbour houses a dozen or so old lake boats.

The A592 which goes along the east side of the lake cuts well inland in many places, but there are still some excellent viewpoints. Among the best of these is the 1054ft peak of Gummer's How, 6 miles south of Windermere, which can be reached by taking the side road at Fell Foot. There is a climb of about half a mile to reach the top.

There are also splendid views from the terraces of Brockhole, the Lake District National Park Visitor Centre, which stands in 30 acres of lakeside grounds 2 miles northwest of Windermere, and is open daily from late March until early November.

WINSTER

Cumbria
3 miles south of Windermere

Almost hidden among the folds of the wooded hillsides that border an upper reach of the River Winster lies the hamlet of Winster, a cluster of whitewashed cottages of rough-hewn stone, mostly 18th century or earlier. A 17th-century cottage, with a magnificently studded front door and a multicoloured rockery, houses the village post office. Its tinkling shop bell evokes memories of the days when shopping was a time for gossip as well as for buying provisions.

Throughout the area are rocky knolls and moss-banked waterfalls and tarns. Crook, a hamlet 3 miles east, is equally attractive.

WITHERSLACK

Cumbria
3 miles north of Lindale

The 17th-century church and school at Witherslack were gifts from John Barwick, a local man who was made Dean of St Paul's in 1661. The $3\frac{1}{2}$ mile long limestone Whitbarrow Scar that strikes northwards is a spectacular crag with slopes covered in holly, hawthorn, wild strawberries and rock-roses.

On the rocky common spreading out at the top, footpaths and stone stiles lead into a wooded world of crab-apple trees, rose hips, juniper, bracken, gorse and bramble – a delightful blaze of colour in autumn.

WORKINGTON

Cumbria
17 miles west of Keswick

A wooded park, set back from the sea and high above the River Derwent, surrounds the impressive and extensive ruins of Workington Hall. In 1568 the Hall was a temporary refuge for Mary, Queen of Scots when she arrived in an open boat with 30 fellow refugees from the Battle of Langside, at the start of a long road which ended at the executioner's block 19 years later. An elegant house on the corner of Park End Road houses the Helena Thompson Museum where clothes, furniture, photographs and sketches recall the town's Victorian heyday.

Traces of the Roman fort of Gabrosentum overlooking the harbour recall Workington's importance in earlier times, while Georgian houses line the cobbled Portland Square. St Michael's Church, rebuilt in 1887, has fragments of 8th-century crosses, and a large Norman arch.

The Derwent flows to the sea through a harbour where more than 200 ships were built between 1839 and 1938. Pubs with names such as the Ancient Mariner and the Sailor's Return underline the town's seafaring heritage. Coal has been mined locally for centuries, seams are still worked far out under the sea, and coal and steel are still exported from here.

WORSTHORNE AND HURSTWOOD

Lancashire
3 miles east of Burnley

The small green of the old village of Worsthorne is overlooked by the Victorian Church of St John and a number of inns. Wander around the 17th-century shops and cottages, then drive the half mile to Hurstwood, or better still stroll to it from Worsthorne's village green along a clearly marked path through the meadows. Near this village in the valley of the River Brun, according to legend, the Anglo-Saxons defeated the Danes in the 10th-century Battle of Brunenburk.

Overlooking the narrow village street is a hall built in 1579 and still a private residence, as is the ivy-clad Spensers House to its right. There, for a while, the poet Edmund Spenser lived before going to London to make his fortune writing *The Shepheardes Calender* and then to Ireland, where he wrote the *Faerie Queene*. Both poems contain more than a trace of north-country dialect. Just beyond the poet's house is a stable yard overlooked by an early 16th-century cottage. The stables, still used today, were once owned by Richard Tattersall, founder in 1766 of the London horse sales, now held at Newmarket.

WRYNOSE PASS

Cumbria
Between Skelwith Bridge and Seathwaite

From the summit of Hardknott Pass, the road tips violently down to the long, lovely valley of the Duddon, then shoots up again to the 1281ft summit of Wrynose Pass, the western gate to Langdale and Ambleside. It is also the eastern gate to Eskdale and Ravenglass, and therefore one of the reasons for the Roman fort on Hardknott.

GREEN VALLEY *Patched by sunlight the soaring flanks of Wrynose Pass dwarf the meandering River Duddon.*

It is not too stiff a climb — for those who have just accomplished Hardknott Pass, at any rate — and it reaches up to Three Shire Stone, the boundary marker of the three old counties of Cumberland, Lancashire and Westmorland, which lies just below the summit. Through a gap in the wild hills the serene, civilised acres of Little Langdale can be seen. The descent to the valley is equal to Hardknott standards — a narrow ledge angling to a steep dive down the mountainside.

WYTHENSHAWE HALL

Greater Manchester
5¼ miles south of Manchester

Wythenshawe Hall is a half-timbered manor house built in the early 16th century with Georgian brickwork extensions. Since 1926 it has been owned by the City of Manchester and is open to the public from

spring to autumn, except on Tuesdays. It contains 17th-century furniture, arms and armour and oil paintings, and 20th-century ceramics, including a fine collection of Royal Lancastrian pottery.

WYTHOP MILL AND WYTHOP WOODS
Cumbria
4 miles east and 5 miles east of Cockermouth

Wythop is an enchanting village, its blue-and-white houses huddled round an old bridge beneath which the Wythop beck chatters over a pebbled bed. From the bridge in a dip to the left is an old mill, while a right turn leads to Wythop Hall, which is open from Tuesday to Sunday in summer and at weekends in winter.

East of the village are Wythop Woods, where visitors are welcome provided that they keep to the footpaths. Occasionally, there are views through the silver birches across Bassenthwaite Lake.

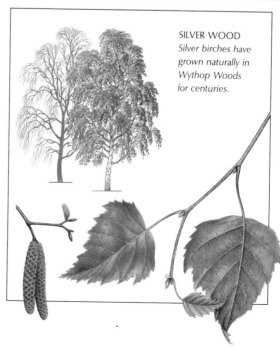

SILVER WOOD
Silver birches have grown naturally in Wythop Woods for centuries.

INDEX

Page numbers in **bold** type refer to main entries in the book. Page numbers in *italic* refer to illustrations.

ACKNOWLEDGMENTS

Photographs in this book were supplied by the following photographers and agencies. Work commissioned by Reader's Digest is shown in italics.

6–7 Jon Wyand; **8–12** (top) Neil Holmes; **12** (centre) Trevor Wood; **13** Jon Wyand; **14, 15** Neil Holmes; **16–17** Jon Wyand; **18–19** Lucinda Lambton; **20** Neil Holmes; **22** By permission of the Trustees, National Portrait Gallery, London; **22–23, 25** Neil Holmes; **27** John Sims; **28–29** Brian Shuel; **30–31** John Sims; **32** Jon Wyand; **32–33** Neil Holmes; **35** Jon Wyand; **36** Colin Molyneux; **37** (top) Philip Llewellin; **38** (bottom) Neil Holmes; **38–39** John Sims; **40–41** Neil Holmes; **42** (top) Philip Llewellin; **42** (bottom) The Mansell Collection; **42–43** Neil Holmes; **44** Trevor Wood; **45** Michael Harris; **46** Neil Holmes; **47** Trevor Wood; **48** Colin Molyneux; **50** Neil Holmes; **50** (inset) BBC Hulton Picture Library; **52–53** Neil Holmes; **54** (left) The Manx Museum; **55** Patrick Thurston; **56–69** Neil Holmes; **70** (top) Trevor Wood; **70** (bottom) Neil Holmes; **72** Aerofilms; **73** David Gallant; **74–75** Patrick Thurston; **76** (top) Philip Llewellin; **76** (bottom) Ian Howes; **78–79** Neil Holmes; **80** Colin Molyneux; **81** (left) Mary Evans/Harry Price Coll., Univ. of London; **81** (right) BBC Hulton Picture Library; **83** Neil Holmes; **84–85, 86** Jon Wyand; **87** John Sims; **89** (top) Philip Llewellin; **89** (bottom) David Gallant; **90** Neil Holmes; **91** John Sims; **92, 94** Neil Holmes; **96–97** Trevor Wood; **99** Mike St Maur Shiel; **100–101** Neil Holmes; **101** Trevor Wood; **102–103** Jon Wyand; **104–105** Trevor Wood; **105** (insets), **106** Neil Holmes; **106** (inset) From 'The Tale of Mrs Tiggy-Winkle' by Beatrix Potter. Reproduced by permission of Penguin Books. **108–109** Andy Williams; **110, 111** Neil Holmes; **112–113** Trevor Wood; **114–115** Reader's Digest; **116** Jon Wyand; **118–119, 120** Trevor Wood; **121** (bottom) Ronan Picture Library; **122** Trevor Wood; **123, 124** Neil Holmes; **125** A. Howarth; **127** Jon Wyand; **129** Neil Holmes; **130** (top) John Sims; **131** (bottom) Neil Holmes; **132–133** Trevor Wood; **134–135** Neil Holmes; **137** Jon Wyand; **138** Titanic Photography; **140** Mary Evans Picture Library; **141** Neil Holmes; **142–143** Ian Howes; **144–145** Neil Holmes; **147, 148–149** Jon Wyand; **150–151, 152** Neil Holmes; **154–155** David Gallant.

Artwork in this book was commissioned by Reader's Digest from the following artists.

8 Ann Savage; **12** (top) Liz Peperell; **12** (bottom) David Nockels; **15** Peter Barrett; **18** Robert Morton; **22** Mick Loates; **24** (Tawny Owl) Trevor Boyer; **24** (left) Eric Robson; **24** (centre) Marjory Saynor; **24** (right) Brian Delf; **26** (top) Roger Hughes; **26** (bottom) Stuart Lafford; **37** (left) John Francis; **37** (right) Ann Savage; **40** Brian Delf; **43** Trevor Boyer; **44** (left) Shirley Hooper; **44** (right) Frankie Coventry; **48** Reader's Digest; **49** Tim Hayward; **51** Mick Loates; **54** Robert Micklewright; **57, 59** Peter Barrett; **62** David Nockels; **66** Phil Weare; **67** (left) Shirley Hooper; **67** (right) Brenda Katté; **72** Barbara Brown; **73** Richard Bonson; **77** Robert Micklewright; **78** Gillian Platt; **80** (Sycamore) Shirley Felts; **80** (Elm) Ian Garrard; **80** (Others) Brian Delf; **83** (top) Ken Wood; **83** (bottom) Gill Tomblin; **90** Helen Cowcher; **92** David Baird; **93** Colin Emberson; **95** John Francis; **97** Ian Garrard; **98** David Baird; **100** Trevor Boyer; **101** Stuart Lafford; **107** Brian Delf; **111** (top) Brian Delf; **111** (bottom) Paul Wrigley; **114** Pauline Ellison; **115** David Nockels; **117** Robert Morton; **120** (top) Andrew Riley/Garden Studios; **120** (bottom) Sue Wickison; **121** (top) Mick Loates; **121** (bottom) Ronan Picture Library; **123** (left) Sarah Fox-Davies; **123** (right) Shirley Hooper; **125** Robert Gillmor; **128** David Nockels; **131** (top) John Francis; **131** (bottom), **135** Stephen Adams; **139** Richard Bonson; **141** Robert Morton; **146** Tim Hayward; **150** Peter Barrett; **152** (left) Trevor Boyer; **152** (right) Colin Emberson; **155** Richard Bonson.

The publishers would like to express their thanks to the local authorities, Tourist Boards and Tourist Information Centres for their help, and to Hilary Bird who compiled the index.

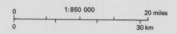
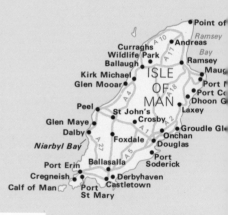